Directors' Dealings and Insider Trading in Germany

Corporate Finance and Governance

Herausgegeben von Dirk Schiereck

Band 2

PETER LANG

Frankfurt am Main · Berlin · Bern · Bruxelles · New York · Oxford · Wien

Patrick Ams

Directors' Dealings and Insider Trading in Germany

An Empirical Analysis

PETER LANG
Internationaler Verlag der Wissenschaften

Bibliographic Information published by the Deutsche Nationalbibliothek
The Deutsche Nationalbibliothek lists this publication in the Deutsche Nationalbibliografie; detailed bibliographic data is available in the internet at http://dnb.d-nb.de.

Zugl.: European Business School, Univ., Diss., 2009

Cover design:
Olaf Glöckler, Atelier Platen, Friedberg

D 1540
ISSN 1869-537X
ISBN 978-3-631-60391-8

www.peterlang.de

Vorwort

Directors' Dealings werden in vielen Ländern schon seit geraumer Zeit Beachtung seitens des Gesetzgebers geschenkt und deren Einfluss auf Aktienkurse auch in der akademischen Literatur analysiert. In Deutschland hingegen wurde bis etwa zur Jahrhundertwende den gesetzlichen Regelungen nur wenig Beachtung geschenkt. Erst seit Mitte 2002 sind Emittenten verpflichtet, Aktientransaktionen ihres Führungspersonals und ihnen nahestehenden Personen zu melden und ein Insiderregister zu führen. Durch diese Aufzeichnungs- und Meldepflicht ist es erst möglich, in wissenschaftliche Studien zu Directors' Dealings für den deutschen Aktienmarkt durchzuführen.

Zielsetzung dieser Arbeit ist es, neben der Analyse der kurzfristigen Effekte von Directors' Dealings, Langzeit-Effekte mit Hilfe von Langzeit -Ereignis-Studien zu untersuchen. Zusätzlich wird erstmalig für den deutschen Markt der Zusammenhang bzw. die Interaktion von Directors' Dealings und Corporate Actions untersucht. Die Arbeit knüpft an die ersten Untersuchungen zum deutschen Markt an und möchte Impulse für weitere Forschungsarbeiten zu Directors' Dealings in Deutschland liefern.

Diese Arbeit wäre ohne die Unterstützung durch eine Vielzahl von Personen nicht möglich gewesen. Meinem Doktorvater Prof. Dr. Lutz Johanning danke ich sehr sowohl für die Betreuung und Unterstützung dieser Arbeit als auch die herzliche Aufnahme am Lehrstuhl. Mein Dank gebührt auch meinem Zweitkorrektor Prof. Dr. Dirk Schiereck für Übernahme des Zweitgutachtens, der durch zahlreiche Hinweise maßgeblich zum erfolgreichen Abschluss der Arbeit beigetragen hat.

Weiterhin möchte ich mich bei der Bundesanstalt für Finanzdienstleistungsaufsicht bedanken, die mir durch die Bereitstellung verschiedener Datensätze die Untersuchungen zu illegalem Insiderhandel in Deutschland erst ermöglicht hat.

Besonderer Dank gilt auch Mark Mietzner, Christian Funke und Timo Gebken, die mir während der Fertigstellung der Arbeit mit vielen Anmerkungen und Hinweisen geholfen haben. Für die erholsamen Ablenkungen danke ich Johannes Schmittat, Marc Schuhmacher, Kay Benk, Gaston Michel, Christian Voigt, Sebastian Werner und Felix Zeidler.

Abschließend möchte ich meiner Familie großen Dank aussprechen, die mich während meines Promotionsvorhabens kontinuierlich unterstützt hat, und mir jederzeit mit Rat und Tat zur Seite stand.

Patrick Ams

Table of Contents

List of Figures

List of Tables

List of Equations

I. Introduction

I.A Overview and Research Objective

> „Our era has been styled, and well may be remembered as, the "age of information". Francis Bacon recognized nearly 400 years ago that "knowledge is power," but only in the last generation has it risen to the equivalent of the coin of the realm. Nowhere is this commodity more valuable or volatile than in the world of high finance, where facts worth fortunes while secret may be rendered worthless once revealed."[1]

This citation pinpoints a major concern in financial markets. Corporate insiders have by the virtue of their position an extensive business insight and can assess their firm's value by far better than other market participants. Since these insiders have access to such precious information, it puts especially a firm's managing employees in a delicate situation. Such material information may secure a firm's leading position amongst its competitors or put the firm at the edge of bankruptcy. Managers can exploit this information with ease and turn their knowledge into fortunes or prevent immense personal losses. Therefore, when directors privately purchase or sell their firm's stock, it seems at hand they do not fade out their inside knowledge and base their decision solely on publicly available information and the outside world's perception of their firm. However, it is not appropriate to assume they exploit inside information every time they trade. To protect outside market participants and equal out informational asymmetries between insiders and outsiders, financial regulators all over the world seek to impede trading on inside information without generally banning corporate insiders from purchasing or selling their firm's stock. In several countries regulators introduces besides insider dealings regulations also an obligation to disclose insider transactions. In Germany, regulators introduced the duty to disclose insider transaction comparatively late. While insider dealings had been regulated for many years, insiders were required by law to disclose their *directors' dealings* as recently as in 2002.

Studies on directors' dealings in the US market are broad and well-known patrons in international empirical literature. Lorie & Niederhoffer find it profitable watching directors' dealings as their results show firms with insider purchases outperform the market subsequently for six months.[2] A few years later, Finnerty (1976b) confirms these findings and concludes "...Insiders are able to outperform the market. Insiders can and do identify profitable as well as unprofitable situations within their corporations."[3] In an more extensive study, Seyhun (1986) analyzes roughly 60,000 insider transactions from 1975 to 1981 and finds "...insiders can predict abnormal future stock price changes. Insiders purchase stock prior to an abnormal rise in stock prices and sell stock prior to an abnormal decline

1 Circuit Judge Kaufman in his opinion on SEC v. MateriaSecurities and Exchange Commission, Plaintiff-Appellee, v. Anthony Materia, Defendant-Appellant, 745 F.2d 197 (1984), p. 198.

2 Cf. Lorie and Niederhoffer (1968), pp. 8-10.

3 Finnerty (1976b), p. 1148.

in stock prices."[4] Certainly, these excerpts reflect only a tiny part of the wide research literature on directors' dealings in the US though it shows the keen interest of researchers in this topic over the last decades. Besides studies discussing only directors' dealings, other authors analyzed also these transactions in conjunction with corporate actions like share repurchases or seasoned equity offerings. Chan, Ikenberry, & Lee (2003) report managers do generally not intensify their trading activity around share repurchases. Moreover, the authors find a counter-intuitive result insofar as long-term performance is higher when insiders sell stock. Lee (1997) investigates directors' dealings around seasoned equity offerings and finds increasing insider sales prior seasoned equity offerings (SEO). Unfortunately, studies on German directors' dealings are rare and less comprehensive; this situation is certainly caused by the fact that directors' dealings are only disclosed and recorded since July 2002. Since then, a few authors conducted short-term studies yet basically all of them suffer from relatively small sample sizes. Tebroke & Wollin (2005) conduct a long-term study measuring the buy-and-hold abnormal return over 100 days; they find significant positive and negative abnormal returns after purchases and sales, respectively.

Now, directors' dealings are recorded for more than six years in Germany and the number of available directors' dealings has increased significantly. Thus, the motivation for this thesis is threefold. Firstly, this thesis aims to answer the question whether corporate insiders are able to time their transactions and exploit short-term under- or overvaluations of their firms. Secondly, I will investigate whether these transactions are profitable over a prolonged time period and therefore are of interest for outside investors following a mimicking-strategy. Finally, this thesis seeks to investigate whether corporate insiders exploit their informational advantage on upcoming corporate actions and trade on this information.

Thus, I control in a short-term study whether directors' dealings are surrounded by abnormal returns. So far, Dymke & Walter (2006) use the largest dataset for Germany with 1,624 directors' purchases and 1,436 directors' sales. In this study, I include 6,054 purchases and 4,268 sales, covering a time span from July 2002 to December 2008. Therefore, I conjecture my results may differ substantially from previous studies and are, due to the increased sample size, more informative.

Findings from earlier literature lead to my first research question:

> Do directors exploit short-term price movements, i.e. do directors purchase after a price decline and sell after a price increase?

This research question addresses the timing ability of directors and whether they know if their firm is under- or overvalued. Assuming directors do time their transactions and know whether their firm is under- or overvalued, the second research question is consequently:

> Do prices rise or decline after directors' purchases or sales, respectively?

4 Seyhun (1986), p. 210.

With this question, I focus on the post-publication period. When directors consider their firm undervalued and purchase stock, one should presume rising prices afterwards and vice versa for sales.
The second block of research questions is based on above two questions yet it is more detail orientated. Intuitively, one would assume corporate insiders in smaller firms have easier access to inside information and can in general judge more precisely on the firm's value. Thus, my third research question is:

Do directors in smaller firms have higher abnormal returns than in larger firms?

Finally, one can assume directors have, depending on their position within a corporate organization, different levels of information. Therefore, my final research question in the short-term study is:

Do abnormal returns vary among different insider groups?

Previously, I claim the long-term performance after directors' dealings as the second research block. Thus, based on above research questions, I formulate the research questions for the long-term study:

Do directors' purchases and sales have long-term above average returns?

Are long-term above average returns higher in smaller firms?

Are long-term above average returns higher for insiders in higher positions?

Obviously, these questions tie in with those from the short-term analysis.
In the corporate actions study, I consider three different types of corporate actions. First, I consider share repurchases, second mergers and acquisitions, and finally seasoned equity offerings. Naturally, expectations for these different events should differ. While share repurchases may increase a firm's market value and thus should trigger directors' purchases, M&A as well as SEOs could have an adverse effect on shareholder value and thus trigger directors' sales.[5] However, all these corporate actions are usually very carefully watched by financial regulators. Hence, it seems questionable if directors trade on inside information and whether firms with directors' dealings perform better or worse than those without directors' dealings. Bearing this in mind, I formulate my research question for the final study as follows:

Are abnormal returns higher after a corporate action when directors' dealings are present?

Over the last decade, the German regulator worked hard to improve investor protection and raise market transparency. One part of these efforts is the documentation of directors' dealings. While previous research questions use these documented directors' dealings, one important question has not been addressed so far:

5 Cf. Chan, Ikenberry and Lee (2003), p. 1, Lee (1997), pp. 1439-1440.

Do insiders in Germany trade in inside information?

To tackle this special topic, I include a short excursus on insider trading in Germany. For outsiders it is close to impossible to judge whether a directors dealing is based on inside information, and thus illegal, or not. To fight illegal transactions, the German supervisor BaFin ("Bundesanstalt für Finanzdienstleistungsaufsicht") follows very closely all transactions and investigates suspicious transactions. Fortunately, BaFin made a set of investigated insider cases accessible to me. The small sample covers three main types of market misconduct, i.e. trading on inside information, market manipulation, and finally price manipulation.
Certainly, the necessary documentations associated with directors' dealings have increased substantially and many still question the necessity. However, my findings show directors earn abnormal returns. In consequence, disclosing these transactions may raises the personal threshold to trade on inside information unobserved by outside market participants. Also, the excursus confirms the existence of market misconduct, which further requests strong market supervision.

I.B Summary of Results

The final sample of directors' dealings in this study a sample of 12,519 documented directors' dealings in Germany is this study's basis. The sample covers a time period from July 2002 till December 2008.
My findings in the short-term study are the following:

Significant negative abnormal returns occur before directors purchase stock. Cumulative abnormal returns (CAR) measured over 20 days before the transaction accumulate to 2.74%. The event day abnormal return is 0.13%.

Significant positive abnormal returns occur before directors sell stock. CAR measured over 20 days before the transaction accumulate to 3.39%. Mean abnormal return on the sell day is 0.37%.

After the publication of these transactions, the return pattern swaps between purchases and sales:

A significant mean abnormal return of 0.38% is measured on the day directors' purchases are published. CAR measured over 20 days following the publication is significant and accumulate to 0.40%.

A significant mean abnormal return of 0.08% is measured on the day directors' sales are published. CARs measured over 20 days following the publication are highly significant and accumulate to 3.18%.

To further investigate these results, I divide the directors' dealings sample into quartiles based on firm size on the transaction as well as on the publication day. My results show:

Firms in the lowest quartile have a significant CAR of 1.57% over 20 before purchases. Pre-event CARs increase for quartiles two and three. Post-publication CARs are highest for smallest firms at 1.98%

Firms in the lower three quartiles experience significant highly significant pre-sales CARs of 7.02%. Largest firms show significant CARs of 2.35%. Post-publication CARs are highest in magnitude for smallest firms (4.80%) and smallest for largest firms (1.19%).

Sorting for different insider groups, I find:

Executive board members have the lowest pre-purchase CAR at 3.81% while the highest post-publication CAR after purchases is in the group of closely related persons at 1.45%.

Prior sales, closely related persons have the highest CAR at 4.72%. After the publication day, only executive board members and legal entities have negative CARs.

The long-term study, also tripartite in general, firm size, and directors' position, brings up the following results:

Buy-and-hold abnormal returns (BHAR) following the publication of directors' purchases observed over holding periods ranging from 3 to 24 months are positive and highly significant. Accounting for overlapping transactions, BHARs are even higher. Following sales, BHARs have over holding periods from three to nine months positive returns yet become negative afterwards.

Sorting for firm size, I find significant BHARs of 25.88% after purchases for firms in the first quartile, while firms in quartiles two and four accumulate only 9.24% and 5.12%, respectively; firms in quartile three have a negative BHAR. Considering sales, I find a less distinctive pattern. Smallest firms have from the 6-month holding period onwards positive BHARs. Higher quartiles show both, positive and negative BHARs.

Sorting results for insider positions, I find supervisory board members have after 18 months of their purchases the highest BHAR at 22.49%. After sales, executive board members transactions show the highest negative BHAR at 19.27%.

The last empirical study covers directors' dealings around corporate actions. My findings for repurchases are:

Firms with directors' dealings have higher pre-event and higher post-event BHARs than those firms without directors' dealings. Share volumes and Euro value of transactions indicate directors sell long before the event and purchase again once the event day comes closer.

My findings for M&A and SEOs are:

For both event types I find higher pre-event BHARs for firms with directors' dealings than for those without. However, results do not allow concluding whether directors' dealings are trigger by the upcoming event or not.

The corporate actions study closes with an ordered-probit model analyzing the amount of quarterly directors' dealings and corporate actions from previous quarters. Results show that the major trigger for directors' purchases and sales is the previous 1-year BHAR while other factors have no major impact.

Overall, I conclude from my findings that directors are able to time their transaction and exploit temporarily under- and overvaluations of their firms. Both, results from the short- and long-term analysis confirm these. Results from the corporate actions study are vague yet they point into a similar direction.

I.C Research Framework and Course of Investigation

The introduction showed the long tradition and diverse aspects of insider dealings. These different aspects are the basis of my research questions. Afterwards, I join these miscellaneous considerations in my research framework, which is also the basis for previously presented research questions.

Figure 1 illustrates major topics connected to directors' dealings. Empirical studies on directors' dealings exist in the Unites States since several decades. Besides empirical studies, legal scholars discuss this topic as it is probably the topic with the highest number of touch points between finance and law. Several theoretical models of insider dealing evolved over time. Since 2002, a few studies on directors' dealings in Germany came up as well. Thus far, empirical studies and theoretical models on insider dealing shaped my research framework, illustrated on the left side in subsequent the figure. The right side, i.e. the actual legal and regulatory framework in Germany and the European Union, shape the remaining half of the research framework. One part of these legal and regulatory aspects is certainly the German supervisor BaFin ("Bundesanstalt für Finanzdienstleistungsaufsicht").

Finally, these manifold aspects meet in research on directors' dealings. Based on this research framework I developed the research questions for this work. From there, I structured the empirical study, illustrated below.

Figure 1: Research Framework

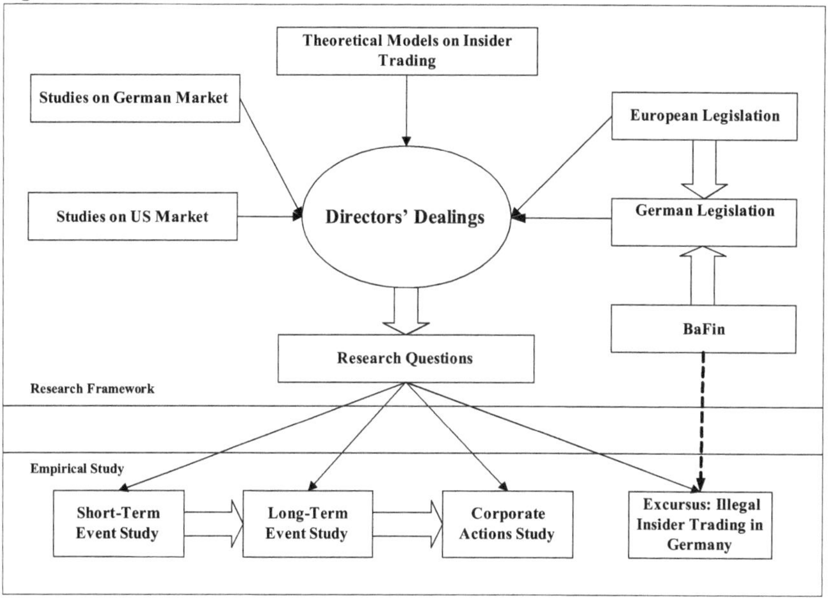

As I previously pointed out, the empirical study's structure is based on the above research framework. Moreover, this framework leads to the overall structure of this thesis in which I imbed the empirical study.

After presenting the objective and research questions of this doctoral thesis in the first chapter, I proceed in the second chapter with the legal and theoretical framework. After introducing the main European financial regulations, I discuss legal landscape in Germany. I stress this part in particular since laws and regulations directly influence directors' dealings. Moreover, the European Union strives for an integrated financial market. Thus, EU regulations directly affect the legal setting in Germany; hence, I consider it important to discuss both the pan-European and national legal framework regulating directors' dealings. Naturally, another important aspect is that these laws constitute directors' dealings; without any regulations, transactions by corporate insiders would be just a few among many other transactions. Above research framework showed also the influence of US studies on the discussion of directors' dealings; thus, I close the legal introduction with a short excursus on US regulations on insider dealing and a summary of probably the most well-known case of insider dealing in US history. The remainder of the second chapter discusses the theoretical framework. Starting with a description of market efficiency, I discuss legal and economic aspect of insider dealing.

The third chapter presents important empirical literature on insider dealing. Starting with the most prominent works on US insider dealing, the chapter closes with

studies on the German market. Chapter four introduces the empirical methodologies and discusses the datasets used in the empirical study.
Chapter five presents findings from the empirical study. At first, I discuss results from the short-term study. Afterwards, I report findings on the long-term study, and finally, I close the chapter with findings from the corporate actions study.
In chapter six, I present the excursus on illegal insider dealing in Germany. Finally, I conclude this thesis in chapter seven.

II. Legal and Theoretical Framework

Directors' dealings are in general transactions executed by corporate insiders. Naturally, this special group of market participants has by the virtue of its position within a firm access to confidential information. While financial regulators do not want to exclude these persons from purchasing or selling their firm's stock, they are eager to prevent insiders from trading on confidential information. For this purpose, the European and German legislators established over the recent years several regulations and laws to govern these transactions. Certainly, this issue is also widely discussed among academics. Unlike most other areas in financial research, this topic brings financial and legal aspects very close together. Therefore, I present in this chapter at first the legal framework in the European Union and Germany, followed by an excursus to US insider dealing laws. Thereafter, I discuss the theoretical framework. Following an introduction to efficient capital markets, I close this chapter with a discussion of insider trading models and legal views on this topic.

II.A Legal Framework

Financial research is usually independent of legal rules. However, research on directors' dealings is probably one of the few topics in financial research that is closely related to the laws governing a financial market. First of all, without any requirement for insiders to disclose their transactions, it would be almost impossible to identify these transactions among others and research on directors' dealings had no basis. Second, depending on the local rules, information on directors' dealings differs in terms of who is required to publish transactions, when must trades are published, and several other aspects. Therefore, I considered it inevitable to start this thesis with a sound introduction to the specific regulations. I choose to commence the discussion with European regulations; my rational is that EU regulations set the standards for an integrated European Financial Market and are then implemented in national laws. Afterwards, I continue with German laws on insider dealing, which are the most relevant ones for this thesis. Finally, conclude this sub-chapter with a short excursus on US insider laws. The US has a long tradition in securities regulation and probably the highest number of research papers on directors' dealings uses US data; thus, I considered it more than reasonable to discuss the major parts of US law as well.

II.A.1 European Financial Regulation

This sub-chapter gives a brief overview on European Union's financial regulations on market abuse and insider dealing. The European legislator plays an important role for Germany, especially when it comes to financial market regulation and restrictions concerning insider dealing. Compared to other countries, Germany enacted laws governing insider trading and market manipulation very late. Today, most of these laws and regulations are based on EU legislation. Therefore,

it is essential to understand the principles of European financial regulation before moving on to German financial market laws.
At first, I summarize the development of the Single Financial Market followed by the historical development of the Market Abuse Directive. Finally, I briefly present the most important parts of the directive.

II.A.1.1 Historical Development of a Single European Financial Market

In 1957, Belgium, France, Italy, Luxembourg, the Netherlands, and West Germany signed the Treaties of Rome, thus creating the first Internal Market with the so-called European Economic Community (EEC). The removal of trade barriers and a closer cooperation between the different industries of each Member State was the underlying aim. Ten years later, in 1967, the European Commission, the Council of Ministers, and the European Parliament were created. The Treaty of Maastricht in 1992 achieved an even higher level of economic integration. The same year also marked the formal completion of a Single Market and the Member States emphasized joint policy decisions. Furthermore, it was the genesis of the European Union. Coevally, free movement of goods and services as well as the free movement of citizens between the Contracting States became easier. The creation of the European Monetary Union (EMU) was not only a step towards the integration of financial markets but also complemented cross-border business transactions. In 2002, the Euro was introduced as a single European Currency in twelve Member States. Today, in 2009, 16 Member States have adopted the Euro as their currency.[6]
A blatant requirement to support flawless business within the European Union was certainly not only the elimination of trade barriers and the introduction of a single currency but rather the creation of an integrated financial system as cross-border business transactions trigger cross-border cash flows. Easing only transnational banking would not have been an option since the idea of foregoing political steps demanded a pan-European financial market. Corporations and individuals would gain access to financial services and capital markets across the EU through such a single financial market.[7]Benefits for the financial market are at hand; besides a widened array of services, an increasing number of participants along the value chain boosts competition and lowers costs through economies of scale. Also, if there are more participants, it lowers the liquidity risk. Certainly, an integrated market would be of use to corporations and consumers in particular. Both groups should experience lower transaction costs, a more extensive range of investment opportunities and thereby superior possibilities to diversify their portfolios. In addition, the rising numbers of market participants should facilitate market efficiency and thus reflect prices more accurately.[8] To accomplish this ambitious

6 Cf. EU (2008).
7 Cf. European Commission (1999b), p. 1.
8 Cf. London Economics (2002), pp. 8-10.

goal, the European Commission released the Financial Services Action Plan in 1998, laying out major milestones towards an integrated financial market and the necessary measures.[9]

The Financial Services Action Plan covered three main subjects, i.e. the wholesale market, the retail market, and regulation and supervision.[10] A single wholesale market was deemed a necessity to give institutions EU-wide access to capital markets. To pave the way for such a market, a first step was to level differences between jurisdictions by setting up a common legal framework.[11] Part of this effort was to clarify regulatory and supervisory competences as well as to formulate rules concerning investor protection and market abuse.[12] Also, pan-EU security offerings and capital rising were eased by a unified prospectus guideline and the introduction of the International Accounting Standards (nowadays International Financial Reporting Standards 'IFRS'). Especially small and medium-sized enterprises were supposed to profit from access to a broader and more diverse base of investors. As mentioned before, investors could also profit from manifold investment options. To facilitate this in practice, it was necessary to simplify cross-border security trading, corporate acquisitions and takeovers. Likewise, raising transparency and legal certainty (e.g. counterparty risk, enforceability of collaterals) to the same level was a prerequisite.[13]

Without doubt, similar changes had to follow in the retail market. With these, financial institutions could not only offer their services to firms and governments but also to individual consumers. Actions in the retail market were aimed in particular at enhancing investor protection and increasing consumer confidence. Here, major obstacles were different levels of investor protection as well as legal and regulatory issues concerning financial retail products. Legal impediments, as an aspect of investor protection, included varying recourse procedures in each Member State.[14]

The third important topic of the Financial Services Action Plan was regulation and supervision. Naturally, these relate to both the wholesale and the retail market. A single European market called for a comprehensive supervision. Regulatory standards and investor protection amongst all partaking countries had to be aligned. A first step to accomplish this goal was certainly an improved information flow between national banking and financial supervising authorities.[15] Consistently, the general structure of the national supervisors had to be discussed. This was considered to be important as not only the European financial markets were in flux but

9 Cf. European Commission (1998b).
10 Cf. European Commission (1998a).
11 Cf. Stern and Beresford (2001), pp. 67-69.
12 Cf. Clifford Chance_LLP (2005), pp. 285-286.
13 Cf. European Commission (1999a), p. 6.
14 Cf. Ibid., p. 9., Stern and Beresford (2001), p. 76.
15 Cf. European Commission (1998a), p. 4.

financial markets world-wide got closer and became more connected.[16] Thus, not only competition within the single market was an issue but also the competitiveness of this market with other markets all over the world.[17] An important milestone in this process was the Market Abuse Directive, covering amongst other financial market abuses directors' dealings. Afterwards, I will shortly introduce this directive, which constitutes the basis for current German directors' dealings regulations.

II.A.1.2 Market Abuse Directive

The first pan-European directive on insider dealing was enacted on November 13, 1989. Directive 89/592/EEC was meant to coordinate national insider regulations. Member States were required to enact laws prohibiting insider dealing (article 2 para. 1). There were also calls for establishing a national supervising authority.[18] In Germany, representatives from the banking industry denied the need for such a regulation and found a voluntary code of honor enough.[19] In 2001, more than ten years later, the Commission presented a proposal for a directive on insider dealing and market manipulation (market abuse). Herewith, already existing regulations concerning insider dealing were complemented by regulations on market manipulation. This proposal was part of the Financial Services Action Plan that was discussed earlier.[20] Following the tragic events on 9/11, there was a strong drive for a more rigorous regulation of insider dealing and market manipulation.[21] To regain market confidence and protect markets against such a tremendous destabilization, the Commission's proposal replaced the existing directive 89/592/EEC on insider dealing and included market manipulation in their new directive.[22] The directive 2003/6/EC was enacted on April 12, 2003. It replaced the directive 89/592/EEC and articles 68(1) and 81(1) of the directive 2001/34/EC on the admission of securities to official stock exchange listing and on information to be published on those securities. The deadline for implementation of the new directive was scheduled for October 12, 2004, thus leaving ample time for the Member States to include the CESR's recommendations in their national implementation.[24]

16 Cf. Lastra (2003), p. 50.
17 Cf. European Commission (1998a), p. 19.
18 Cf. European Council (1989).
19 Cf. Paefgen (1991), p. 385.
20 Cf. Reynolds and Rutter (2004), p. 307.
21 Cf. European Council and European Parliament (2003).para. 14.
22 Cf. Ferrarini (2004), p. 711.
23 Cf. European Council and European Parliament (2003).Article 20.
24 CESR is the Committee of European Securities Regulators. Its three main areas of work are the improvement of coordination among the EU's national securities regulators, advice to the EU Commission, and the supervision of national implementation of Community legislation. For more details refer to the CESR homepage (http://www.cesr-eu.org/index.php?page=cesrinshort&mac=0&id).

II.A.1.2.1 Aim and Scope of the Market Abuse Directive

As stated before, the goal of the Financial Services Action Plan was an integrated market for financial services. The importance for the EU of an integrated financial market was codified in directive 2003/6/EC:

> *"A genuine Single Market for financial services is crucial for economic growth and job creation in the Community."*.

Without doubt, such a single functioning market was and is an utmost priority for a strong and competitive Community. Certainly, confidence of all market participants in the market's integrity and flawless functioning was considered a building block of paramount significance. To accomplish this goal, the directive 2003/6/EC covered several issues beyond insider dealing and tried to include a broad range of fraudulent actions in financial markets. Market abuse was seen as jeopardy to investor confidence and hence as a source of irritation to a smooth functioning of financial markets. Therefore, to promote economic prosperity in the European Union, the directive should contribute to a market with integrity to assure its efficiency and to safeguard all participants. Particularly after the terrorist attacks on September 11, the prevention of external market disturbances and the preservation of public confidence in financial markets had reached a new level of relevance. The European legislator combined both insider dealing and market manipulation in one single directive to assure similar national rules based on a common framework.

Another measure to enhance market efficiency and boost investor confidence was definitely the emphasis on transparency. Under the new Directive, issuers were obligated to extensive disclosure, i.e. any material information had to be made publicly available immediately. Of course, the quickest possible disclosure was meant to reduce the possibility of insider trading.[26] In addition, the new legislation focused more than ever on the protection of private investors and those without direct access to relevant financial information. Safe-harbor provisions were only included with respect to price stabilization and share buyback programs. Besides, any research or recommendation on financial instruments now had to be presented in a fair manner and any possible conflicts of interest had to be disclosed.[27] In general, the directive focused on a higher level of transparency to minimize possible fraud.

To achieve this aim, the directive's scope covered all financial instruments traded on at least one Member State's market. Apart from instruments that are traded on a regulated market, the directive's reach extended also to financial products traded over the counter or via alternative trading systems.[28] Further, the directive's territorial scope increased as well; market abuse could be avenged in both the Member

25 European Council and European Parliament (2003).para. 1.

26 Cf. Fergusson (2005), p. 4, Ferrarini (2004), p. 731.

27 Cf. European Council and European Parliament (2003).Art. 6 para. 5.

28 Cf. Fergusson (2005), p. 2.

State in which the market abuse occurred and the Member State in which the affected financial instrument was admitted to trade or had its origin.[29]

II.A.1.2.2 Market Abuse Definitions

Following the historical development of European directors' dealings regulations, I briefly present in this paragraph the most important definitions from the market abuse directive on inside information and insiders.

(a) Inside Information

The Directive commences with a detailed definition of 'Inside Information'. According to article 1, the definition reads:

> *"'Inside information' shall mean information of a precise nature which has not been made public, relating, directly or indirectly, to one or more issuers of financial instruments.*[30] *or to one or more financial instruments and which, if it were made public, would be likely to have a significant effect on the prices of those financial instruments or on the price of related derivative financial instruments.".*

This connotes that information must be concrete and purposive to be considered as *inside information*. Directive 2003/124/EC. particularizes this as follows: "(…) information (…) indicates a set of circumstances which exists or may reasonably be expected to come into existence (…)".. One is supposed to be able to draw a conclusion about a price impact on a financial instrument or a related derivative.[33] Thus, information has to relate to an event which has already happened or which is reasonably likely to occur. However, determining the possibility of a price impact is rather complicated. Often, a small group within a firm has access to a vast quantity of information while other market participants do not. Even though such inside information might be of interest for outsiders, its publication would not affect share prices in most cases.[34] It is important to notice that the Directive uses this wording in an attempt to differentiate between information based upon existing facts and that based on rumors.[35] CESR also gives further guidance on material information relating to the issuer, which could be changes in controlling

---

29 Cf. Reynolds and Rutter (2004), p. 307.

30 According to Art. 1 para. 3, Financial Instruments include: transferable securities, units in collective investment undertakings, money-market instruments, and financial-futures contracts including equivalent cash-settled instruments, forward interest-rate agreements, interest-rate-, currency-, and equity-swaps, options on aforementioned instruments, derivatives on commodities, and any other instrument admitted to trading on a regulated market in a Member State.

31 Directive 2003/124/EC is a so-called implementing directive, i.e. a directive specifying issues from a previous directive. An implementing directive also gives guidance to Member States on how to implement certain paragraphs.

32 Cf. European Council and European Parliament (2003).Art. 1 para. 1.

33 Cf. Hansen (2004), p. 194.

34 Cf. Ferrarini (2004), p. 718.

35 Cf. CESR (2003), p. 8.

ownership, changes in management, changes in share capital, significant legal disputes and so forth.[36]

CESR defines precise information based on two conditions. The first condition states: "The underlying matter or event to which the information refers is true or could reasonably be expected to become true in the future.". Thus, information must relate to issues or events that either already exist or are likely to eventuate. The second condition reads: "The information is specific enough to allow a conclusion to be drawn about its impact on prices.". Bringing both conditions together, it is clear that information is only precise when it relates to true matters or events that already exist or that are likely to come into existence and when it allows a reasonable investor to judge its impact on prices.[39]

(b) Insider

Beyond the general provisions regulating insiders, the Directive 2003/6/EC also differentiates between *primary insiders* and *secondary insiders*, just like the Investment Services Directive from 1989.

According to Art. 2 para. 1 of the Directive 2003/6/EC, a primary insider is a person who possesses inside information by "*virtue of his membership of the administrative, management or supervisory bodies of the issuer; or by virtue of his holdings in the capital of the issuer; or by virtue of his having access to the information through the exercise of his employment, profession or duties; or by the virtue of his criminal activities.*[40] The latter relates on the one hand to upcoming external events with a significant price impact, i.e. terrorist attacks, and on the other hand to a person gaining illegal access to inside information, e.g. theft.[41]

A secondary insider is a person who is not a primary insider and who is in possession of inside information and knows or should be aware of the fact that the information in question is inside information.[42] This article seems to render Article 2 of the Directive unnecessary in that a secondary insider has not necessarily obtained the inside information form a primary insider.[43] To constitute the corpus delicti of a secondary insider, the person just has to be in possession of inside information. Hence, a primary insider could also be considered a secondary insider and therefore a catch-all clause would have been sufficient without limiting the scope of the Directive.[44]

36 Cf. Ibid., p. 12.
37 Cf. CESR (2002), p. 9.
38 Ibid.
39 Cf. Ibid., p. 10, Ferrarini (2004), p. 719.
40 Cf. European Council and European Parliament (2003).Art. 2 para. 1 lit. a-d.
41 Cf. Ferrarini (2004), p. 722, Hansen (2004), p. 197.
42 Cf. European Council and European Parliament (2003).Art. 4.
43 Cf. Hansen (2004), p. 197.
44 Cf. Ferrarini (2004), p. 723, Hansen (2002), p. 257.

II.A.2 German Insider Dealing Laws

European legislation certainly has a great influence on German legislation. Laws in form of directives and regulations issued by the European institutions either must be converted into German law within a predefined transition period or they are directly enacted. Hence, European laws concerning the European financial market are of paramount importance to the German financial market. Based on the European developments in financial laws, which were laid out in previously, this chapter describes German laws and regulations covering financial markets, in particular directors' dealings and insider transactions. A brief synopsis describing the major historical developments in Germany is followed by the description of the Investor Protection Enhancement Act of 2004, which introduced the directive 2003/6/EC into the German Securities Trade Act. Afterwards, the articles covering insider dealing and market manipulation in Germany are described. This chapter concludes with a short description of fraudulent behavior in financial markets and an introduction to the Bundesanstalt für Finanzdienstleistungsaufsicht (BaFin), i.e. the German financial supervising authority.

II.A.2.1 Historical Development

The federal ministry of economics established in 1968 an expert commission on the German stock market. One major aspect of their final report, submitted in 1970, were recommendations to solve the insider dealing issues. They proposed rules for voluntary self-monitoring, which were enacted in 1972 and stayed in place until 1988. Throughout this period, these rules were revised.[45] Major criticism concerned the narrow group of persons covered by the insider dealing rules, as external groups with access to inside information were not included.[46] In 1989, Germany had to revise its insider dealing regulations as the European Council adopted the Council Directive to coordinate insider dealing.[47] In 1994, the German legislator enacted a law to boost the country's financial market. With article 1, the law established the German Securities Trading Act (Wertpapierhandelsgesetz - WpHG) and integrated the Directive 89/592/EEC.[48] In this directive, insider trading was strictly forbidden for the first time by law. After several revisions, the German insider dealing regulations experienced major amendments in 2004. Germany adopted the directive 2003/6/EC into German law with the "Gesetz zur Verbesserung des Anlegerschutzes – AnSVG".

II.A.2.2 Investor Protection Enhancement Act

One of the latest parts in German financial regulation and law making is the Investor Protection Enhancement Act of 2004. On October 30, 2004, the Inves-

45 Cf. Assmann (1994), p. 197.
46 Cf. Hienzsch (2006), p. 29.
47 Cf. European Council (1989).
48 Cf. Zweites Finanzmarktförderungsgesetz (1994).
49 Henceforth: AnSVG or Investor Protection Enhancement Act.

tor Protection Enhancement Act (Gesetz zur Verbesserung des Anlegerschutzes – AnSVG) was enacted in Germany. Directive 2003/6/EC, which was discussed earlier, was implemented into German law together with the AnSVG. Furthermore, Commission Directives concerning the implementation of 2003/6/EC were introduced into German law as well. The Commission Regulation No. 2273/2003, concerning share buyback programs and price stabilization of financial instruments, was enacted directly without modification through the German legislator.[50] With the implementation of the Market Abuse Directive into the WpHG, Germany modernized especially its insider dealing rules. Certainly, the denomination of the law showed the general intention, i.e. increasing investor protection in Germany. The law therefore covered several aspects in the WpHG. The term "financial instrument" was introduced into German law; the legislator wanted to cover all existing and possible future financial instruments with this term.[51] Beyond this, the term inside information was reformed, changes in the definition of insiders were implemented, and insider lists were introduced. Next, publication of ad-hoc news was revised as well as regulations concerning directors' dealings. Also, articles covering market manipulation were changed. Several regulations concerning financial analysts and their recommendations were broadened.[52] Of course, these amendments did not find acceptance by many groups. Especially the greater information and investigation rights of the German supervising authority were criticized. Also, many found fault with increasing costs and administrative efforts.[53]

II.A.2.3 Insider Dealing and Market Manipulation in Germany

In the following paragraphs, I shortly describe important changes and definitions from the Investor Protection Enhancement Act. Measures concerning directors' dealings and insider trading were implemented in the WpHG.

II.A.2.3.1 Inside Securities

The Market Abuse Directive introduced the term "financial instruments", which encompasses a wide variety of securities, financial and commodity derivatives and other instruments traded in regulated markets and over the counter.[54] The WpHG picks up this term in §12. It defines insider securities[55] as financial instruments that are admitted to trading on a domestic regulated stock exchange, in a regulated market or over the counter.[56] Therefore, the new wording does not only cover ordinary stocks and bonds but any tradable financial instrument. Its flexibil-

50 Unlike directives issued by the EU institutions, a regulation is not implemented into a Member State's legal system but is enacted without modification.
51 Cf. Bürgers (2004), p. 204.
52 Cf. Pluskat (Ibid.), p. 467.
53 Cf. Kreditausschuss and BVI (2004), pp. 2-4.
54 Cf. European Council and European Parliament (2003).Art. 1 para. 3.
55 In German, the official technical term for insider securities is "Insiderpapiere".
56 Cf. WpHG (2007).§12 No. 1

ity allows including not yet existing financial instruments as well.[57] Inside securities also compromise financial instruments that are admitted to trading in another Member State and other contracting States of the European Economic Area. Further, the law covers also financial derivatives with underlying inside securities.[58] As the legislator aimed for utmost investor protection, even financial instruments that were announced to be registered for trading and financial instruments in the admittance process were regarded as inside securities.[59]

II.A.2.3.2 Inside Information

Today, the German Securities Trade Act uses the term inside information[60] to denominate facts or information known to insiders. This term was introduced in the WpHG among other things with the enactment of the AnSVG, and thus with the implementation of the Market Abuse Directive. According to §13 WpHG, inside information is information that is either related to an issuer of insider securities or insider securities themselves. It is precise and not public. Also, it must be able to influence the price of an insider security significantly.[61] This capability is given if a competent investor[62] includes this information in his decision process. Also, future events that are likely to happen with a sufficient probability are circumstances considered as inside information. Hence, the legislator also includes subjective judgments and future prospects.[63] Furthermore, knowledge of trading orders of financial instruments, either insider securities or derivative financial instruments relating to insider securities, is also regarded as inside information.[64] Recommendations or other information relating to an issuer of insider securities or insider securities themselves are not considered as inside information if they are based solely on facts and circumstances that are publicly known.[65]

II.A.2.3.3 Disclosure of Directors' Dealings

Certainly, employees are allowed to purchase, sell, and own shares of their employers. This right also includes any financial instrument related to their employer. Nevertheless, employees must adhere to the insider dealing regulations described above, regardless of their position within the firm. The German legislator pays special attention to those employees in managing positions. The WpHG covers

---

57 Cf. Bürgers (2004), p. 424.
58 Cf. BaFin (2005), pp. 15-16, WpHG (2007).§12 No. 2-3
59 Cf. WpHG (2007).§12
60 The German official name is „Insiderinformation"; cf. Ibid.§13
61 Ibid.§13 para. 1
62 The term competent investor was introduced by directives 2003/6/EC and 2003/124/EC, describing a rational investor who integrates all public information into his investment decision.
63 Cf. Bürgers (2004), pp. 424-425, WpHG (2007).§13 para. 1.
64 Cf. BaFin (2005), p. 22, WpHG (2007).§13 para.1 No. 1-2
65 Cf. WpHG (2007).§13 para. 2, Ziemons (2004), p. 538.

directors' dealings in §15a. This article also implements the Commission Directive 2004/72/EC.

Particularly employees with management responsibilities have access to inside information by virtue of their position. In addition to managers, the WpHG includes employees with decision-making power.[66] Furthermore, the German legislator also included a manager's close relatives, i.e. spouse or children, and any person living in the same household for more than one year.[67] To minimize the threat of insider dealing and to prevent the use of inside information in trading decisions, §15a WpHG requires all persons belonging to one of the groups described above to disclose their transactions within five working days to both the issuer and the competent authority.[68] Not only transactions in the respective issuer's shares must be reported but also transactions with related financial instruments.[69] An exemption for the reporting duties is made for persons whose transactions do not exceed an annual value of €5,000. This value includes not only the director's transactions but also those of closely related persons. This threshold is a strong accentuation compared to the regulations before the AnSVG. Before, directors had a limit of €25,000 during a four-week period before they had to report their transactions. According to the Commission Directive 2004/72/EC, the threshold introduced through the AnSVG is optional.[70]

Notification of directors' dealings should consist of precise information on the trading person, inter alia his relationship to the issuer and his role within the issuer's organization. Also, order details should be disclosed in the notice.[71] The notice has to be published on the issuer's website or, if the issuer does not have an online presence, in an official newspaper. Foreign issuers are permitted to publish their communication in English as long as investors are not misled.[72]

Failure to disclose directors' dealings or reporting directors' dealings incorrectly, incompletely, not in time, or not in the required form, either intentionally or imprudently, is punishable. If the publication slip is not transmitted to the BaFin or if it arrives late, the WpHG allows for a fine of up to €50,000.. If a publication is missing, wrong, or incomplete, the fine is set at €100,000..

Another innovation in the course of the implementation of the Market Abuse Directive was the introduction of insider registers. §15b WpHG requires all issuers to maintain such a database and register all persons with access to inside information. Entries should consist of personal details, reasons for registration, and dates

---

66 Cf. BaFin (2005), p. 69, Diekmann and Sustmann (2004), p. 936.
67 Cf. BaFin (2005), p. 70, Heiring (2005), p. 36.
68 In Germany, the competent authority is the BaFin.
69 Cf. WpHG (2007).§15a para. 1.
70 Cf. European Commission (2004).Art. 6 para. 2, WpHG (2007).§15a para. 1.
71 Cf. BaFin (2005), p. 80, WpAIV (2004).§§10,12.
72 Cf. BaFin (2005), pp. 79-80.
73 Cf. Pluskat (2004), p. 473, WpHG (2007).§39 para. 1 No. 1 lit. d.
74 Cf. Bürgers (2004), p. 428, WpHG (2007).§39 para.4.

of access to inside information.[75] Not only employees with access to inside information must be registered in the database but also external consultants with access to inside information. The database must be updated whenever a new person gains access to inside information or when an already registered person does no longer have access to inside information.[76]

II.A.2.3.4 Market Manipulation Laws

Market manipulation is addressed in §20a WpHG. As in the Market Abuse Directive, the German legislator differentiates between information-based and transaction-based manipulation in §20a WpHG. After the changes of the AnSVG, the revised §20a WpHG now includes changes and new requirements from the Market Abuse Directive. In addition, Commission Directives 2003/124/EC on market manipulation and 2004/72/EC on accepted market practices were implemented with the reformed §20a WpHG. To clarify questions that are left open by §20a WpHG, the German ministry of finance issued a by-law in March 2005 to concretize the article.[77]

Before the revision in 2004, the WpHG prohibited only false statements. With the amendments in 2004, §20a WpHG now covers not only false but also misleading statements and misleading information, which are able to influence the value of a financial instrument. This minor change is far-reaching. Looking closer, one finds that even if an issuer of financial instruments disseminates information or makes a statement correctly as regards content, he may be convicted under §20a WpHG based on a misleading phrasing.[78] Vice versa, it is also prohibited to conceal information[79] if it is able to influence a financial instrument's price.[80] According to BaFin, statements from the issuer always refer to a verifiable fact. Thus, this includes both facts and value judgments. Also, they might be based on forecasts as long as they rely on plausible facts.[81] Statements are considered to be false if they are either based on faulty or untrue facts or if they cannot be justified by the prevailing facts. In addition, one must ensure that a statement is complete. Otherwise, it is also considered as misleading and thus prohibited. This is similar to information or statements which are correct as regards contents but have a misleading phrasing.[82] Finally, one has to determine whether information or a statement might be able to influence the value of a financial instrument. Here, the German legislator concretizes such circumstances in §2 MaKonV. Again, the

75 Cf. WpAIV (2004).§14.
76 Cf. Ziemons (2004), p. 540.
77 Cf. BaFin (2005), p. 86.
78 Cf. Bisson and Kunz (2005), p. 187, WpHG (2007).§20a para. 1 No. 1.
79 Such information may include a vast array of possible circumstances or events. Further guidance is given in MaKonV (2005).§2. (Marktmanipulations-Konkretisierungsverordnung).
80 Cf. BaFin (2005), p. 91, WpHG (2007).§20a para. 1 No. 1.
81 Cf. BaFin (2005), p. 89.
82 Cf. Ibid., pp. 89-90.

term "competent investor" is used to define a person who uses this information or statement in his investment decision process. Circumstances that would make a statement or information valuable for a competent investor can relate to upcoming insolvency, M&A transactions, important patents, strategic decisions, and several other things.[83] Certainly, inside information is such a circumstance.

As described before, §20a WpHG differentiates between information-based and transaction-based manipulation. Thus, in addition to false or misleading information and statements, it is strictly prohibited to engage in transactions of financial instruments that might give out misleading signals. Transactions with the purpose to maintain an artificial price level are not permitted either.[84] Misleading transactions or transactions that are supposed to maintain or achieve a certain price level include purchases and sales that constitute a significant amount of the daily trading volume or trades with a significant impact on prices including related financial instruments.[85] Reversing significant positions within a short time or closing a high number of trades within a short time, which might trigger a price change or lead to a price reversal, is not permitted.[86] As with inside information, the legislator asks only for a possible price impact but not for an actually occurred impact.[87] Beyond these actions, it is also strictly prohibited by §20a WpHG to engage in any other deceiving actions. Spreading false recommendations and warnings or devising rumors is considered as a deceiving action. This is especially true if they are not based on verifiable facts and if they can mislead investors, as they are then able to manipulate the price of financial instruments. The German legislator names the use of online communities and forums in particular, because they are mostly unregulated and can be misused for such purposes.[88] Moreover, it is not permitted to attain a dominant position which might influence the demand or supply of financial instruments and as a result maintain artificial price levels.[89] Exemptions are made for share buyback programs and price stabilizations in accordance with Commission Regulation No. 2273/2003. As EC regulations have a direct effect, they are not transformed into national law.[90]

Violations against §20a WpHG are either offenses or misdemeanors. An offense is committed if the person acts with intention and if the market price effectively influences the price of a financial instrument. A misdemeanor is committed when a person acts without intention, or if he acts with intention but the price is not ef-

83 Cf. MaKonV (2005).§2.
84 Cf. Bürgers (2004), p. 428, WpHG (2007).§20a para. 1 No. 2.
85 Cf. Bisson and Kunz (2005), p. 187, MaKonV (2005).§3 para. 1 lit. a-b.
86 Cf. MaKonV (2005).§3 para. 1 lit. c-d.
87 Cf. Bisson and Kunz (2005), p. 187, Bürgers (2004), p. 428.
88 Cf. MaKonV (2005).§4.
89 Cf. Bisson and Kunz (2005), p. 188, MaKonV (2005).§4 para. 3 No. 1.
90 Cf. WpHG (2007).§20a para. 3.

fectively influenced.[91] Penalties for offenses are up to five years of imprisonment or fines and misdemeanors can be fined with up to €2,000,000..

II.A.2.4 Federal Financial Supervisory Authority

Founded in May 2002 through the law to constitute an integrated financial supervisory office (Gesetz über die integrierte Finanzdienstleistungsaufsicht – FinDAG), the German Federal Financial Supervisory Authority[93] (Bundesanstalt für Finanzdienstleistungsaufsicht – BaFin) is responsible for the supervision of financial service providers (including banks), insurances, and securities trading.[94] The BaFin is an autonomous authority, ancillary to the Federal Ministry of Finance in terms of §87 para. 3 GG. It emerged from the Federal Banking Supervisory Office (BAKred), the Federal Supervisory Office for the Insurance Industry (BAV), and the Federal Securities Supervisory Office (BAWe). With this merger, the legislator intended to create a supervisory office that would match the needs of a more and more integrated financial market with those of integrated financial service providers. Hagemeister mentions especially the merger of Allianz AG and Dresdner Bank AG in 2001 as a trigger, as it was a first great step towards more integrated financial service firms ("Allfinanzdienstleister") in Germany.[95] Certainly, the British Financial Services Authority FSA was an archetype for the BaFin. Founded in 1998 through the Bank of England Act and further empowered through the Financial Services and Markets Act of 2000 (FSMA), the British FSA combined several financial supervisory authorities under one roof. Unlike its British counterpart, the BaFin was not established as a legal entity under private law but as an authority in terms of §87 para. 3 GG as described above. As a legal entity based on private law, the FSA – unlike the BaFin – is able to pay competitive salaries and thus attract highly motivated and qualified personnel.[96]

BaFin has two headquarters in Germany, one in Bonn and one in Frankfurt, where Bonn is responsible for banking and insurance supervision and Frankfurt handles all supervisory activities for securities and asset management in Germany. The organizational structure is comparable to the prior institutions. The BaFin is headed by a president and a vice-president; its three divisions (banking, insurance, securities and asset management) are managed by a director ("Erster Direktor"). Also, the BaFin has a governing board ("Verwaltungsrat"), which consists of 21 members (§7 FinDAG). The Ministry of Finance delegates four members, including the chair and his deputy, the Federal Ministries of Justice and of Economics and Technology delegate one member each. In addition, five members of the Bundestag, four representatives of the credit industry, five representatives of the

91 Cf. BaFin (2005), pp. 94-95, WpHG (2007).§38 No. 2.
92 Cf. BaFin (2005), p. 95.
93 Hereinafter: BaFin.
94 Cf. BGBl. (2002), p. 1310.
95 Cf. BT-Drucksache (14/7033), pp. 31-32, Hagemeister (2002), p. 1773.
96 Cf. Binder (2001), p. 2232, Hagemeister (2002), p. 1775.

insurance industry, and one representative of the investment industry are part of the governing board (§7 para. 3 lit. a-g FinDAG). The German Central Bank may attend meetings even though their representative does not have a voting right.[97] The BaFin and its about 1,700 employees are wholly financed through fees and cost allocation paid by the governed firms.[98]

II.A.3 Excursus US Laws

The US financial market is probably the most important financial market in the world. With its leading position, US financial market regulations have a long history and world-wide impact. Long before Germany established dedicated insider and directors' dealings regulations, the US legislator had clear rules governed by the Securities Exchange Commission (SEC). This comparatively long tradition of dedicated insider dealings regulations certainly fostered early research on directors' dealings. Therefore, I will briefly introduce these regulations and present in short on of the most prominent cases of insider dealing in the US.

II.A.3.1 US Insider Regulations

The financial market in the United States has experienced strong regulation since the Wall Street Crash on October 24, 1929. Major reforms of American financial regulation followed in 1933 with the Securities Act and in 1934 with the Securities Exchange Act, which were both aiming to stabilize the market and protect investors against fraud.

The objective of the Securities Act was to increase the information flow to investors and enhance transparency throughout the market. The preamble of the act reads:

> "AN ACT to provide full and fair disclosure of the character securities sold in interstate and foreign commerce and through the mails, and to prevent frauds in the sale thereof, and for other purposes.".

Section 17 of the Securities Act prohibits fraudulent actions concerning the sale of financial instruments. SA Sec. 17 (a) states that it is unlawful "...to employ any device, scheme, or artifice to defraud, or to obtain money or property by means of any untrue statement of a material fact". The more prominent parts of U.S. insider regulation followed in the Securities Exchange Act of 1934. As the title implies, its main objective focused on the security exchanges. Here, it aimed to "prevent inequitable and unfair practices".[100]

Section 10 of the Securities Exchange Act promulgates the anti-fraud provisions. In here, rule 10b-5 is presumably the most cited as it prohibits – like Sec. 17 of the SA 1933 – the use of any fraudulent device, the dissemination of misleading and the reservation of material information, or engaging in any other fraudulent

97 Cf. BaFin (2006), pp. 221-225.
98 Cf. Ibid., p. 212., BT-Drucksache (14/7033), pp. 2,9.
99 Cf. SA (1933).Preamble.
100 Cf. SEA (1934).Preamble.

action. Hence, this rule serves to protect investors against defraud when purchasing or selling shares or other financial instruments.
The main three elements of the U.S. insider regulations are the persons governed by these rules, i.e. insiders, the definition of "material information", and the abstain-or-disclose rule.

II.A.3.2 Insiders under US Regulations

Insiders in the U.S. can be divided into two main groups.[101] The first group consists of persons with continuous access to material, non-public information. These are persons in managing positions and with fiduciary responsibilities towards the firm and its shareholders. Directors, officers, and major shareholders belong to this group of insiders. By virtue of their position they are not allowed to purchase or sell shares of the firm on the basis of non-public information for their own benefit without disclosing this information.[102] Furthermore, persons with a close relationship (e.g. spouse or husband, children) to these insiders may also be classified as insiders. In addition, employees can also be treated as insiders when they have access to material information.[103] The second group is made up of temporary insiders, i.e. persons with temporary access to material, non-public information. A large number of external service suppliers may be classified as temporary insiders, for example accounting firms, lawyers, and investment banks. It is necessary to employ an "access test" when defining insiders, i.e. testing who has access to material information. Hence, the list of potential insiders can be much longer.[104]

II.A.3.2.1 Material Information

Defining material information is not easy, especially as most information evolves into the status of materiality. Therefore, responsible personnel must watch the organization where such information may be generated. Lorie defines information in this context as "anything that changes the investor's subjective probability distribution with respect to future market prices or return.". Consequently, materiality is present when an investor would include the information in his investment decision process. From a market perspective, information is material when it can have a significant impact on the firm's share price. Examples include financial statements and forecasts, information on the firm's prospective (important contracts or mandates, Chapter 11 filings), and many others; in principle anything that can have an impact on the company's operations.[106] Negotiations on mergers or acquisitions are strictly confidential in most cases but they involve a variety of persons. Hence, it seems crucial to analyze merger talks and their encompass-

101 Cf. Greene (2005), pp. 10-11.
102 Cf. Bromberg (1970), p. 1142.
103 Cf. Anonymous (1966), p. 470.
104 Cf. Bromberg (1970), p. 1143.
105 Lorie (1980), p. 820.
106 Cf. Bromberg (1970), p. 1151.

ing actions to determine "the importance of the transaction to the issuer".[107] The seminal insider case Texas Gulf Sulphur which will be presented later gives an example of when information is material. The chemical analysis of a drilling probe showed high concentrations of copper ore. Further probe drillings showed similar results, giving the firm access to a 25 million tons copper ore mine. The results of the probe drilling were kept secret for several months while involved employees bought stocks and options. This information was considered material during the later lawsuits.[108]

II.A.3.2.2 Abstain or Disclose Rule

One of the most prominent rules in US insider trading regulations is the so-called "abstain or disclose" rule. The general idea is that insiders may only trade in their company's stock or related derivatives if they either trade solely on public, non-private information or, if they intend to trade on material inside information that is unknown to the public, disclose this information before trading or refrain from trading. Certainly, in most cases an insider cannot disclose material inside information and thus he has to refrain from trading.[109]

The rule itself evolved over several different cases from 1960 on, with its origin in re Cady, Roberts & Co. In this case, a person serving as a director passed on the information of a dividend reduction to his own brokerage firm, which sold shares of the respective company. The SEC demanded that an insider who is trading securities based on material information must disclose this information to his counterparty. In this case, the intention was twofold. First, the legislator wanted to reduce the threat of unfair to trades based on information asymmetries and second, the legislator wanted to prevent the use of corporate material information for personal benefit.[110] Of course, although it is impossible to achieve absolute information parity, the SEC tried to maintain market integrity with its fairness approach.[111] Second, the SEC's argument that corporate material information cannot be used for personal benefit shows that such information is regarded as business property under rule 10b-5. Using such material information for one's own benefit would be considered as an agency cost in the principal-agent context.[112] The frequently cited insider dealing case of Texas Gulf Sulphur, which was often referred to as seminal for the "abstain or disclose" rule, finally lead to the birth of the rule in 1964.

107 Ferrara and Crespi (1988), p. 330.
108 Cf. Greene (2005), p. 26.
109 Cf. Brudney (1979), p. 322.
110 Cf. Ickler, Schultz and Yates (1982), p. 133.
111 Cf. Scott (1980), p. 806.
112 Cf. Jensen and Meckling (1976), p. 308, Scott (1980), p. 814.

II.A.3.3 SEC v. Texas Gulf Sulphur Co.

One of the most prominent insider cases in the United States is certainly "SEC v. Texas Gulf Sulphur Co.".[113] In November 1963, Texas Gulf Sulphur (TSG) started drilling in Ontario during an exploration effort. Shortly after samples were taken, their analysis showed high amounts of copper and zinc in the ground. The results of the analysis were kept confidential. Only directly involved TSG employees knew about the results.[114] Following the probe drilling, TSG acquired the exploration rights of the surrounding land and in March 1964, the company started drilling. One employee bought shares and calls on TSG before March 1964 and recommended stock purchases. On April 11, 1964, newspapers published articles on major resource discoveries by TSG, which were played down by the company.[115] One day later, another involved employee bought the firm's shares, and on April 16, the secretary of an informed employee bought shares when the market opened. Shortly after, at 10 a.m., TSG announced the discovery of a 25 million tons copper ore mine in a press conference.[116] Overall, several insiders and persons with hints from insiders bought shares or options between the discovery in November and the public announcement the following April. During this timeframe, the TSG share price fluctuated between $18 and $25. After the announcement in April, the TSG share price rose to over $58 on April 30, 1964..

After these transactions had become public, the Securities and Exchange Commission (SEC) filed complaints. The employees and TSG were charged for purchasing shares or options on the basis of material information, thus violating rule 10b-5. Furthermore, they were charged for tipping others and disseminating misleading information when they played down the discovery of a copper ore mine. During the following lawsuit, the Second Circuit Court of Appeals held the opinion that an insider must reveal material information to the public before trading the firm's stock. Otherwise the insider must abstain from trading. Based on this, the so-called "Disclose or Abstain" rule was formed. The SEC wanted to boost market transparency and efficiency with its strict prosecution in the TSG case.[118] Certainly, the same principle applied to those who gave hints to others. Hence, those persons must have had either not given hints at all or disclose the material

113 Cf. Securities and Exchange Commission, Plaintiff-Appellant, v. Texas Gulf Sulphur Co., a Texas Corporation, Charles F. Fogarty, Richard D. Mollison, Walter Holyk, Kenneth H. Darke, Francis G. Coates, Claude O. Stephens, John A. Murray, Earl L. Huntington, and Harold B. Kline, Defendants-Appellees. Securities and Exchange Commission, Plaintiff-Appellee, v. David M. Crawford and Richard H. Clayton, Defendants-Appellants (1968).

114 Cf. Bainbridge (1999), p. 42.

115 Cf. Reiling and Camargo (2004), p. 1.

116 Cf. Anonymous (1969), p. 939, Bainbridge (1999), p. 43, Reiling and Camargo (2004), p. 4.

117 Cf. Bainbridge (1999), p. 43, Reiling and Camargo (2004), p. 4.

118 Cf. Anonymous (1969), pp. 940-941, Bainbridge (1999), p. 45.

information to the public. In contrast, tippees are only liable if they were aware that the informant was breaching his duty by passing on material information.[119] The courts also argued that material information must be disseminated in a way that it is generally available to the public. Of course, the time between publication and the moment when trading is no longer illegal has shortened since Texas Gulf Sulphur. Today, such information is available all over the world within minutes after disclosure while in 1964; information certainly took more time to spread among market participants.[120]

Texas Gulf Sulphur represents one of the most prominent cases in US insider dealing legislation and was seminal for further development of US securities legislation and its associated case law.

II.B Theoretical Foundations

After describing the important German and European legal framework in which this work is embedded, and after a roundup of equivalent US rules, this chapter now sets out to present the theoretical and economic framework of insiders' and directors' dealings.

II.B.1 Market Efficiency

The legal introduction already showed the essential role of information in financial markets. Naturally, this is true for any market setting. The general idea of a market is to establish a place where subjects can trade all kinds of goods and services. In principle, prices are determined by supply and demand. The price is then set at the point where supply and demand meets, and thus the market is cleared. Financial markets are not different. Changes in demand and supply can have a many different reasons. Varying beliefs in future development of firms or rather their securities can influence supply and demand of financial instruments. Also, information asymmetries have an impact on supply and demand. Of course, one needs to distinguish between general information on overall economic development and specific inside information. Thus, financial instruments are not only priced in accordance with firm-specific news but also in accordance with systematic economical information.[121] From a regulatory perspective, equal knowledge among all market participants is desirable for an efficient and frictionless market. Legislators all over the world try to pursue this goal through supervision and appropriate regulations. Efficient markets react quickly to new information and incorporate them into the prices of financial instruments. Hayek already addressed the major problem of an efficient market in 1945: "The peculiar character of the problem of a rational economic order is determined precisely by the fact that the knowledge of the circumstances of which we must make use never exists in concentrated or integrated form, but solely as the dispersed bits of incomplete and

119 Cf. Greene (2005), p. 19.

120 Cf. Bainbridge (1999), pp. 84-85.

121 Cf. Chen, Roll and Ross (1986), p. 402.

frequently contradictory knowledge which all the separate individuals possess.”. Thus, regulators are keen to ensure a fast flow of information to the market participants. Also, they have a great interest in monitoring the use and dissemination of information as it plays a major role in market manipulation and insider trading. Following this quick overview, I will proceed with an introduction to the Efficient Market Hypothesis (EMH)

II.B.1.1 Efficient Market Hypothesis

In an efficient capital market, prices react quickly to new information and level off at the appropriate price. Thus, it is assumed that current prices reflect all available information of a financial instrument if the efficient market hypothesis is valid.[123] Prices always reflect the correct value for a financial instrument, hence neither undervaluation nor overvaluation exist on efficient markets. Based on this assumption, market participants cannot systematically achieve returns that are above average if they use publicly available information. Also, information is available for free in an efficient market and there are no transaction costs.[124] Certainly, real financial markets cannot be as perfect as this model. Fama considers these conditions as sufficient but not necessary. He claims that transactions still take place when costs occur if all information is processed by the market participants.[125] The following figure illustrates an efficient market response when new information arrives.

Figure 2: Market response to new information[126]

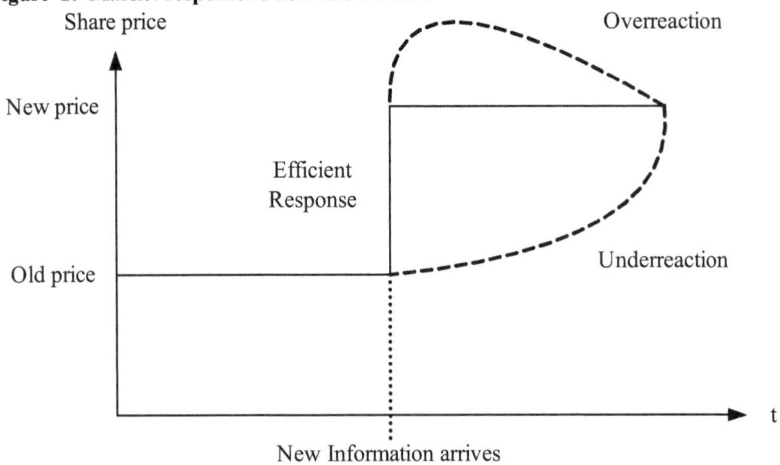

122 Hayek (1945), p. 519.
123 Cf. Fama, Fisher, Jensen and Roll (1969), p. 20.
124 Cf. Fama (1970), p. 387.
125 Ibid., pp. 387-388.
126 Source: Ross, Westerfield and Jaffe (2002), p. 344.

Figure 2 assumes positive information as the price rises. Clearly, an efficient response should yield an immediate correction of the stock to an appropriate level. An overreaction occurs when market participants react to new information with overestimation. The stock price then reverses to the appropriate level after a certain time. In contrast, if market participants underestimate or do not notice new information, the stock price may move to the new level very slowly.

The efficient market hypothesis (EMH) can be broken down into three forms: weak, semi-strong and strong EMH. First, the weak-form EMH assumes that a market is weak-form efficient when all historical information is incorporated into the current price of a financial instrument. Thus, it is not possible to earn above-average returns through historical analysis since the current stock price is the most appropriate forecast of the future stock price. Naturally, this assumption requires that stock prices are independent.[127] Although perfect independence is very unlikely, stock prices may be assumed to be independent as long as dependence in serial stock returns is minimal.[128] Based on these assumptions, the path of prices in the weak-form EMH can be modeled as a random walk.

Equation 1: Random Walk

$$P_t = P_{t-1} + E(R) + \varepsilon$$

In equation II-1, P_t represents the price of a security on day t as a function of its price one period before t plus the expected return R and a disturbance term ε, which can be interpreted as unknown information.[129] Thus, each return is a random variable with an independent distribution. Louis Bachelier was the first academic to consider stock returns as an independent process.[130] Certainly, this does not imply that the price building process itself is random. Stock prices are still based on the rational behavior of the market participants.

Testing for the weak-form EMH is rather simple. According to the weak-form EMH, market participants cannot achieve above-average returns with the analysis of past returns. Thus, applying trading rules for when to purchase or sell a financial instrument is not very helpful. Based on these assumptions, several authors investigated the profitability of such trading rules. The results of these studies vary, even though most findings show no profits if trading costs are considered. After carrying out several studies, Alexander (1964) advises "any reader who is interested only in practical results, and who is not a floor trader and so must not pay commissions, to turn to other sources for advice on how to beat buy and hold".[131] Other authors arrive at the same conclusion in their studies. They support the random walk model as a sufficient description of the price movements. Also,

127 Cf. Fama (1970), p. 386.
128 Cf. Fama (1965), p. 35.
129 Ross, Westerfield and Jaffe (2002), p. 344.
130 Cf. Bachelier (1900), pp. 31-32.
131 Alexander (1964), p. 33.

mechanical trading rules do not beat simple buy-and-hold strategies after accounting for transaction costs.[132] The second possibility to test for weak-form EMH is to test for statistical independence. This is already implied in the assumptions for the weak-form EMH, which state that securities' return series are independent.[133] Several tests can be used the weak form EMH. The first is a runs test, which tests for statistical independence by analyzing changes in sign.[134] The second option is to test return series for autocorrelation. A test for serial correlation tests whether returns are either independent or correlated over a specified time window. Fama uses this test in his work and only finds "extremely slight or completely non-existent[135] serial correlation"[136]

The second form is the semi-strong-form EMH. Like the weak-form EMH, it is assumed that past information is known and incorporated in the stock price. In addition, the semi-strong-form EMH says that stock prices reflect all publicly available information, too. Thus, any information in the market, for example dividend or earnings announcements and other information concerning the firm but also general economic and political information with impact on the firm and therefore on its value, are quickly priced in.[137] Testing for the semi-strong form of the EMH is by far more complex than for the weak-form EMH. As stock prices do not only reflect past stock prices but also current public information, testing must take this fact into account. The method at hand is the event study methodology, which tries to analyze the impact of new information on a firm's stock price. For this purpose, one forecasts stock returns and compares them with the actual returns during the time period in question. The semi-strong form of the EMH cannot be tested with one single test; several tests are conducted to get a more complete picture.[138] One major source of publicly available information is of course accounting data. One seminal study again comes from Fama, together with Fisher, Jensen and Roll. They investigated the effect of stock splits on stock prices. Their results, based on a large sample of stock from the New York Stock Exchange, show that information is absorbed quickly by the market and incorporated into the stock price very fast.[139] Once again, market participants should not be able to yield above-average returns over a longer time period since stock prices incorporate new information rapidly. Thus, actually realized returns should not differ very long from forecasted returns.[140]

The strong-form EMH includes both the weak and the semi-strong form of the EMH. In addition, the strong-form EMH includes private information. Thus, not

---

132 Cf. Fama and Blume (1966), p. 240.
133 Cf. Fama (1970), p. 396, Reilly and Brown (2003), p. 179.
134 Cf. Akhter and Misir (2005), pp. 41-42, Fama (1965), p. 80.
135 Fama (1965), p. 74.
136 Cf. Fama (1970), pp. 393-394.
137 Cf. Ibid., p. 383.
138 Cf. Ibid., p. 404.
139 Cf. Fama, Fisher, Jensen and Roll (1969), p. 21.
140 Cf. Brown and Warner (1980), p. 208.

even insiders can profit from their proprietary knowledge since this information is already contained in the stock price.[141] Naturally, testing markets for the validity of the strong-form EMH is far more challenging than both previous forms. The four main groups with access to private information are directors, large shareholders such as mutual funds, professional traders, and financial analysts.[142] Thus, one major data source that is used to test the strong-form EMH is directors' dealings databases, documenting exactly when corporate insiders have traded stock. Another possibility is to analyze stock price behavior around the publication of analysts' recommendations. Since their recommendations can have a significant impact on stock prices, knowing a recommendation's content before it is published can be considered as inside information. Furthermore, all persons involved in security transactions, especially those with access to order books, can also use their private information to yield above-average returns. Thus, these groups of non-directors strive for collecting information and combine it with the information they already possess in order to yield higher returns.[143] However, research has found more support for the strong-form EMH than against it.[144] I will discuss in more detail research results concerning insiders' profits in the subsequent literature review.

II.B.1.2 Criticism on the Efficient Market Hypothesis

Of course, several authors also criticized the Efficient Market Hypothesis. A more general point for criticism is the loose definition of the framework. Since a tighter definition would lead to a more complex structure, the number of hypotheses would increase. Then, more tests of single hypotheses would be the result. Finally, drawing conclusions from a larger set of hypotheses would not put the EMH on a firmer basis.[145] In addition, there are studies with differing results. For example, Lo & MacKinlay (1988) tested the random walk hypothesis. Their study does not validate the random walk hypothesis for weekly data covering all weeks from 1962 to 1985.[146] Based on these findings, Fama suggests that nonsynchronous trading might induce the serial correlation in their results.[147] Another point for criticism comes particularly from financial analysts who focus on fundamental analysis. They have difficulties to accept the underlying assumptions. Since all the information they reveal with their analyses is already contained in the stock price, their work becomes almost worthless.[148] Finally, ever since the Efficient Market Hypothesis exists, some researchers have found results confirming it while many

141 Cf. Fama (1970), p. 383, Reilly and Brown (2003), p. 193.
142 Cf. Akhter and Misir (2005), p. 44.
143 Cf. Levmore (1984), p. 649.
144 Cf. Reilly and Brown (2003), p. 196.
145 Cf. Lo and MacKinlay (1999), p. 6.
146 Cf. Lo and MacKinlay (1988), p. 52.
147 Cf. Fama (1991), p. 1578.
148 Cf. Shostak (1997), p. 28.

others found arguments against its validity.[149] Certainly, the discussion will continue and find valid arguments on both sides.

II.B.2 Economic and Legal Perspectives on Insider Dealing

Both, the introduction to the legal framework on insider dealing regulation in the European Union as well as Germany and the presentation of the Efficient Market Hypothesis lay the foundation for the further discussion. This chapter gives an overview on economic and legal views of insider dealing. Over the last decades, two primary models of insider trading have emerged. The first model regards insider transactions as signals to the market. The second model views insider dealing from an asymmetric information perspective. The model assumes information asymmetries between corporate insiders trading in their firm's stock and other market participants. Over the last decades, legal scholars developed various theories about whether insider dealing should be prohibited or not. Thus, this chapter gives an essential input to the discussion of the empirical results of this work, namely whether directors' dealings and insider trading in the German market earn above-average returns and whether changes in insider dealing regulation may improve market integrity.

II.B.2.1 Inside Information and Insider Trading

The term inside information was already introduced during the discussion of the legal framework. In general, what differentiates public from inside information is the group which has access to the information. Thus, information that is freely available to the public (i.e. to all market participants) is considered public information. On the other hand, information that is not available to the public is considered inside information or, more precisely, private information. Some authors differentiate between inside and private. In their reasoning, private information can be seen as superior information, which was for example produced through intense research on a firm. In contrast, inside information is available solely to persons with direct access to firm-specific, non-public facts. Furthermore, inside information has to satisfy the concept of materiality. In this context, information is only considered material and thus inside information when a reasonable investor would use it in his investment decision.[150]

II.B.2.2 Insider Trading Models

Over the last decades, two major streams of models explaining insider dealing have been developed. One group of scholars explains their trading behavior with signaling models. Corporate insiders communicate private information via signals to the market and increase indirectly their welfare. The second group also has the underlying assumption of asymmetric information, even though insiders do not

---

149 Cf. Findlay and Williams (2000), p. 197.
150 Cf. Bainbridge (2001), p. 34.

signal their knowledge to market participants but rather exploit their privileged position and trade on inside information.

II.B.2.2.1 Signaling Equilibrium Models

Signaling models assume asymmetric information between corporate insiders and outside market participants. Even though the theory of signaling models is based upon information asymmetries, it does not assume that insiders capitalize their superior informational position directly. Signaling models rather assume that insiders will convey information to the market through their actions, which would then be considered as a signal. Indirectly, they will signal the true value of their firm to the market and bring prices to equilibrium.[151] Certainly, such a model can be applied to many different situations. In his seminal work, Akerlof (1970) uses the automobile market as a situation where information asymmetries exist.[152] Spence shows in his work on "Job Market Signaling" how applicants incur signaling costs through their education and how they try to maximize the difference between these costs and wages offered at the market.[153] His model describes a hiring cycle in which employers revise their beliefs and thus alter the offered wages; applicants in turn change their choices in signals (i.e. behavior). At the end of such a cycle, employers have gained new information, they can once again change their beliefs, and a new equilibrium is achieved.[154] Of course, such a model can be applied to financial markets as well. Higher information transfer should boost efficiency in markets. Even though, investors have to rely on the information that is disseminated by the firm or an insider. Hence, if an insider personally invests in his firm, an outside investor receives a signal on the firm's true value. Leland & Pyle (1977) use the example of an entrepreneur looking for funding for a project. Certainly, the entrepreneur has superior information on the project's quality and is interested in positive information about the project in order to increase the market value. Since investors cannot differentiate between the qualities of projects, entrepreneurs would benefit from potentially overvalued low-quality projects. However, if insiders invest in their projects themselves, this could be considered as a clear signal of true project quality.[155] John and Williams designed a signaling equilibrium model where insiders signal a firm's value by adjusting dividends. Firms are assumed to raise cash either via issuing new stock or retiring less stock from trading. Thus, current shareholders will experience dilution. Since insiders know the firm's true value, they will adjust the dividend, which in turn motivates outside investors to buy stock and similarly drive up the stock prices.[156] Their findings show that firms with more valuable inside information will

151 Cf. Leland and Pyle (1977), p. 372.
152 Cf. Akerlof (1970), pp. 490-491.
153 Cf. Spence (1973), p. 358.
154 Cf. Ibid. 360
155 Cf. Leland and Pyle (1977), p. 371.
156 Cf. John and Williams (1985), p. 1054.

increase their stock price to a new equilibrium and current shareholders are compensated for a dilution effect. This signaling equilibrium is achieved through the dividend announcement effect.[157] Also, with higher purchasing of insiders prior a dividend announcement, price effects become smaller.[158] Another interesting example of communicating private information exists among real estate investment trusts (REIT), since they can choose outside appraisers to value their real estate investments.[159] Thus, when insiders see their REIT as undervalued, they can ask for reappraisal. Damodaran & Liu (1993) found increased insider purchases before favorable revaluations.[160] Further examples for information asymmetries are initial public offerings. Investors have an informational disadvantage compared to the issuer. When an issuer does not try to maximize the capital inflow at the IPO but sees potential to raise further capital in secondary offerings, an outsider can see this as a signal for positive future prospects.[161]
Signaling equilibrium models see insiders' actions, especially their trading activity, as signals to the market. Insiders can therefore communicate directly with the market and reveal their superior information. They can certainly increase their personal wealth through their signaling activity.[162] Signal equilibrium models assume that they will choose the most cost-efficient way to signal their private information to outsiders.[163] Also, joint signals have a high impact. Thus, even if dividends increase, insider sales can trigger negative price effects. Therefore, insiders can directly influence the credibility of their signals.[164]

II.B.2.2.2 Asymmetric Information Models

Like in signaling models, asymmetric information models have the underlying assumption of information asymmetries between corporate insiders and the outside world. In contrast to signaling equilibrium models, where insiders signal their superior information to the market and indirectly increase their wealth, insiders in asymmetric information models use their superior knowledge directly. Even though the efficient market hypothesis suggests that insiders are unable to profit from their superior information, asymmetric information models find that insiders can increase their wealth when trading on private information.[165] Sometimes, information asymmetries are caused by the structure of the firm or project. For example, the entire venture capital industry is built on information asymmetry. Venture capital firms provide financing for entrepreneurs with often brand-new product or service ideas without any historical record. In these situations, entre-

157 Cf. Ibid., p. 1065.
158 Cf. Fuller (2003), pp. 403-404.
159 Cf. Damodaran and Liu (1993), p. 84.
160 Cf. Ibid., p. 115.
161 Cf. Garfinkel (1993), p. 80, Su (2004), p. 13.
162 Cf. John and Mishra (1990), p. 836.
163 Cf. Ambarish, John and Williams (1987), p. 338.
164 Cf. John and Lang (1991), p. 1385, John and Mishra (1990), p. 836.
165 Cf. Güth, Krahnen and Rieck (1997), p. 253.

preneurs have a significant informational edge. Two forms of informational asymmetry are described in this context. The first is the direct information asymmetry between an investor and an entrepreneur concerning the product. The second information asymmetry concerns the entrepreneur's actions, i.e. whether he really wants to succeed with his product or whether he is only interested in the investor's money.[166] Venture capitalists act as intermediaries since they have a special capability to identify and select successful entrepreneurs. Also, they pick firms with small information asymmetries.[167]

Certainly, information asymmetries between insiders and other market participants have been modeled in theory. When insiders engage in trading activities on financial markets, they have an imminent interest to trade incognito. Glosten & Milgrom (1985) conjecture that traders who are recognized as insiders will receive larger bid-ask spreads than uninformed traders. Dealers offer these less favorable spreads to compensate their expected losses when trading with informed investors.[168] Insiders seek to maximize their welfare in asymmetric information models by directly exploiting their private information. Thus, an insider will break up his trade into smaller portions for several reasons. First, as already mentioned, he will get more favorable bid-ask spreads if he trades anonymously and at small volumes.[169] Second, since insiders reveal parts of their private information to the market when trading, they are interested in a slow disclosure to maximize their profits with each transaction.[170] On the other hand, insiders do not necessarily get better prices by splitting their trades. If insiders are uncertain about future price movements, they can eliminate the risk of unfavorable price movements and maximize their profits by trading one large block instead of several small ones.[171]

II.B.2.2.3 Relevance of Insider Trading Models

The relevance of signaling and asymmetric information models to directors' dealings and insider dealing is clear. Insider dealing, which is regarded as illegal and prohibited in the context of this work, can be seen in the light of the asymmetric information models. To ensure market integrity and investors' confidence, it seems necessary that insiders who are in possession of material information either abstain from trading or disclose their information. Since in many cases disclosure is not possible without harming business, insiders must abstain.

Directors' dealings, which I regard as legal in the context of this work, are therefore rather interpreted in terms of signaling models than pure asymmetric information models, where insiders strive to exploit their inside information for personal benefit. In the context of directors' dealings, outside investors perceive disclosed

166 Cf. Amit, Brander and Zott (1998), p. 443.
167 Cf. Ibid., pp. 457-462.
168 Cf. Copeland and Galai (1983), pp. 1460-1468, Glosten and Milgrom (1985), p. 91.
169 Cf. Glosten and Milgrom (1985), p. 91.
170 Cf. Kyle (1985), p. 1326.
171 Cf. Easley and O'Hara (1987), p. 72.

insider transactions as a signal. Furthermore, insiders who have personally invested in their firm have a higher incentive to increase the firm value.[172]

II.B.2.3 Regulation of Insider Trading

Financial researchers have studied insider trading for many years. Even though they analyzed the impact of informed traders on financial markets, they lack a general economical and legal discussion of this topic. However, this discussion whether insider dealing is fair, useful or harmful to financial markets has a long tradition among legal scholars. Besides these more theoretical discussions, financial regulators also found their way to this topic. On the one hand, they tried hard to open their financial market to more and more investors. On the other hand, as part of their duty to safeguard the proper functioning of financial markets, they generally aimed to establish a framework of laws and regulations in order to protect market integrity, to guarantee a certain level of investor protection, and to limit information asymmetries. Thus, insider dealing is a major point of concern for regulators as well.

In his seminal article from 1966, Manne (1966) names three main questions concerning insider trading which are still unanswered. He asks: "Who gains and who loses from insider trading?", "What are the long-run consequences of disallowing insider trading?", and "Can insider trading be prevented, and at what financial and social cost?".

Financial markets are more and more accessible for private investors. Thus, financial regulators have to meet objectives that are often diverging when they establish a regulative framework for financial markets. In recent years, investor protection came to the fore and regulators tried hard to reduce insider dealing to minimize information asymmetries. Regulators often find that investor protection will increase when insiders are not allowed to trade. Thereby, long-term investors do not necessarily suffer when selling to or buying from insiders. First, since transactions on financial markets are carried out in anonymity, regular investors do not know their counterparty. Second, it is unlikely that they would not close a contract with an insider. Investors usually select their investments very carefully rather than trading on short-term price movements. In contrast, speculators often have a very short investment horizon and could therefore suffer from insider trading. When insiders sell on or purchase private information, which might trigger short-term price adjustments if it was disclosed, their counterparty could experience a loss. Thus, speculators may be directly affected.[174]

II.B.2.4 Regulation Shareholder and Insider Dealing

172 In this context, I focus on stock purchases and not on stock or option granted as part of management remuneration.

173 Manne (1966), p. 113.

174 Cf. Ibid.

Finally, financial regulators need to find an optimum that satisfies many diverse objectives. Shareholders and insiders are two main groups affected by insider dealing regulations. Thus, it is necessary to analyze possible effects of insider trading bans. The following two figures show the impact of insider trading bans when positive or negative shocks to the firm value occur.[175]

Figure II2 presents a situation where an event has a positive impact on a firm's value. When the event takes place, the company's stock is traded at a level that is marked "Old price". If regulators ban insider dealing completely, the share price will stay at the same level until information on the event is disclosed on the announcement date. This case is presented by the solid line marked "completely effective ban". When insider trading is restricted but only partially effective, some insiders will trade on their privileged information and the firm's stock price will change before the announcement date. The final case assumes no insider dealing restrictions at all and is marked in the figure as "no ban". Here, insiders will exploit their informational edge and the share price will adjust to the new price level. Clearly, the cases where there is a limited ban or no ban at all signal the market that something important has happened to the firm's value, while in situations with a completely effective ban, no signal is transmitted to the market prior to the announcement.[176]

Figure 3: Positive Shock to Firm Value[177]

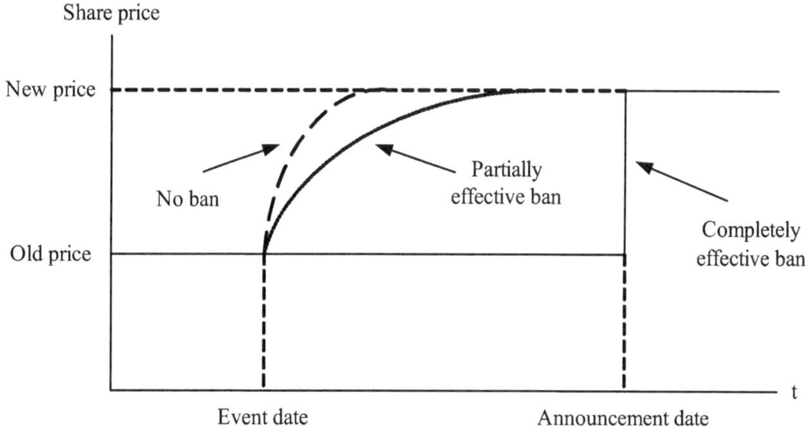

With a completely effective ban, outsiders cannot change their investment decisions. When they purchase shares between the event date and the announcement date, they are clearly in a better position since they can buy at the "old price" and participate in the price jump. In contrast, when outsiders sell their shares between

175 These graphics are adopted from Haddock and Macey (1986), p. 1469.

176 Cf. Ibid., p. 1452.

177 Source: Ibid., p. 1469.

the event date and the announcement date, they have a disadvantage as they sell at the lower price level. If an insider trading ban is only partially effective or inexistent, outside investors can sell at an increasing price. Of course, outsider buying in these two cases would occur at an increasing price.[178]
Figure 4 presents the opposite case, i.e. when a negative event takes place. Here, the picture is just inverted. Without an insider trading ban, prices will move quickly from the old price level to the new, lower price level when a negative event takes place. With a partially efficient ban, this process is slower but prices will converge towards the new price level before the announcement date. In cases where there is a completely effective ban, the share price will stay at the higher level until the information on the negative event is announced.[179]

Figure 4: Negative Shock to Firm Value[180]

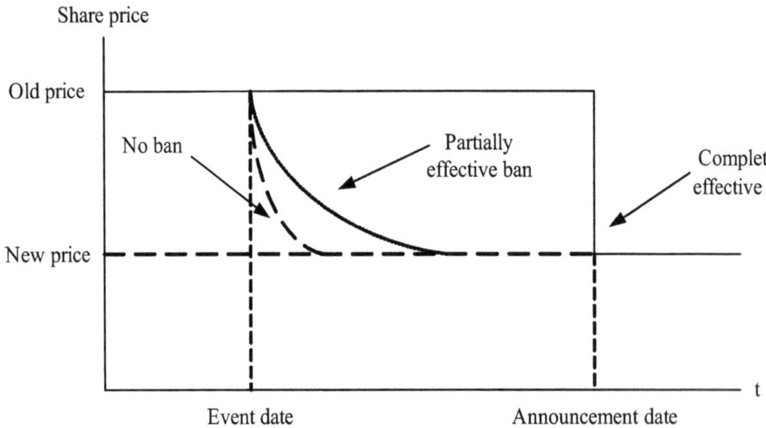

When outsiders purchase shares between the negative event and the announcement, they pay a higher price when there is a completely effective ban compared to both other cases. On the other hand, outside shareholders will suffer from insider trading when they sell between the event and the announcement because insider selling will lower prices.[181]
Certainly, these figures raise some questions. Even if stock prices reflect a firm's current value more accurately and faster when insider trading is allowed, some will still feel treated unfair. Shareholders are interested in low uncertainty concerning their investment. The more they know about the firm, the better they can judge and value their investment. To a certain part, they receive information from the firm directly, in form of annual reports, quarterly earnings announcements or

178 Cf. Ibid., p. 1452, Levmore (1982), p. 125.
179 Cf. Haddock and Macey (1986), p. 1453.
180 Source: Ibid., p. 1469.
181 Cf. Macey (1991), p. 28.

any other sort of information disseminated by the firm. On the other hand, they can conduct research on their own or receive research information from financial analysts, media reports and similar sources. Unfortunately, information generated through private research is in most cases costly. Thus, investors can lower their costs when a firm discloses more information. Of course, many events are crucial for a firm and might harm the business if they were disclosed too early. Hence, outside investors have to watch for other signals from a firm. One such signal can be insider trading; firms can use it as another way to communicate with shareholders and increase the amount of information included in share prices.[182]

But then, insider trading seems unfair with respect to information asymmetries.[183] Even if outside investors benefit on some occasions when trading with insiders, opponents of insider trading demand equal informational levels for all market participants. However, this argument is quite shortsighted. It is very unlikely that absolute informational equality will ever exist among market participants, even if insider trading was completely banned. Traders will always differ in their personal level of knowledge.[184] Furthermore, if the use of private information is constrained, everyone will experience disadvantages since the stock price is set less efficiently. Informed traders will push the share price either up or down and prevent the price from deviating too far from the equilibrium. Therefore, outside investors benefit from accurate prices. Also, their information costs decrease when private information is already contained in the share price.[185] The more insiders trade, the faster their knowledge is conveyed to the market and the faster prices will move. Thus, their potential benefit is limited.[186]

Certainly, this discussion is always based on principles. However, it is difficult to argue that a demand for informational equality in financial markets implies informational equality in all other areas.[187] Furthermore, financial regulators do not necessarily want to eliminate all information asymmetries; they rather try to protect outside investors. Even if outside investors increase their knowledge with intense research, they may not achieve the same level of knowledge as insiders. For this reason, it is considered unfair when insiders exploit their superior knowledge.[188]

Another line of argument regards insider information as a business property, or more precisely as part of a firm's intellectual capital. Of course, it also relates to

---

182 Cf. Carlton and Fischel (1983), p. 868.

183 Defining fair and unfair in the light of insider trading is very difficult. Many different aspects and views come into play during the discussion and they result in very vague definitions for what is fair and what is not. In general, it is inherently regarded as unfair if insiders exploit their superior informational position, since in turn it is regarded as "fair" not to harm others. Cf. Bainbridge (2001), p. 71, Easterbrook (1981), p. 324.

184 Cf. Macey (1991), p. 28.

185 Cf. Easterbrook (1981), pp. 329-330.

186 Cf. Manove (1989), p. 828.

187 Cf. Boyle (1992), p. 1496.

188 Cf. Schoen (1999), pp. 246-247.

previous fairness arguments in such a way that inside information can also be regarded as a public good, and thus it must be disclosed to the public before trading on it.[189] When inside information is regarded as intellectual property of a firm, managers would use valuable corporate resources for their own benefit. Certainly, it is questionable whether the material information loses value when insiders trade on it. However, when property rights are regarded as inside information, a conflict arises from the legal obligation to disclose material information as soon as possible.[190] Also, firms should clearly regulate who holds the rights on such inside information. When firms transfer the property rights to inside information to their employees, insiders can no longer exploit firm property. Nevertheless, care must be taken since insider trading may also serve as a signaling instrument and thus material information may be disclosed unintentionally.[191]

II.B.2.5 Harms and Benefits from Insider Trading

Arguments for and against insider regulation are manifold. Beyond the points that were presented above, the following discussion shows other potential benefits and threats of insider dealing.

From a company perspective, it can be cost-efficient to allow insiders to trade on material information. When property rights are assigned to inside information, firms can offer these rights as part of a compensation package to managers. The intention behind this approach is to lower the fixed salary of insiders and to give them a high incentive to increase the firm value. Of course, the compensation of managers already includes stock options and performance based bonuses in most cases. However, they are related to short-term achievements and rarely to true innovations. When insider trading is allowed, managers can participate directly when they create values that were not defined previously.[192] Also, insiders and firms can save costs because they do not have to negotiate on performance bonuses. With insider trading, managers can in part negotiate their salary themselves.[193]

This potential benefit in turn faces strong arguments opposing insider trading. When insider trading is allowed, managers can of course not only purchase shares on "good news" but also sell shares on "bad news"; thus, a moral hazard is created and insiders can either prevent incurring a personal loss by selling shares or even yield a positive return when selling shares short. Also, insiders can exclude parts of their compensation when selling short their negotiated stock compensation.[194] As a consequence, managers will take on greater risks when insider trading is allowed since they can increase their personal welfare while only the firm's risk increases. As insiders are a special group of shareholders, they can either increase

189 Cf. Krawiec (2001), p. 466.
190 Cf. Ibid., pp. 456-457.
191 Cf. Carlton and Fischel (1983), pp. 878-879.
192 Cf. Manne (1966), pp. 117-118.
193 Cf. Posner (2003), p. 433.
194 Cf. Carlton and Fischel (1983), pp. 870-871.

or decrease their personal investment in the firm's stock before the outcome of a risky project is made public. Easterbrook (1981) calls this a "perverse incentive" and assumes that this is not in the best interest of shareholders.[195] Macey (1991) points out that outside investors can diversify their portfolios and thus reduce the impact of such "perverse incentives". Therefore, when insider trading is not allowed, managers may opt for a project with lower risk and lower expected value than outside investors would.[196]

Haft contributes another interesting opinion. He points out the effects of insider trading on a firm's organizational efficiency. Material information is usually generated within the firm and passes through several hierarchical levels. Once insider trading is allowed, employees who receive this information as part of their work will delay the transmission until they exploited the information for their own benefit.[197] As a result, the efficiency within the organization will decrease and the decision-making process will be prolonged and potentially influenced in favor of personal welfare.[198]

195 Cf. Easterbrook (1981), p. 332.
196 Cf. Macey (1991), p. 33.
197 Cf. Haft (1982), p. 1055.
198 Ibid., p. 1071.

III. Related Literature

Empirical studies on directors' dealings and insider trading in the United States date back much further than studies on this subject in Germany. One major reason for this is certainly that the SEC has already demanded the filing of directors' dealings for a very long time while records for Germany have only been filed since July 2002. Hence, the database for the US securities market is significantly larger. Also, concerning illegal insider transaction, US supervisors seem to be better equipped than their German counterparts and thus simply have more manpower to monitor stock trading and to identify fraudulent activities.

III.A International Literature

This subchapter will start out with a short overview on two very prominent pieces of on illegal insider transactions in the US followed by a brief discussion of the most important studies on US directors' dealings.

III.A.1 Studies by Meulbroek and Cornell

Lisa Meulbroek published her study in the Journal of Finance in December 1992. She analyzed a sample of illegal insider transactions based on civil and administrative cases from 1980-1989. The study includes non-public material from the SEC. Since most cases (about 70%) are settled and not brought to court, a substantial part of information on insider cases is freely available.[199] All in all, the study sample covers 320 of 464 available cases and relates to 218 different firms. Most of these cases are related to M&A situations.[200] Statistics show that the median profit is $24,673 and the median avoided loss is $23,575. Furthermore, the average penalty resulting from these cases is $19,349 with a maximum of $5,100,000.[201] The empirical analysis reveals an average abnormal return of 3.06% when insiders trade and 18.50% on the day the inside information becomes public. For takeover-related insider cases, Meulbroek shows an average abnormal return on the announcement day of 17.46% and 2.55% on trading days. Cases of bankruptcy show a sharp price drop of -40.96% on average with average abnormal returns of -5.65% on insider trading days. In contrast, positive, non-merger-related news lead to an average abnormal return of 14.43%; here, average abnormal return on the insider trading days is comparably high at 9.47%.[202] One might conjecture that general "good" news can be more easily detected from outsiders through detailed research than merger-related news and thus lead to higher pre-publication abnormal returns. Insiders' transactions show a cumulative abnormal return of 32.2% over an average holding period of 13.7 days.[203] Insider trading cases in her sample

---

199 Cf. Meulbroek (1992), p. 1665.

200 Cf. Ibid., pp. 1666, 1669, 1670.

201 Cf. Ibid., p. 1992

202 Cf. Ibid., p. 1676.

203 Cf. Ibid., p. 1680. Meulbroek defines the time from the first insider trade to the day of publication as holding period.

all come from transactions that were identified as illegal by the SEC and one can therefore assume a selection bias in the sample. Therefore, she analyzes the SEC's selection method and finds that the commission focuses on the legal circumstances and not on specific price patterns when cases are prosecuted as insider dealing. Also, Meulbroek finds that 41% of all insider cases are triggered by public complaints, followed by 31% of complaints given by exchanges. Afterwards, 9% of all cases are triggered by SEC's internal investigations and another 9% by press stories. The remaining 10% come from different sources like brokers or issuers.[204] A further analysis based on these figures shows that her results are robust and not really affected by a selection bias.
Meulbroek concludes that securities that are affected by insider trading have more accurate prices since insider trading can move prices. Furthermore, she finds that most inside information is incorporated into the price through higher volumes during insider trading days. The study implicates that future regulation should consider the informational function of insider transactions. Also, research connecting insider transactions with the probability of mergers and acquisitions might be of future interest.[205]
In contrast to Meulbroek, Cronell and Sirri focused their study on a single insider case. The takeover of Campbell Taggart by Anheuser-Busch in 1982 was accompanied by insider trading. The authors used court records to identify individual share purchases by a small group of informed investors.[206] Overall, a group of 38 insiders purchased 265,600 shares in 124 transactions over a period of 23 days. Their detailed analysis shows the flow of information between different insiders and how the target's firm share volume rose to 121% of the previous average monthly volume during insider buying.[207] During the entire insider trading period, Campbell Taggart's stock price rose by more than 20%. The SEC closed the case when Paul Thayer, a director at Anheuser-Busch and main tipper, agreed to pay $550,000.[208] Furthermore, Cornell and Sirri were able to prove that insider trading in this particular case affected neither the bid-ask-spread nor the liquidity.[209]

III.A.2 First Studies on Directors' Dealings in the United States

Lorie & Niederhoffer (1968) were among the first to conduct an empirical analysis of insider dealing in the US market. Their dataset comes from the Official Summary of Stock Transactions issued by the SEC and covers insider transactions from 1950 to 1960. The authors selected a random sample of 105 firms with 3,973 purchases and 3,277 sales.[210] In their first analysis, they investigate whether insid-

204 Cf. Ibid., pp. 1680, 1682.
205 Cf.Ibid., pp. 1696, 1697.
206 Cf. Cornell and Sirri (Ibid.), p. 1031.
207 Cf. Ibid., pp. 1034, 1035.
208 Cf. Ibid., pp. 1033, 1053.
209 Cf. Ibid., pp. 1047, 1050-1051.
210 Cf. Lorie and Niederhoffer (1968), pp. 38, 45.

ers purchase or sell shares before news announcements. The authors concentrate on trading activities prior to large price movements[211]. Their findings suggest that insiders are able to foresee such large price movements. Chances of a large price increase after purchases are 2.5 to 1, while chances after sales are only 1.1 to 1. [212] The second part of their study investigates price movements after intensive insider trading activities. For this purpose, they use a random sample of 30 firms from a different dataset.[213] After calculating end-of-month prices for months with two or more insider purchases or sales, they found a significant relationship between insider trading and stock price movement when they compared transaction prices with end-of-month prices. Lorie and Niederhoffer found that firms with two or more insider purchases have a 60% probability to outperform the Dow Jones; for two or more sales, they found a 64% probability for these firms to generate returns below the index.[214] Their third and final part analyzes the consistency of price movements after insider transactions. Again, their sample comes from Rogoff's thesis. Here, they cannot identify insiders who consistently outperform the market. Lorie and Niederhoffer finally conclude that the SEC should disseminate insider trading data faster and regard a mimicking strategy as profitable for outsiders.[215]

Jaffe (1974) was the second author who tested the informational content of insider transactions recorded in the SEC's Official Summary. For his work on "Special Information and Insider Trading",[216] Jaffe used a random sample of 200 firms covering roughly 1,000 trading months from 1962 to 1968. Total sample size is 952, consisting of 466 purchases and 486 sales.[217] His results show a cumulative abnormal return of 0.6% after one month, 1.18% after two months and 1.36% after eight months. Jaffe analyzes large transactions, i.e. transactions with a volume of over $20,000, in a subsample and finds cumulative abnormal returns of 0.62%, 1.34%, and 1.84% after one, two and eight months respectively. In a second subsample, Jaffe analyzes intensive trading months. For this purpose, he defines any month in which either buys outnumber sales by three or vice versa as an intensive trading month. Cumulative abnormal returns for this subsample over one, two and eight months are 0.98%, 2.09%, and 5.07% respectively. Jaffe's rationale for intensive trading months is that material information should cause more insiders to trade.[218] In order to determine the informational content of the Official Summary, the author subsequently presents similar analyses after the publication. The first sample shows cumulative abnormal returns of 0.87%, 0.27% and 0.70% after

211 Ibid. define a price movement greater than 8% as large.

212 Cf. Ibid., pp. 46, 47.

213 The dataset for this study comes from D. Rogoff's thesis "The forecasting properties of insiders' transactions", dissertation at Michigan State University.

214 Cf. Lorie and Niederhoffer (1968), pp. 49, 51.

215 Cf. Ibid., pp. 52, 53.

216 Jaffe (1974).

217 Cf. Ibid., p. 412.

218 Cf. Ibid., pp. 420, 421.

one, two and eight months. Within the same time frames, Jaffe measures CARs of 0.98%, 1.34% and 1.84% respectively for the large transactions sample. For the intensive trading sample, Jaffe measures cumulative abnormal returns of 0.74%, 1.24% and 4.94%.[219]
Jaffe concludes that insiders in the intensive trading sample earn abnormal returns even after accounting for transaction costs, thus he regards this intensive trading as a violation of security laws. Also, his analyses show the informational content of Official Summary's records and regard this information valuable for trading rules.[220]
Finnerty's study on "Insiders' Activity and Inside Information"[221] analyses the relationship of insider trading and announcement of financial results. Using a multivariate analysis, Finnerty builds a prediction model for insider purchases and sales based on financial and accounting data. The study covers the year 1971 and data on insider transactions comes from the Official Summary together with financial data from Compustat. Finnerty analyzes six periods and allocates insider transactions in buyer or seller groups in each of these periods. Finnerty uses 32 variables from the Compustat database and condenses them into six factors using a principal component analysis, thereby explaining 67.4% of dataset variance.[222]
His model shows that purchases took place in smaller firms with large earnings and large dividends, and vice versa for the selling group. Furthermore, Finnerty's model predicts that purchases and sales are better in later periods of the year. Thus, insiders have more certainty on their firm's performance at the end of the year than at the beginning.[223]
Finnerty's second article on "Insiders and Market Efficiency" tests whether markets incorporate all public and private information.[224] The study covers the time from 1969 to 1972 and uses 9,602 purchases and 21,487 sales from the Official Summary. Overall, Finnerty constructs 36 monthly buy and sell portfolios. Finnerty uses the CAPM as the model of choice in his event study, which yields similar results to Jaffe's study. The empirical results show that securities bought by insiders performed significantly better than the market while securities sold by insiders performed worse than the market in months subsequent to the transaction.[225] During the first month, Finnerty finds abnormal returns of 3.68% for purchases and 0.90% for sales. After the transactions, the abnormal returns in the buy portfolio drop to 1.01% and to 0.45% in the sell portfolio. Afterwards, for up to eleven months after the transaction, monthly abnormal returns in the sell portfolio vary between 0.26% and 0.47%. Monthly abnormal returns in the

219 Cf. Ibid., p. 426.
220 Cf. Ibid., pp. 427, 428.
221 Finnerty (1976a).
222 Cf. Ibid., pp. 206, 209.
223 Cf. Ibid., p. 213.
224 Finnerty (1976b).
225 Cf. Ibid., pp. 1144, 1146.

buy portfolio vary between 0.85% and 0.16%. With his empirical study, Finnerty verifies previous authors' results and confirms insiders' ability to generate above average returns.[226]

III.A.3 Studies by Seyhun

Seyhun is one of the most prominent authors in the field of insider trading research. In 1986, he published his article "Insiders' Profits, Costs of Trading, and Market Efficiency".[227] The study aims to verify previous findings on profitable mimicking strategies by outsiders. Overall, data from 769 US firms is included, covering the period from 1975 to 1981. Within this time span, 59,148 transactions by insiders (directors' dealings) were recorded. The study analyzes an event window of 199 days before until 300 days after the event.[228] Purchases show a cumulative abnormal return of -1.4% from 100 days before the event to the event day, -0.7% of which are accumulated during the last 20 days. For sales, he records 2.5% and 1.7% respectively over the same periods. Following the event, purchase and sale abnormal returns change signs. From days 1 to 20, purchases gain a CAR of 1.1% on average while sales' CAR drops to -0.9%. Over 50 and 100 days after the event purchase, CARs climb to 1.9% and 3.0%; sales CARs continue their negative trend with -1.5% and 1.7%. For a period of 300 days after the event, Seyhun measures a cumulative abnormal return of 4.3% for purchases and -2.2% for sales. Also, Seyhun analyzes the insiders' profits in relation to firm size and finds a negative relationship. Insiders trading in firms below $25 million have an average cumulative abnormal return of 4.5% while those trading in firms over $1 billion can bring in only a cumulative abnormal return of 0.9% over 50 days following the event. Further, Seyhun investigates several variables to find determinants for insiders' profits.[229]

Another important finding is certainly that outsiders investing in larger firms have a lower probability to engage in a transaction with an insider than in smaller firms.[230] He also concludes that directors and officer-directors with a close involvement in operations possess more valuable information than officers. Furthermore, insiders trading in smaller firms have higher profits. Finally, Seyhun finds in this study that insiders know when to purchase or sell their firm's stock; in addition, Seyhun cannot confirm the profitability of mimicking strategies by outsiders after transaction costs, which in turn confirms the efficient market hypothesis.[231]

Roughly two years later, Seyhun published a study on aggregate insider trading.[232] This study uses the same dataset as the previous one; however, the emphasis in

---

226 Cf. Ibid., pp. 1147, 1148.
227 Seyhun (1986).
228 Cf. Ibid., pp. 193-194.
229 Cf. Ibid., pp. 198, 200, 206.
230 Cf. Ibid., p. 201.
231 Cf. Ibid., pp. 210, 211.
232 Seyhun (1988).

this study is on the information content of aggregate insider trading as a response to firm- and economy-specific factors influencing stock prices.[233]
Seyhun uses monthly insider purchases and sales to construct a proxy for aggregate insider trading and builds firm-size portfolios. For his empirical study, he hypothesizes that aggregate insider trading based on firm-specific information is not related to excess market returns, while he expects a positive relationship when aggregate insider trading is based on economy-specific factors.[234] Findings suggest that some insiders are able to foresee changes in economic factors, since aggregate insider trading occurs about two months prior to such unanticipated economical changes. Seyhun conjectures that insiders may use changes in their firm's cash-flow as an indicator. He also finds that insiders in smaller firms earn higher abnormal returns than in larger firms, which is in line with his previous study. Furthermore, insiders in larger firms can rely more on economic factors, which he attributes to higher diversification in larger firms.[235] He concludes that many insiders trade on firm-specific information, which is in fact economy-specific information. He regards aggregate insider trading as an indicator of overall economic activity.[236]
In a third study, Seyhun and Bradley investigate insider trading and bankruptcy filings.[237] They include 314 firms, which filed 324 petitions from 1975 to 1992. They emphasize that in contrast to Meulbroek, their dataset is from the official summary; hence, it contains legal insider transactions.[238] The empirical study deviates from the standard event study design in that the authors use the avoided loss by insiders who sold their shares before a bankruptcy filing. The study's results indicate that investors experience a capital loss of about 70% over two years before the bankruptcy filing.[239] Insiders are grouped according to their position, i.e. officers and top executives. Overall, they find insiders avoid significant losses and start selling stock up to five years before the filing. Finally, they question whether insiders would better protect shareholders' interests when they were not allowed to sell stock prior to bankruptcy filings.[240]

III.A.4 Study by Rozeff & Zaman

In 1988, Rozeff and Zaman published their study on "Market Efficiency and Insider Trading: New Evidence", confirming the existence of abnormal profit opportunities for outsiders mimicking insider transactions.[241] In their study, Rozeff and Zaman try to find explanations for the insider trading anomaly and assume a

233 Cf. Ibid., p. 1.
234 Cf. Ibid., p. 10.
235 Cf. Ibid., pp. 15, 16.
236 Cf. Ibid., pp. 22, 23.
237 Seyhun and Bradley (1997).
238 Cf. Ibid., p. 200.
239 Cf. Ibid., pp. 197,198.
240 Cf. Ibid., pp. 214, 215.
241 Cf. Rozeff and Zaman (1988).

mismeasurement of abnormal returns due to size and price-earnings effects.[242] The study covers a ten-year time span from 1973 to 1982 and includes all transactions, thus fulfilling an intensive trading criterion, i.e. at least three insiders purchase shares and no insider sold shares and vice versa. For this purpose, Rozeff and Zaman looked at two samples, one with transactions by outsiders and one with transactions by insiders. The former consists of 318 purchases and 322 sales while the latter consists of 365 purchases and 333 sales. The outsider sample is constructed by simulating previous insider transactions with a delay of two months.[243]

Instead of using a market portfolio as a reference like in other studies, Rozeff and Zaman construct control portfolios based on size and e/p-ratio. Abnormal returns are then measured with a market model. To test whether insider transactions are profitable over a longer time period, they use holding periods of 1, 3, 6 and 12 months.[244] For the outsider sample, their results show abnormal returns of 0.59% after one month, followed by 0.55%, 0.44% and 0.47% for longer holding periods. For the same holding periods, Rozeff and Zaman measure abnormal returns of 1.40%, 1.13%, 0.81% and 0.72% in the insider sample. Thus, insiders' profits diminish over time; however, they have a higher initial gain on their transactions. After adjusting the sample for size and e/p-effects, results for the outsider sample over the same holding periods change to -0.18%, 0.37%, 0.23% and 0.19%. Adjustments in the insider sample show a sharp drop in abnormal returns in the first month. Abnormal returns in this sample are then at 0.70%, 0.86%, 0.47% and 0.43%.[245]

Their results suggest that abnormal returns are largely dependent on size and e/p-effects. Rozeff and Zaman conclude insiders buy especially in small stocks and sell in large stocks. However, they cannot strongly support the general notion that insiders exploit material information and thus earn abnormal returns. After including transaction costs, abnormal returns should experience a significant drop close to zero.[246]

III.A.5 Studies on Directors' Dealings and Corporate Actions

Chan et al. (2003) analyze in their study the interaction of corporate share repurchases and directors' dealings. The authors analyze a set of 5,508 share repurchases in the US form 1980 to 1996 and significant long-term return drifts around repurchase announcement dates. In contrast to previous studies, they find no evidence that insiders exploit their informational advantage and trade for their benefit. Much more, their findings show the opposite of general expectations. BHARs are higher when insiders sell stock.[247] Lee (1997) analyzes relationship

242 Cf. Ibid., pp. 26, 27.
243 Cf. Ibid., pp. 28, 29.
244 Cf. Rozeff and Zaman (1998), p. 33.
245 Cf. Rozeff and Zaman (1988), p. 37.
246 Cf. Ibid., pp. 42, 43.
247 Cf. Chan, Ikenberry and Lee (2003), pp. 2, 15.

between the long-term performance of seasoned equity offerings and directors' dealings. He concludes that directors' dealings are in general a useful signal in terms of future development. However, he reminds that top executives may biased by high pre-issue returns or that directors are not able fully estimate the effects of an upcoming SEO. His findings show a general increase of insider sales before the issue, which is consistent with existing literature.[248]

III.B Studies on the German Market

Following international studies on directors' and insider dealing, this part presents recent studies on the German market. Since official records of directors' dealing started in Germany on 1 July 2002, all pieces of work cover only a short period of time compared to other international studies. The research is presented in chronological order.

III.B.1 The Study by Heidorn, Meyer, Pietrowiak

This was the first study conducted on the German market, even though it also covers Italy and the Netherlands.

For the Netherlands, they include 743 transactions in their sample after adjusting their original sample of 825 transactions. The sample covers the time from April 1999 to March 2004. 153 of these transactions are purchases and 587 are sales. The average transaction volume is 720,480 Euro with a median of 188,367, with 625,620 for purchases and 747,344 for sales respectively. For Italy, they include 2,850 transactions in their sample after adjusting the original sample of 3,448 transactions. The sample covers the time from January 2003 to March 2004. 2,067 of these transactions are purchases and 783 are sales. The average transaction volume is 109,560 Euro, with 45,859 for purchases and 277,504 for sales respectively. The median for the average transaction is 12,033 Euro. Their German sample consists of 1,382 transactions after adjusting the original sample of 2,704 transactions. The sample covers the time from July 2002 to March 2004. 731 of these transactions are purchases and 651 are sales. The average transaction volume is 371,553 Euro, with 206,197 for purchases and 557,231 for sales respectively. The median for the average transaction is 20,088 Euro.[249]

In their event study, they employ the market model to measure abnormal returns.[250] They also use a control-portfolio model to adjust for firm size effects. Statistical significance is tested with a Student-t-Test as a parametric and a Wilcoxon-Signed-Rank test as a non-parametric test.

Their results for German directors' dealings purchases show a cumulative abnormal return of -0.96% five days prior to the transaction followed by a cumulative abnormal return of 0.57, 1.65 and 3.79% after five, ten and 20 days. For two, three and six months after the transaction, they find CARs of 3.95, 4.36 and 9.30% for

248 Cf. Lee (1997), pp. 1463-1464.
249 Cf. Heidorn, Meyer and Pietrowiak (2004), p. 9.
250 Cf. Ibid., pp. 11-13.

purchases, which are all significant at the one percent level. For sales, they identify CARs of 1.35% five days before the event and -0.72, -1.75 and -2.99% after the transaction. Long-term CARs for two, three and six months after the transaction are -1.69, -0.35 and 15.30% respectively.[251]
For Italy, they measure a CAR of 0.39% five days prior to the event for purchases and 3.97% for sales. After purchases, they find CARs of 0.57, 1.09 and 2.32% after five, ten and 20 days respectively. For two, three and six months after the transaction, they find CARs of 5.02, 7.53 and 11.72% respectively. All post-event CARs are significant at the 1%-level while CARs before the event are not significant. Cumulative abnormal returns after sales reach -2.61, -3.20 and -5.08% after five, ten and 20 days. Long-term CARs for sales amount to -10.46, -10.45 and -15.15% after two, three and six months.[252]
For the Netherlands, they find a CAR of -1.89% five days prior to the event for purchases and 1.08% for sales. After purchases, they find CARs of 1.35, 1.66 and 2.76% after five, ten and 20 days. Both pre- and post-event CARs are highly significant at the one percent level for purchases. For two, three and six months after the transaction, they find CARs of 10.37, 8.33 and 21.73%. CARs after sales are 0.42, 0.5 and 0.91% after five, ten and 20 days respectively. Long-term CARs for sales build up to 0.36, 1.49 and 4.08% after two, three and six months. None of the post-event CARs are significant for the Dutch sample.[253]
With their empirical analysis, the authors show that insiders can earn abnormal returns in all three countries. Interestingly, Dutch directors' dealings show much higher cumulative abnormal returns on purchases compared to transactions in Germany. Heidorn, Meyer and Pietrowiak conclude that their results have a similar pattern to studies in the US and the Netherlands. Furthermore, they conjecture that outsiders can profit from a mimicking strategy especially for purchases. Sales are not so much caused by firm-specific events but rather by personal needs, such as diversification or liquidity needs.[254]

III.B.2 The Study by Rau

Together with Heidorn, Meyer and Pietrowiak, Rau was among the first to analyze directors' dealings in Germany. The study uses datasets from the BaFin and the Deutsche Gesellschaft für Ad-Hoc Publizität, a private financial news service.[255]
His sample covers the time from July 2002 until December 2003. The initial sample consists of 3,083 observations. After adjustments, his final sample compromises 2,507 transactions with 1,675 purchases and 1,229 sales. In his empirical analysis, Rau uses the market model as event study methodology with an estima-

251 Cf. Ibid., p. 16.
252 Cf. Ibid., p. 21.
253 Cf. Ibid., p. 25.
254 Cf. Ibid.
255 Since the DGAP must transmit all published directors' dealings to the BaFin, the DGAP sample is naturally a subset of the BaFin sample.

tion window of 230 days and an event window of 21 days centered on the transaction day.[256]
Abnormal returns on the event day are 0.60% for purchases, followed by a cumulative abnormal return over ten day of 0.96%. Sales have an abnormal return on the event day of 0.47% and a CAR over ten days of -2.56%. Long-term CARs show 3.05% for purchases after 120 days and -20.80% for sales.[257] Furthermore, Rau analyzes firm size effects. Here, his findings show a cumulative abnormal return of 28.3% after purchases over 120 days in the lowest quartile, followed by 0.6%, -5.5%, and finally -12.9% in the biggest quartile. Over the same time, sales show -52.3%, -31.6%, 15%, and -14.2% of cumulative abnormal returns.[258]
The empirical analysis also includes abnormal returns after public announcement of directors' dealings. Purchases show an AR of -0.21% on the publication day and accumulate over ten days to a CAR of 1.22%. Sales have an abnormal return of -0.49% on the event day and a ten day CAR of -3.03%.[259]
Rau showed with one of the first empirical studies on directors' dealings in Germany that insiders can earn abnormal returns and outside investors can use the publication of these transactions to mimic insiders' trading patterns.

III.B.3 The studies by Betzer and Theissen

Betzer & Theissen (2005) investigate directors' dealings in Germany with the intent not only to identify abnormal returns but also to analyze the potential impact of UK-like blackout periods for directors' dealings prior to corporate events.[260] Their expectation is to find that abnormal returns in Germany are higher than those documented for the UK and US markets. This idea is driven by differences in national accounting standards. In the UK and the US, accounting standards call for a high degree of transparency, which leads to a more equal distribution between insiders and outsiders. In contrast, they expect a higher degree of information asymmetry for German firms applying the national accounting standard "HGB". Thus, transactions initiated by directors of these companies should yield a higher abnormal return.[261]
In their study, they analyze a sample of 2,522 transactions during July 2002 and June 2004. 1,379 of these trades are purchases and 1,143 are sales. The average Euro volume of all trades is 725,817 Euro, 382,217 for purchases and 1,141,151 for sales. The medians are 40,000 for all transactions, 23,496 for purchases and 89,899 for sales respectively.[262] The authors also state the average size as the per-

256 Cf. Rau (2004), pp. 127, 138-139, 180.
257 Cf. Ibid., pp. 189,192.
258 Cf. Ibid., pp. 194-195.
259 Cf. Ibid., p. 204.
260 The blackout period in the UK is two months before final or interim earnings announcements and in the month preceding the announcements of quarterly earnings according to Betzer and Theissen (2005), p. 3.
261 Cf. Ibid., pp. 2-3.
262 Cf. Ibid., p. 28.

centage of share outstanding, thus giving an indication of possible impact. The average for all transactions is 0.82% of outstanding shares, with 0.46% for purchases and 1.24% for sales. The median for all transactions is 0.04% for outstanding shares, with 0.02% for purchases and 0.07% for sales. In their analysis, they also differentiate trades executed by the chair of the executive or the supervisory board, other executive or supervisory board members, including representatives from banks and employees, and other persons obliged to register their transactions.

For purchases, they find a cumulative abnormal return of 3.69% over an event window of -20 to +20 days around the transaction and 9.29% for trades equal to or above 0.1% of shares outstanding. CARs for 20 and ten days prior to events are 0.09% and -0.15% respectively. Ten and 20 days after the event, CARs amount to 2.18% and 3.60%. For large trades, the values are 3.28% and 1.93% before and 4.36% and 6.01% after the event.[263]

For sales, they measure CARs of 2.19% over an event window of -20 to +20 days around the transaction and 4.25% for trades equal to or above 0.1% of shares outstanding. Over a period of 20 and ten days before the sale, CARs are 5.73% and 4.57% respectively. Ten and 20 days afterwards, CARs fall to -1.99% and -3.54%. For large trades, values are 9.22% and 7.17% before the event and -3.37% and -4.97% afterwards.[264]

In addition, Betzer & Theissen (2005) perform a cross-sectional analysis.[265] They divide their analysis into ownership structure, position of insider, and blackout period. Results for management-controlled firms show that these trades earn CARs[266] of 4.34% on purchases and -2.05% on sales. For family-controlled firms, they find CARs of 3.82% on purchases and -5.29% on sales. Transactions in widely-held firms achieve CARs of 5.79% for purchases and -5.40% for sales. Industry- and other controlling shareholders achieve 1.30% and 1.37% on purchases respectively. On sales, both of these two groups achieve -0.57%. Their cross-sectional analysis of differences in insider positions shows CARs of 2.20% on purchases and -3.14% on sales for CEOs. Other executive board members earn higher CARs of 4.12% on purchases while sales drop to -2.59%. Their counterparts from the supervisory board earn CARs of 4.36% and 4.80% on purchases respectively. Bank representatives earn about five percent more, i.e. 9.45%.[267] CARs for sales are -12.3%, -1.84% and 5.18% for the chair, other members and bank representatives respectively.[268] For trades within the two months before earnings announcements, Betzer and Theissen find CARs of 5.26% and -4.85% for purchases and

263 Ibid., p. 30. consider trades incorporating shares equal to or above 0.1 percent of shares outstanding as large trades.

264 Cf. Ibid.

265 Cf. Ibid., p. 31.

266 Ibid. only document CARs covering days zero to 20 in their cross-sectional analysis.

267 Only ten observations are available for this group, hence this CAR may be skewed.

268 Cf. Betzer and Theissen (2005), p. 30.

sales respectively. Transactions outside this blackout period earn only 1.96% on purchases and -2.75% on sales.[269]

Betzer and Theissen conclude that a blackout period comparable to the UK regulations can be useful since their findings show higher abnormal returns for trades within a potential blackout period than at other times.[270]

III.B.4 The Study by Klinge, Seiffert, and Stehle

Klinge, Seifert, & Stehle (2005) include directors' dealings from 1 July 2002 until 30 June 2004 in their analysis. Apart from an event study that is similar to previous ones, the authors conduct a cross-sectional analysis with a "net trading intensity" measure following empirical studies in the US.[271]

Their initial sample consists of 4,273 observations. After adjustments, the final sample contains 2,938 transactions, with 1,434 purchases and 1,504 sales. Abnormal returns on the event day are 0.43% for purchases and 0.18% for sales. Cumulative abnormal returns covering the entire event window of 41 days sum up to 1.29% for purchases and 0.69% for sales. From 20 days until one day before the event, they measure CARs of -1.43% and 7.92% for purchases and sales respectively. While purchase CARs are only significant on the ten percent level, sale CARs are highly significant on the one percent level. Post-event CARs for five, 20 and 30 days are 1.10%, 2.29% and 2.90% after purchases and -0.70%, -7.41% and 9.71% after sales respectively. Long-term CARs for 60 and 100 days after the transaction amount to 5.26% and 7.59% for purchases and drop to -12.56% and -18.99% after sales.[272]

Following Lakonishok & Lee (2001) , they use net trading intensity as an important explanatory variable. In addition, they include historical market return (CDAX performance index) for six and twelve months, log of market value, market to book ratio, log of transaction volume in Euro, relative size of the transaction to total equity, and position of insider in the firm. As dependent variable, they use CARs around the event, i.e. [-1; +1] and [0; +5] days. Findings are anti-cyclical investments by insiders because negative short-term market movements precede purchases and vice versa. The authors measure this effect with a six-month market return prior to the event; also, net trading intensity is highly significant, with more impact on sales than purchases. Other variables such as firm size or the insider's position within the firm are significant, too.[273]

---

269 Cf. Ibid., p. 31. The period of two months corresponds to the blackout period set in the UK regime.

270 Cf. Ibid., p. 25.

271 Cf. Klinge, Seifert and Stehle (2005), pp. 5-6.

272 Ibid. seem to provide cumulative abnormal returns and not buy-and-hold returns for long-term performance.

273 Cf. Ibid., pp. 16-19.

Klinge, Seifert and Stehle find the German capital market has a semi-strong efficiency. Also, they attribute a high signaling character to insider purchases and sales, although the signal becomes less evident with larger transactions.[274]

III.B.5 The Study by Tebroke and Wollin

Tebroke & Wollin (2005) analyze in their study directors' dealings spanning from July 2002 to July 2003. Their sample is among the smallest and consists only of 847 transactions, thereof 612 purchases and 235 sales. They are to my knowledge the only authors for the German market to employ the BHAR methodology for long-term abnormal returns. They report findings for up to 100 days; purchases gain after 20 days 4.55%, after 60 days 9.12 %, and after 100 days 16.34%. All BHARs are highly significant. For sales, Tebroke and Wollin find over the same holding periods 2.42%, 0.92%, and 3.40%. All sales BHARs are insignificant. They conclude from their findings directors' dealings are not efficiently priced in and that outsiders can even with an assumed transaction cost of 2% achieve significant gains.[275]

III.B.6 The Study by Stotz

Stotz (2006) follows previous German authors by covering four main research questions in his article. First, he explores whether German directors can achieve an above average return and second he tries to find out whether outside investors can reach similar returns by mimicking insider trades. His third research question focuses on the point in time when insiders invest or divest. Finally, he takes a closer look on transaction costs.[276]

The empirical study uses a sample consisting of 979 transactions, with 787 purchases and 189 sales. The sample covers the time from 1 July 2002 until 7 July 2003. The sample is adjusted for offsetting transactions, multiple entries on one day and penny stocks. His methodology is in line with other authors; he uses a standard event-study approach with an estimation window of 250 days and an event window of 25 days before and after the transaction. Also, Stotz investigates effects after the disclosure of the transaction, thus measuring abnormal returns also for 25 days after the reporting day.[277]

His results show no direct price reaction after the transaction, although CARs rise constantly during the 25 days after purchases and peak at 2.73%. After including one percent transaction costs, he concludes that insiders can still earn an abnormal return of about 1.73%, which is significantly different from an expected zero percent abnormal return. CARs after sales have their trough at -2.85% after 25 days post transactions; hence, one can conjecture that insiders may prevent

274 Cf. Ibid., pp. 20-21.

275 Cf. Tebroke and Wollin (2005), pp. 40-42, 50-51.

276 Cf. Stotz (2006), pp. 450-451.

277 Cf. Ibid., p. 453.

losses.[278] For his third research question, he explores the first 25 days of the event window, i.e. the time before the event. Similar to authors investigating US stock markets, he finds evidence proving that directors in Germany sell securities after prices have risen and purchase securities after shares have fallen. CARs amount to 5.55% before sales and drop to -0.42% before purchases.[279]
Outsiders can only mimic insider transactions with a certain time lag, since directors do not have to file their transactions immediately in Germany. Stotz (2006) finds a median time span of five days between the actual transaction and the disclosure, i.e. the reporting of the transaction.[280] Results are comparable to those where the transaction date is considered as event. On average, outsiders can earn 2.81% after purchases excluding transaction cost; assuming one percent transaction cost, outsiders still earn 1.81% with a mimicking strategy. Outsiders who follow insiders when they sell stock can avoid losses of about -2.20% and thus about -1.20% after transaction costs.
For the final research question, large-volume trades are defined as trades with a volume of 25,000 Euro or more. In contrast to prior research, Stotz finds lower CARs for these large-volume trades. Purchases in this group show pre-event CARs of 0.69% and 2.34% after the transaction. After the reporting date, these trades earn CARs of 2.15% or 1.15% after transaction costs respectively. Still, sales accumulate higher negative CARs in large-volume trades. On the transaction day, sales drop to 3.45%, and to -2.89% after the reporting date.[281]
For firms with an equity value above 100 million Euro and firms with a combined equity and debt value above 100 million Euro, CARs for purchases are 3.75% and 3.54% after the date of purchase and 4.71% and 4.81% after the reporting date. Firms below 100 million Euro show CARs of 2.18% and 2.25% after the transaction date and 1.83% and 1.63% after the reporting date. For sales, there are CARs of -2.49% and -2.19% for firms above 100 million Euro after the date of sale, and -2.36% and 1.64% after the reporting date. For firms below 100 million Euro, Stotz finds CARs of -3.39% and -4.43% after the transaction date, and -1.95% and -3.36% after the reporting date.[282]
His findings show that directors' dealings in Germany are profitable with roughly 3% abnormal returns after purchases. Even with a delayed publication, outside investors can participate by mimicking directors' purchases.[283]

III.B.7 The Study by Dymke and Walter

One of the most recent studies about the German market comes from Dymke & Walter (2006) . Their work is in line with other German authors but they extend

278 Cf. Ibid., p. 455.
279 Cf. Ibid., p. 456.
280 Cf. Ibid., p. 457.
281 Cf. Ibid., p. 458.
282 Cf. Ibid., p. 460.
283 Cf. Ibid., p. 459.

the analysis by linking directors' dealings to ad-hoc news disclosures. Their study includes directors' dealings from 1 July 2002 until 30 April 2005. The authors try to link directors' dealings with ad-hoc news disclosures; however, this part of their work is not reliable since they cannot determine whether the directors traded before or after the news disclosure.[284]

After adjusting their initial sample of 7,543 transactions, they have a final sample of 3,079 transactions. This sample is then split into two sub-samples, one containing 767 trades associated with news releases (as ad-hoc news) and one containing 2,312 transactions without a direct connection to a news release. The final sample consists of 1,643 purchases and 1,436 sales from 241 and 250 firms respectively, with a total number of 351 firms under investigation.[285]

The event study uses standard market models with an estimation window of 180 days and an event period of 20 days before and after the event. The CDAX is used as reference index in the regression. They test for abnormal returns using a t-test and the Corrado rank-test for significance.[286]

The first part of their empirical analysis addresses the question whether insiders earn above average returns. Immediately on the event, they find abnormal returns of 0.25% for purchases and 0.57% for sales. The cumulative abnormal return for 20 days before the event is at -1.10% for purchases and 8.91% for sales, which seems very high compared to 5.55% stated by Stotz[287] but only slightly higher than the values given by Klinge, Seifert and Stehle, who find a CAR of 7.92% for the same period. Ten days after the transaction, Dymke and Walter find cumulative abnormal returns of 2.19% for purchases and -0.69% for sales. After 20 days, CARs increase to 3.76% for purchases and drop to -1.37% for sales.[288]

Dymke & Walter (2006) second research question, i.e. whether insiders exploit material information and which type of insiders do so, is addressed in the second part of their empirical analysis. As mentioned earlier, they use ad-hoc news disclosures by the firm as an indicator for whether material information exists and link it to directors' dealings that occur at the same time. Unfortunately, they cannot identify the time of trading; thus, it is unclear whether the director traded before or after the news announcement. For directors' dealings with a news event, they measure an abnormal return of 0.16% for purchases and 0.27% for sales on the event date. Transactions without news disclosure show higher ARs in both cases, i.e. 0.28% for purchases and 0.68% for sales. CARs for transactions with news disclosure yield abnormal returns of 3.33% after ten days and 5.05% after 20 days for purchases. Sales' CARs are 1.35% and -2.05%. Interestingly, transactions without news disclosure show lower CARs. Purchases accumulate

284 Cf. Dymke and Walter (2006), p. 6.
285 Cf. Ibid., p. 21.
286 Cf. Ibid., p. 8.
287 Note: Stotz (2006). measures the CAR over 25 days and not over 20 days.
288 Cf. Dymke and Walter (2006), p. 23, Klinge, Seifert and Stehle (2005), p. 31, Stotz (2006), p. 460.

1.81% over ten and 3.34% over 20 days. CARs from sales are -0.47% and -1.14% over ten and 20 days respectively.[289] Though CARs for directors' dealings have a greater absolute value, Dymke and Walter point out that this does not necessarily prove that insiders exploit superior information since several news disclosures like quarterly earnings do not necessarily provide new information. On the other hand, directors' dealings with a news event should not yield different abnormal returns than those transactions without an ad-hoc disclosure.[290] In the second part, they split the subsamples further to distinguish between members of the executive board, members of the supervisory board and other insiders. In the executive group, they find abnormal returns of -0.36% with and 0.42% without news release after purchases on the transaction day. Sales show abnormal returns of 0.65% and 0.89%. In the supervisory group, they measure abnormal returns of 0.48% and 0.01% for trades with and without news disclosure respectively. For sales, they actually measure negative abnormal returns of -0.19% with disclosure but a positive abnormal return of 0.53% without ad-hoc news. The third group of insiders yields abnormal returns of 0.67% with and 0.41% without news disclosure on purchases. For sales, ARs are 0.44% and 0.59%.[291]

Dymke and Walter conclude supervisory board members and non-executive insiders exploit material information and engage in front-running activities. For outside investors who are interested in a mimicking strategy of directors' dealings, they suggest following trades in the vicinity of ad-hoc news disclosures in particular.[292]

289 Cf. Dymke and Walter (2006), p. 24.
290 Cf. Ibid., p. 12.
291 Cf. Ibid., p. 26.
292 Cf. Ibid., p. 16.

IV. Methodology and Data

Foregoing chapters covered the legal grounds for this study, the theoretical framework, and lastly summarized important international and German literature related to this thesis. This chapter will introduce the methodologies and datasets for the empirical study. The first sub-chapter starts with a more general introduction to the event study methodology and closes with the methods used for the short-term study. Afterwards, sub-chapter two explains the methodologies employed in the long-term study. Finally, the third sub-chapter covers methodological aspects of the corporate actions study. All studies share some of the empirical tests. Therefore, I will describe each test only once albeit it might be employed in more than one study.

IV.A Empirical Methodology Short-Term Study

This sub-chapter explains the general idea of event studies and related price-building models, and finally specific event study methodology used in this work. In general, an event study tries to identify an event's impact on stock prices. This type of study has a long tradition in financial literature for two main reasons. First, event study methodology is simple to implement and researchers will obtain swift results. Second, the event study methodology can be applied to various settings. The basic idea is to choose a price-building model and estimate the event firm's return over a pre-specified event-window. Finally, the estimated return is compared to the actual observed return and the difference is considered the abnormal return.

IV.A.1 Price Building in Capital Markets

The foregoing chapter introduced the idea of efficient capital markets with particular emphasis on the Efficient Market Hypothesis. Naturally, the process how stock prices are built on a market is of great interest in the financial literature. Further, the event study methodology employs price building models to forecast stock prices and compare these forecasts with actually realized prices.

At first, three very common statistical event study models in financial research are presented. The mean adjusted model is the first and most simple model, followed by the market adjusted model and finally the market model, which is also employed in this study. Then, the Capital Asset Pricing Model and the Arbitrage Pricing Theory are presented from the group of economic price-building models.[293]

(a) The Mean Adjusted Model

The mean adjusted model assumes the best forecast of a security's return is the arithmetic mean of its historic returns over a pre-specified estimation period.[294] Thus, the model does not reflect market changes, assuming the security is inde-

293 MacKinlay differentiates these models into statistical and economical models. (cf. MacKinlay (1997), pp. 17-19.

294 Cf. Henderson (1990), p. 285.

pendent from market movements. Only the previous mean return of the investigated security is considered. In practice, one only has to select the number of historic periods to be included in the model.[295]

Equation 2: Mean Adjusted Model

$$E(R_i) = \frac{1}{N}\sum_{n=1}^{n} R_{i,n}$$

$E(R_i)$: Expected return of security i
N: Number of historic periods
$R_{i,n}$: Return of security i in period n

Certainly, the absence of any market influence can be considered a major drawback of this model. Nevertheless, this very simple model proofed its explanatory power in studies and did not show significant disadvantages.[296] Also, its implementation is rather simple and straight forward.

Equation 3: Mean Adjusted Abnormal Return

$$AR_{i,t} = R_{i,t} - E(R_{i,t})$$

$AR_{i,t}$: Abnormal return of security i
$R_{i,t}$: Observed return of security i in period t

The abnormal return is then simply the difference between the observed return and the estimated mean return.[297]

(b) The Market Adjusted Model

In contrast to the previous model the market adjusted model does not rely on the historic prices of a single security. The model rather assumes that all securities have the same expected return ex ante. Thus, the market return is the best forecast of a single security's return even though the return does not have to be constant over time.[298]

Equation 4: Market Adjusted Model

$$E(R_{i,t}) = R_{m,t}$$

$E(R_i)$: Expected return of security i
R_m: Market return

Similar to the mean adjusted model, the abnormal return is calculated as the difference between the observed return of the security and the expected return.

295 Cf. Brown and Warner (1980), pp. 207-208.
296 Cf. Ibid., p. 246.
297 Cf. Peterson (1989), p. 42.; cf. Brown and Warner (1980), p. 250.
298 Cf. Brown and Warner (1980), p. 208.

Equation 5: Market Adjusted Abnormal Return

$$AR_{i,t} = R_{i,t} - R_{m,t}$$

$AR_{i,t}$: Abnormal return of security i in period t
$R_{m,t}$: Observed market return in period t

Implementing this model is even simpler than the mean adjusted model since the only two components necessary to calculate the abnormal return are the security's return and the market return in the period of interest. This model is especially useful when historic data is missing, for example when investigating IPO cases.[299] MacKinlay describes the market adjusted model as a special case of the following market model with preset coefficients, i.e. α_i is set zero and β_i is set one.[300]

(c) The Market Model

The market model simplified the estimation of the efficient line in Markowitz's portfolio model.[301] Originally, Sharpe called it the "Diagonal Model". The model assumes a linear relationship between security's return and the market return.[302] Thus, the market model is also considered a single-factor model. The linear relationship is presented in eEquation 6.

Equation 6: Market Model

$$R_i = \alpha_i + \beta_i \times R_m + \varepsilon$$

R_i: Return of security
α_i: Constant term
β_i: Coefficient
R_m: Return of market portfolio
ε Random variable, normally distributed

The security's return R_i is the dependent variable and explained through the constant component α_i and β_i, times the market return. α_i represents the systematic risk and β_i represents the unsystematic risk.[303] Thus, a security's return is expressed through firm specific factors and general market factors. The necessary parameters are estimated via a linear regression over the estimation period.[304] Also, the general assumptions of the linear regression model, which are the error term's se-

299 Cf. Ritter (1991), p. 8.
300 Cf. MacKinlay (1997), p. 18.
301 Please refer for further information on Markowitz's Portfolio Selection theory to his article."Portfolio Selection", Markowitz (1952)..
302 Cf. Sharpe (1963), p. 281.
303 Cf. Steiner and Uhlir (2001), p. 173.
304 Cf. Sharpe (1963), p. 281.; cf. Perridon and Steiner (1999), p. 258.

rial independence and its distribution's independence of the market return, must be satisfied.[305] The expected return of a security is then expressed as:

Equation 7: Expected Market Model

$$E(R_{i,t}) = \alpha_i + \beta_i \times R_{m,t}$$

Again, the abnormal return is then the difference between the realized return and the estimated return with the parameters from the regression analysis.

Equation I-8: Abnormal Return Market Model

$$AR_{i,t} = R_{i,r} - E(R_{i,t})$$

This model is probably the most suitable model for many applications and was also used by Fama, Fisher, Jensen, and Roll in their seminal work "The Adjustment of Stock Prices to New Information". They did not use the original version but slightly modified the model by employing log returns.[306] Further, since economical models have often restricting assumptions, the market model is more preferable.[307]

(d) The Capital Asset Pricing Model

The Capital Asset Pricing Model (CAPM) is the first of two very often used economical models. Sharpe is together with Lintner and Mossin the founder of the Capital Asset Pricing Model, which is often referred to as the classical model of capital markets theory.[308] Based on the Markowitz's portfolio theory, these authors developed an equilibrium model which formulates the expected return on a security as a linear function of the risk-free rate R_f and a market risk premium adjusted by the security's beta.[309] The following equation describes this model:

Equation I-9: Capital Asset Pricing Model

$$E(R_i) = R_f + \beta \times (E(R_m) - R_f)$$

$E(R_i)$: Expected return of security i
R_f Risk-free rate
β_i: Beta of security i
$E(R_m)$: Expected market return

This model is based on several assumptions. First, it is assumed investor have homogenous expectations on investments' returns.[310] Also, investors choose an

305 Cf. Fama, Fisher, Jensen and Roll (1969), p. 4.
306 Cf. Ibid.
307 Cf. MacKinlay (1997), p. 19.
308 Cf. Perridon and Steiner (1999), p. 260.
309 Cf. Brealey and Myers (2000), p. 195.
310 Cf. Sharpe (1964), p. 433.

optimal portfolio and act risk-averse. Further, they can invest and lend at the risk-free rate without restrictions. The market itself is perfect, always cleared at the equilibrium price and free of any frictions such as taxes or transaction costs. Also, information is available for free and informational efficiency is assumed.[311] Abnormal returns are calculated likewise to afore described models:

Equation 10: CAPM Abnormal Return

$$AR_{i,t} = R_{i,t} - E(R_{i,t})$$

The Capital Asset Pricing Model is vanished almost completely from the event study methodology since its many model assumptions are very constraining. On the other hand the market model is very similar in its structure and is thus an ample alternative.[312]

(e) The Arbitrage Pricing Theory

The Arbitrage Pricing Theory (APT) is an alternative economic model to the CAPM. Ross developed the model in 1976 as an alternative model explaining returns through macroeconomic factors instead of a single coefficient β in the CAPM.[313] Thus, a security's risk can be allocated to different factors. The model itself does not restrict these factors, also they are not explicitly mentioned; it could be for example interest rate, commodity prices, and many others.[314] The APT can be expressed as a linear equation of a constant term β_0 and factor-specific sensitivities $\beta_{1\text{-}n}$. The constant term may be set at the risk-free rate when such an investment exists.[315]

Equation 11: Arbitrage Pricing Theory

$$E(R_i) = \beta_0 + \beta_1 F_1 + \beta_2 F_{21} + \cdots + \beta_n F_n$$

$E(R_i)$: Expected return of security i
β_0: Constant term
β_i: Sensitivity of factor i

Although the APT provides a sophisticated approach to catch different risk premiums of factors influencing security returns other statistical models are preferred in event studies. When this model is use with a single factor, it is of a similar structure like the market model.[316] A major drawback is certainly the higher workload associated with the estimation of the risk premiums and the sensitivities for each single factor.[317]

311 Cf. Ibid., p. 429.; cf. Mossin (1966), p. 780.; cf. Lintner (1965), pp. 15-16.
312 Cf. MacKinlay (1997), p. 19.
313 Cf. Ross (1976), pp. 341-342.
314 Cf. Ross, Westerfield and Jaffe (2002), p. 289.
315 Cf. Perridon and Steiner (1999), p. 278.
316 Cf. Ross, Westerfield and Jaffe (2002).
317 Cf. Brealey and Myers (2000), pp. 207-208.

IV.A.2 Event Study Methodology

For several decades event studies have been employed to measure stock market reactions to new information. As the methodology's name implies, the arrival of new information is considered an event which may or may not triggers a reaction on the stock market. Thus, event studies are a well-known tool in financial and economic policy research. Fama, Fisher, Jensen, and Roll presented in their article "The Adjustment of Stock Prices to New Information" the first seminal study.[318]. Another seminal paper comes from Ball and Brown, who investigate the impact of accounting income figures on stock prices.[319] Even though several variations of their approach were developed over time, the basic methodology has not changed since then. Generally, all models try to explain the relationship between events and price reactions in financial markets. These events include reactions to new information concerning a security, e.g. earnings announcements or announcements concerning mergers and acquisitions.

Event studies try to estimate the impact of an event by measuring the abnormal return, i.e. the difference between the real return of a security and the hypothetic return, which would have occurred without an event. Hence, the price building process of the security under investigation is an essential part to be discussed. Two prominent models trying to explain the price of a security are the Capital Asset Pricing Model (CAPM) and the Arbitrage Pricing Theory (ATP). Both are economic models

In general, event studies consist of four parts.[320] The first part is certainly the identification of the event of interest. As described before, events can range from earnings announcements to changes industry regulations. Once the event itself is identified, it is necessary to collect the appropriate data and prepare it for the study. Since the aim of the study is to detect the event's impact on the stock price, it is vital to find the precise date. The underlying assumption of a semi-strong form of the efficient market hypothesis suggest an immediate influence of new information, thus a wrong event date may render the entire study worthless. Certainly, there is also the possibility of several event dates. In these cases, it is necessary to select the appropriate dates even though this would introduce a selection bias.[321] Also, when events are cluster the forecast models should be selected more carefully since the mean adjusted model may produce inaccurate results compared to other statistical models.[322]

In the second step, stock prices during the identified event periods are measured. Depending on the study design and the availability it may be daily, weekly, monthly, or even yearly data.

318 Cf. Fama, Fisher, Jensen and Roll (1969).

319 Cf. Ball and Brown (1968), p. 161.

320 The number of steps varies depending on how the author splits the study. E.g. Bowman names five steps; cf. Bowman (1983), p. 563.

321 Cf. Bhagat and Romano (2001), p. 6.

322 Cf. Brown and Warner (1980), p. 247.

The third step involves estimation of the expected return and calculation of the abnormal return, which is simply the difference between the measured and the expected return of the stock. In this part one of afore presented economic or statistical models is employed. Generally, the abnormal return is calculated for several days before and after the event, during the so-called event window. Figure 5 shows the sequences in a typical event study.

Figure 5: Time Windows in Event Studies

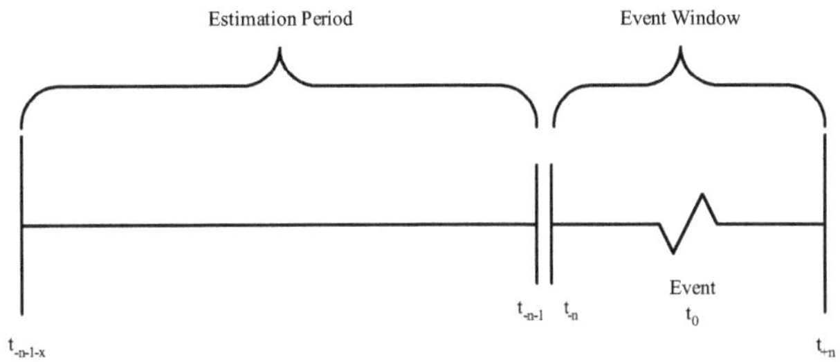

The event window ranges from t_{-n} to t_{+n} with the event on t_0. In most cases, the number of days before and after the event (n) is between 10 and 20 days, thus the total event window's length ranges from 21 to 41 days.[323] The estimation period, used to estimate the coefficients for the forecast model, begins usually one day before the event window, in Figure 5 on day t_{-n-1}. Estimation period and event window should not overlap; otherwise stock price effects around the event date may influence the estimated parameters and thus impact the study's results.[324] The length of the estimation period (x) is typically set between 100 and 300 days.[325] The expected return is then forecasted with the estimated parameters for the entire event window. Finally, the abnormal return is calculated as difference between the measured return and the expected return.

As a final step, the abnormal returns are tested whether they deviate significantly from zero and thus H_0 must be rejected.[326] In many cases cumulative abnormal (CAR) returns, spanning over several days in the event window, are calculated. Since most event studies involve more than one firm, abnormal returns are averaged across firms.[327] Significance of abnormal returns can be tested with a several parametric and non-parametric tests. Usually a Student-t test can be used as first diagnostic test. Some authors suggest varying methods to derive the standard deviation and adjustments for heteroskedasticity.[328] Often, the standard deviation is

323 This assumes a study with daily return figures.

324 Cf. MacKinlay (1997), p. 20.

325 Cf. Peterson (1989), p. 38.

326 The general hypothesis H0 assumes abnormal returns are zero.

327 Cf. Serra (2002), p. 3.

328 Cf. Binder (1998), p. 114.; Binder names many further references in his article.

measured over the estimation period to avoid event-induced distortions.[329] Since abnormal returns are mostly not normal distributed, non-parametric tests enhance the explanatory power of the parametric tests significantly. Thus, non-parametric tests are usually better specified and avoid false rejections.[330] A general sign-test is often used as a standard non-parametric test even though this test assumes symmetrically distributed abnormal returns.[331] Thus, more sophisticated tests like the Corrado-Rank-test are better suited to test abnormal returns for significance, especially when daily data is used.[332]

IV.A.2.1 Short-Term Event Study Methodology

The empirical study of directors' dealings is split into several parts because there are two specific events during directors' dealings. The first event is the director's purchase or sale. The publication of this transaction is the second event. Since these two events do not necessarily occur on the same day but rather with several days in between, it is inevitable to study them as separate events. Although, all parts of the short-term study have the same estimation period of 250 days ending 21 days before a director's purchase or sale takes place. There are two reasons for this set-up. First, the underlying parameters for the abnormal return estimation are the same for the transaction event and the publication event. Second, the publication event's estimation period would overlap the event window of the transaction event whenever transaction and publication are not on the same day.

IV.A.2.2 Pre-Transaction Abnormal Returns

The first part of the empirical study on directors' dealings in Germany measures abnormal returns before the transaction takes place. As already explained, each transaction in the directors' dealings sample has two specific dates, each is considered as an event. The first event is certainly the transaction and the second event is the transaction's publication. To avoid any distortion from overlapping events, the study is arranged in separate blocks. In this first block, returns 20 days before the first event, i.e. the transaction, are check for abnormal returns. The following figure graphically depicts the event study set-up for this block.

329 Cf. Bowman (1983), p. 572.
330 Cf. Ibid., p. 571.
331 Cf. Peterson (1989), p. 54.
332 Cf. MacKinlay (1997), p. 32.

Figure 6: Short-Term Study Set-Up Pre-Trading Period

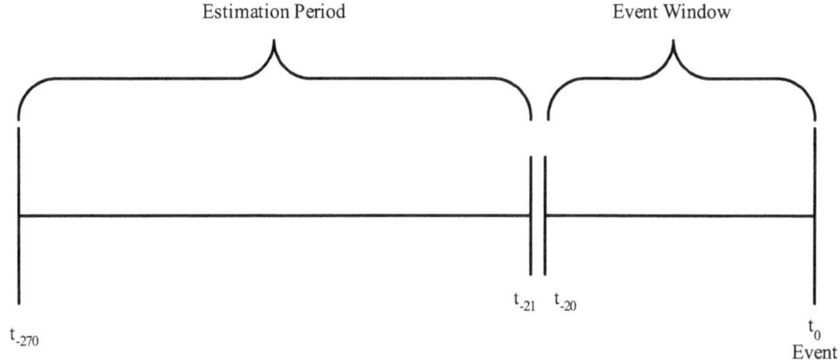

Since the market model is used in the empirical analysis, parameters must be estimated. For this purpose, the estimation period is set at 250 days and ends 21 days before the event. As shown in Figure 6, the event window begins for this block on t_{-20} and ends on t_0, the day of the transaction. With this set-up it is possible to check whether abnormal returns occur prior the transaction.

IV.A.2.3 Post-Publication Abnormal Returns

The second part of the empirical study on directors' dealings in Germany measures abnormal returns after the transaction' publication took place. After measuring abnormal returns before the transaction in the first block, this second block of the study analyzes the returns from the day of publication, which is the second event in each director's dealings transaction. Like in the first block the event window spans over 20 days, even though in this block after the event and not before. The following figure graphically depicts the event study set-up for this block.

Figure 7: Short-Term Study Set-Up Post-Publication Period

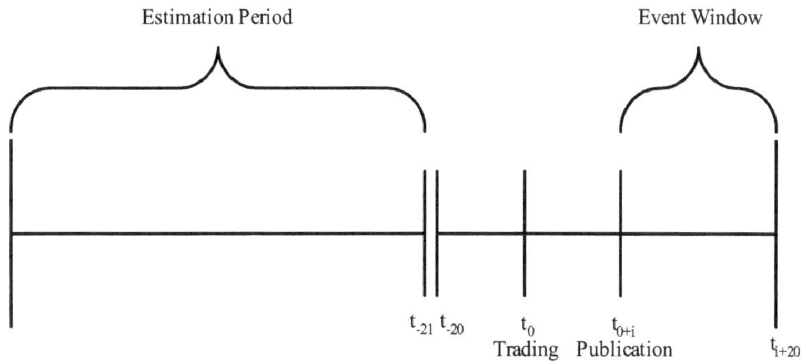

Figure 7 shows the event window starting on the publication day and ending on t_{i+20}. The day of transaction is again marked as t_0, followed by the publication day, marked with t_{0+i}. As directors' dealings must be disclosed according to German law within five business days, interval *i* between the transaction and the publication changes in length. Naturally, one would assume intervals have to be between zero and five days in length but unfortunately German directors seem less meticulous when reporting their transactions. Thus, intervals of more than five days are no rare event despite high penalties. The estimation period in this second block of the empirical analysis is again 250 days. Like in block one, the estimation period ends 21 days before the transaction, i.e. the first event. This set-up ensures the estimation period for the second analysis does not lap over the first event or the first event window.

IV.A.2.4 Hypothesis Tests Short-Term Study

Once the abnormal returns are estimated, I check them for statistical significance. For this purpose, I test the hypothesis whether abnormal returns significantly deviate from zero or not. The null hypothesis is:

H_0: The mean abnormal return is not significantly different from 0.

The alternative hypothesis is:

H_1: The mean abnormal return differs significantly from 0.

The most common hypothesis test in event studies is the Student t-test. The test assumes normal distribution and is usually well-specified to test abnormal returns. Brown & Warner (1980) compare the t-test with non-parametric tests and find the t-test not less powerful. While the t-test requires normally distributed returns, the Wilcoxon sign test requires symmetrically distributed returns. Furthermore, the Wilcoxon test rejects the null hypothesis not often enough. To overcome possible specification problems, I employ both the Student t-test and the Wilcoxon test. I calculate the following t-statistic[333]:

Equation 12: Student t-Test

$$T = \frac{\bar{x} - \mu_0}{s}\sqrt{n}$$

$\bar{x}$: sample mean
s: sample standard deviation
μ_0: expected mean
n: expected mean

333 Cf. Brown and Warner (1980), p. 220, Fahrmeir, Künstler, Pigeot and Tutz (2003), pp. 433-434.

While t-test tests the hypothesis whether the sample mean deviates from the expected mean, the Wilcoxon-test tests both sign and magnitude of abnormal returns.[334] The test-statistic is calculated as follows:

Equation 13: Wilcoxon-Sign-Rank Test

$$W^{+} = \sum_{i=1}^{n} rg\left|D_i\right| Z_i \text{ with } Z_i = \begin{cases} 1 \text{ for } D_i > 0 \\ 0 \text{ for } D_i < 0 \end{cases}$$

While both tests are commonly used to test event study results for statistical significance, criticism on the specification has not ceased. Corrado (1989) introduced a new non-parametric test to overcome major short comings. To increase the general validity of my event study results, I employ this test as well. Afterwards, I shortly described the test-statistics.

At first, the test requires to rank all abnormal for a sample firm.

Equation 14: Rank for Corrado-Test

$$K_{i,t} = \text{rank}(A_{i,t})$$

Afterwards, the test-statistic is calculated as follows:

Equation 15: Corrado-Test Score

$$Z_t = \frac{\frac{1}{N}\sum_{i=1}^{N}(K_{i,t} - \bar{K}_i)}{S(K)}$$

The standard deviation S(K) is derived over the combined period of estimation and event window, i.e. over 291 days:

Equation 16: Standard Deviation Corrado-Test

$$S(K) = \sqrt{\frac{1}{T}\sum_{t=1}^{T}\left(\frac{1}{N}\sum_{i=1}^{N}(K_{i,t} - \bar{K}_i)\right)^2}$$

To derive the Corrado-score for L event days, the formula is adjusted as follows:

Equation 17: Multi-Period Corrado-Test Score

$$Z_L = \frac{\sum_{l=1}^{L}\frac{1}{N}\sum_{i=1}^{N}\left(K_{i,t} - \bar{K}_i\right)}{S(K)\sqrt{L}}$$

334 Cf. Brown and Warner (1980), p. 218, Fahrmeir, Künstler, Pigeot and Tutz (2003), pp. 440-441, Serra (2002), p. 8.

With this test-statistic, the return distribution is no longer restricted as in the t-test or the Wilcoxon test. Through the ranking procedure, all returns are converted into a uniform distribution.[335]

IV.A.3 Empirical Methodology Long-Term Event Study

The long-term event study uses another methodology to measure long-term abnormal returns. Kothari & Warner (2004) name the buy-and-hold abnormal return (BHAR) and the calendar-time portfolio method as the two methods of choice. The BHAR method approaches long-term performance measurement from a more investment orientated angle, while the calendar-time method approaches this issue with monthly rebalanced portfolios.[336] I choose to employ the BHAR methodology as the primary method for the long-term study; however, I will use the calendar-time portfolio method as robustness check. The main reason for this procedure lies in the fact that the BHAR method allows me to consider each event while the calendar-time portfolio method requires me to directors' dealings into event portfolios.

IV.A.3.1 Long-Term Buy-and-Hold Returns

In the first step of the analysis, I form equally-weighted reference portfolios to measure the long-term abnormal return of the event firms. These portfolios are based on CDAX constituents, which are represented in the index from 2000 till 2007.[337] Further, to minimize any delisting or new listing biases, reference portfolios include only firms with available return data over the entire holding period. Firms are ranked based on their market value on each event day. Based on these rankings, I form deciles portfolios. In cases where the event firm is also among the CDAX constituents used for reference portfolios, it is not included in the respective portfolio. Loughran & Ritter (2000) point out benchmarks should not include sample firms as this diminishes the power of the tests to detect abnormal returns.[338] Overall, 371 firms are used to form reference portfolios. Thus, the average reference portfolio is constructed out of 37 firms, equally-weighted. Following Lyon, Barber, & Tsai (1999) , I calculate buy-and-hold returns for reference portfolio by compounding each firm's return over the holding period and then summing across all portfolio firms.[339]

Equation 18: Buy-and-Hold Return

$$BHR_{rp\tau} = \sum_{i=1}^{n} \frac{\left[\prod_{t=s}^{s+\tau}\left(1+R_{i,t}\right)\right]-1}{n}$$

335 Cf. Corrado (1989), p. 388, Serra (2002), p. 9.

336 Cf. Kothari and Warner (2004), p. 28.

337 Constituents' lists are taken from Thomson Financial One Banker.

338 Cf. Loughran and Ritter (2000), p. 364.

339 Cf. Lyon, Barber and Tsai (1999), p. 169.

where BHR_{rp} presents the return on the reference portfolio, n is the number of firms in the portfolio, s is the event day, and τ the length of the holding period in months. Holding period returns for the event firm are then calculated similarly. Finally, long-term buy-and-hold abnormal returns are calculated with the market-adjusted model as follows:

Equation 19: Buy-and-Hold Abnormal Return

$$BHAR_{i\tau} = BHR_{i\tau} - BHR_{rp\tau}$$

$BHR_{i\tau}$ is the buy-and-hold return of the event security i over the holding period τ and BHR_{rp} is the reference portfolio's buy-and-hold return.

IV.A.3.2 Calendar-Time Portfolio Method

As mentioned in this chapter's introduction, I employ a calendar-time portfolio model as a robustness check. Jaffe (1974) and Mandelker (1974) were among the first to employ calendar-time portfolios. Mitchell & Stafford (2000) highlight this approach's advantage of accounting for dependence in event-firm abnormal returns.[340]

While the procedure experienced several variations of the years, the initial idea has not changed. In principal, over the entire sample period K monthly portfolios are formed including all firms with an event within the last $K-1$ months each particular month. Monthly abnormal returns are calculated as the difference of the monthly event portfolio and a reference portfolio.[341] I use as reference the MSCI Standard Index for Germany.

Afterwards, I regress monthly excess returns on the Fama-French Three-Factor model. Different authors suggest various models, inter alia the capital asset pricing model or the arbitrage pricing theory. However, I rely on the Fama-French three factor model, which is probably the most popular.[342]

The three-factor regression model is constructed as follows:

Equation 20: Fama-French Three-Factor Model

$$R_{i,t} - R_{f,t} = \alpha_i + \beta_i \left(R_{m,t} - R_{f,t}\right) + s_i SMB_t + h_i HML_t + \varepsilon_{i,t}$$

where $R_{i,t}$ is the return on the calendar-time portfolio, $R_{f,t}$ is the risk-free rate and $R_{m,t}$ is the market-return. SMB is the difference between in returns on a portfolio of small and big stocks; HML is the difference between in returns on a portfolio with high and low book-to-market firms.[343] The intercept α allows to test whether

340 Cf. Mitchell and Stafford (2000), p. 326.

341 Cf. Lyon, Barber and Tsai (1999), p. 194.

342 Cf. Kothari and Warner (2004), p. 29.; Aboody and Lev (2000), p. 2756.

343 Cf. Fama and French (1993).

abnormal returns of the calendar-time portfolio are significantly different from zero or not.[344]

While historical data on these portfolios is freely available for the US market, it is not for Germany. However, different authors suggest robust proxies for these factors. Following Robert W. Faff (2003) and Pham (2007) , I create proxies for the two Fama-French factors SMB and HML. They construct these two factors by using style indices for large and small caps. Following their approach, I use data from MSCI Global indices for Germany; more specific, I use the MSCI Germany Value and Growth indices for small and large caps, as well as the MSCI Germany Standard index as market reference. Based on these indices, I create SMB and HML as follows:

Equation 21: SML and HML Construction

$$SMB_t = MSCI_{SCt} - MSCI_{LCt}$$
$$HML_t = MSCI_{Vt} - MSCI_{Gt}$$

Where

$MSCI_{SCt}$ is the return on the MSCI Germany Small Cap Index

$MSCI_{LCt}$ is the return on the MSCI Germany Large Cap Index

$MSCI_{Vt}$ is the return on the MSCI Germany Value Index

$MSCI_{Gt}$ is the return on the MSCI Germany Growth Index

Besides these indices I use the MSCI Germany Standard Index as market reference and as risk-free rate the yield on German Federal securities with a one-year maturity, which is the shortest available time-series.[345]

IV.A.3.3 Skewness-Adjusted t-Test

Kothari & Warner (1997) find parametric tests for long-term studies often indicate significant abnormal returns even though they are not significant. They simulate long-term abnormal returns using different abnormal return calculation models and find rejection rates of the null hypothesis of up to 16% in studies using the market-adjusted model and up to 26.8% in event studies using the market model over a period of 24 months when tested at a 5%-significance level.[346] To minimize this effect and increase the overall explanatory power of the study, I employ the suggested skewness-adjusted bootstrapped t-test besides a standard t-test and the Wilcoxon-Sign-Rank test. Many authors use this test for long-horizon studies; for

344 Cf. Lyon, Barber and Tsai (1999), p. 193..

345 Data for MSCI indices is available through www.mscibarra.com, time series for German Federal securities through www.bundesbank.de. As proxy for the risk-free-rate I use time-series WZ3400.

346 Cf. Kothari and Warner (1997), p. 309.

example Ikenberry, Lakonishok, & Vermaelen (1995) study long-term buy-and-hold returns after open market share repurchases and measure significance with such a bootstrapping-method.

Lyon et al. (1999) present such a bootstrapped skewness-adjusted t-statistic based on a transformed t-statistic developed by Johnson.[347] I follow their testing procedure, which I briefly describe below.[348] The skewness-adjusted t-statistic is calculated as follows:

Equation 22: Skewness-Adjusted t-Test

$$t_{sa} = \sqrt{n}\left(S + \frac{1}{3}\hat{y}S^2 + \frac{1}{6n}\hat{y}\right)$$

with

$$S = \frac{\overline{AR_\tau}}{\sigma(AR_\tau)}$$

$$\hat{y} = \frac{\sum_{i=1}\left(AR_{i\tau} - \overline{AR_\tau}\right)^3}{n\sigma\left(AR_\tau\right)^3}$$

Lyon et al. (1999) follow Sutton (1993) in their test set-up, who recommends a bootstrapped test-statistic. In their opinion, only bootstrapped statistics are well-specified and reduce type I error.[349] For that purpose, 1,000 resamples of size n_b of the original sample are drawn. Lyon, Barber, Tsai suggest $n_b = \frac{n}{4}$ based on their empirical analysis. Following t-statistic is then calculated for each of the 1,000 resamples.

$$t_{sa}^b = \sqrt{n_b}\left(S^b + \frac{1}{3}\hat{y}^b S^{b2} + \frac{1}{6n_b}\hat{y}^b\right)$$

with

$$S^b = \frac{\overline{AR_\tau}^b - \overline{AR_\tau}}{\sigma^b(AR_\tau)}$$

$$\hat{y}^b = \frac{\sum_{i=1}^{nb}\left(AR_{i\tau}^b - \overline{AR_\tau^b}\right)^3}{n_b\sigma^b\left(AR_\tau\right)^3}$$

347 Cf. Lyon, Barber and Tsai (1999), pp. 173, 174; cf. Johnson (1978).

348 Following authors give detailed descriptions on this test: Lyon, Barber and Tsai (1999)., Kothari and Warner (1997).;

349 Cf. Lyon, Barber and Tsai (1999), p. 174. Sutton (1993)..

Finally, critical values for the upper and lower bound are determined based on the calculated distribution of bootstrapped t-values for the chosen alpha.

Equation 23: Upper and Lower Bounds

$$\Pr\left[t_{sa}^{b} \leq x_{l}^{*}\right] = \Pr\left[t_{sa}^{b} \geq x_{l}^{*}\right] = \frac{\alpha}{2}$$

Herein, values for the 1%, 5%, and 10% significance level are calculated.

IV.B Data

Following the introduction of this thesis' empirical methodologies, this chapter describes the different datasets for directors' dealings and corporate actions. The first part covers directors' dealings data along with firms' return series and other relevant financial times series. Part two of this chapter introduces the three different datasets for share repurchases, mergers and acquisitions, and seasoned equity offerings. The dataset for the excursus on insider dealing is discussed later on in the excursus.

IV.B.1 Directors' Dealings Data

An essential part of any empirical study is the underlying dataset and its precision is of utmost importance for the final results. While financial data is generally well available from many trusted sources, directors' dealings data for Germany is a novelty and thus only supplied by a few sources. Starting in July 2002, the German legislator introduced with §15a WpHG the obligation for firms listed in Germany to published directors' dealings. Since then, all persons with managerial duties must notify the issuer and the BaFin about all transactions in the issuer's stock or other financial instruments related to the issuer within five working days. Usually, firms disclose these transactions in a special section on their home page. Further, BaFin maintains a public database with all recent directors' dealings. In addition, all transactions are recorded in the Unternehmensregister[350]. Firms may also choose to publish directors' dealings through a third-party service-provider, like Deutsche Gesellschaft für Ad-Hoc Publizität (DGAP). They are specialized in ad-hoc news disclosure and provide also directors' dealings. However, their database covers only firms using their publishing service and not the entire market. While these sources primarily publish directors' dealings, another private service-provider, Insiderdaten[351], maintains a chargeable database containing all directors' dealings since July 2002. On BaFin's recommendation, I use this source as it provides the most complete directors' dealings dataset. In the meantime, a few more

350 Unternehmensregister is an official database containing different financial information and registration details of firms in Germany. It is available at http://www.unternehmensregister.de

351 http://www.insiderdaten.de

data providers emerged, like 2iQ Research and most recently Deutsche Börse, both covering European directors' dealings.

My sample of directors' dealings consists solely of directors' purchases and sales; I exclude any other financial instruments than stock. The starting sample consists of 14,522 purchase and sale transactions spanning over a time period from July 1, 2002 to December 1, 2008. After removing duplicate transactions, entries with publications dates prior the actual transaction, and entries with a lag of more than 30 days between the transaction and the publication, the final sample consists of 12,519 transactions.

The following table shows the actual number from the original sample to the final sample and which of these transactions are included in the short- and long-term study.

Table 1: Directors' Dealings Sample

Original Sample		14.522
	Duplicate Entries	-551
	Publication Date before Transaction Date	-228
	Publication Lag > 30 Days	-1.224
Final Sample		12.519
	Directors' Purchases	7.716
	Directors' Sales	4.803
Short-Term Study		10.322
	Directors' Purchases	6.054
	Directors' Sales	4.268
Long-Term Study		10.795
	Directors' Purchases	6.307
	Directors' Sales	4.488

The return series requirements vary between the short- and long-term studies; thus, the actual number of transactions varies between the studies, due to missing or unavailable return data. For example, the short-term analysis requires return series over 250 days before the transactions, which eliminates those firms with missing data from the short-term study. In contrast, the long-term study requires return data for at least three months after the publication, which reduces the number of included transactions in the long-term study with increasing holding period Table 1

Table IV-2 reports total and annual summary statistics for number of transactions, number of shares traded, and Euro value of transactions. Panels A through C report these figures for the final sample, followed by figures for the short- and long-term study. For both the short- and long-term study, I report additionally firm sizes in million Euro.

Table 2: Directors' Dealings Dataset

This table reports dexcriptive statistics of the directors' dealings dataset. The first column in each panel reports total figure followed by annual figures. Each panel reports totals, followed by purchase and sales figures. Panel A reports the number directors' dealings, panel B the amount of shares traded, and panel C the Euro value of directors's dealings. Panels D through G report these figures for the short-term stuy and respective firm sizes in million Euro, and panels H through K report these figures for the long-term study. The number of directors' dealings varies between the study since the availability of return data varies.

	Total	2002	2003	2004	2005	2006	2007	2008
Panel A: Number of Directors' Dealings								
Total	12519	687	1108	1302	2328	2312	2278	2504
Purchases	7716	535	577	578	1062	1321	1513	2130
Sales	4803	152	531	724	1266	991	765	374
Panel B: Mean Number of Shares								
Total	88,32	69,04	70,06	67,48	99,18	103,45	82,84	93,43
Purchases	60,05	37,78	58,97	44,81	101,17	53,99	53,07	58,28
Sales	133,73	179,09	82,11	85,57	97,51	169,38	141,71	293,63
Panel C: Mean Euro Volume								
Total	1,46	1,06	0,59	0,77	1,59	2,11	1,47	1,59
Purchases	0,89	0,77	0,18	0,19	0,96	0,86	0,97	1,22
Sales	2,38	2,09	1,03	1,23	2,12	3,77	2,44	3,68
Panel D: Number of Directors' Dealings - Short-Term Study								
Total	10322	630	1020	1225	2092	2059	2083	1213
Purchases	6054	489	519	542	967	1183	1349	1005
Sales	4268	141	501	683	1125	876	734	208
Panel E: Mean Number of Shares - Short-Term Study								
Total	84,24	71,20	73,68	68,98	104,99	84,85	80,73	84,49
Purchases	60,15	40,04	65,06	46,33	105,49	59,13	56,82	36,91
Sales	118,40	179,27	82,61	86,95	104,56	119,59	124,69	314,38
Panel F: Mean Euro Volume - Short-Term Study								
Total	1,37	1,15	0,63	0,80	1,63	1,52	1,30	2,10
Purchases	0,95	0,83	0,20	0,20	0,98	0,93	1,04	1,67
Sales	1,97	2,25	1,07	1,27	2,19	2,32	1,79	4,21
Panel G: Firm Size - Short-Term Study								
Total	3025	2033	1879	1583	3053	3629	3744	3656
Purchases	2528	2291	2144	1705	2974	2696	1873	3540
Sales	3730	1140	1604	1487	3121	4888	7181	4214
Panel H: Number of Directors' Dealings - Long-Term Study								
Total	10795	621	1058	1241	2263	2258	2261	1093
Purchases	6307	483	554	551	1020	1307	1490	902
Sales	4488	138	504	690	1243	951	771	191
Panel I: Mean Number of Shares - Long-Term Study								
Total	84,53	72,01	55,85	77,68	98,98	107,57	81,63	55,69
Purchases	58,08	40,33	32,61	66,80	101,30	57,95	52,68	38,18
Sales	121,70	182,91	81,39	86,37	97,07	175,78	137,60	138,35
Panel J: Mean Euro Volume - Long-Term Study								
Total	1,47	1,16	0,59	0,79	1,59	2,15	1,47	1,68
Purchases	0,88	0,84	0,16	0,21	0,93	0,88	0,98	1,53
Sales	2,31	2,29	1,06	1,26	2,12	3,89	2,41	2,40
Panel K: Firm Size - Long-Term Study								
Total	2872	2000	1821	1488	2869	3391	3500	3596
Purchases	2400	2249	2030	1555	2929	2490	1797	3489
Sales	3537	1125	1591	1434	2819	4628	6792	4101

Notes: Number of shares is expressed in thousand.
Euro volume and firm size are expressed in million Euro.

Panel A reports numbers of transactions in the final sample. Interestingly, the number of purchases is relatively stable for 2002 to 2004. That is especially notable because 2002 covers only six months. Subsequent years show substantial increases for purchases; sales peak in 2005 and go down afterwards. Though the number of sales is in most years below the number of purchases, the Euro value of directors' sales is always higher than for purchases. These figures change slightly for the short- and long-term study yet the pattern remains.

The following figure shows the relationship between the number of monthly directors' purchases and sales and the CDAX index.

Figure 8: Monthly Directors' Dealings & CDAX

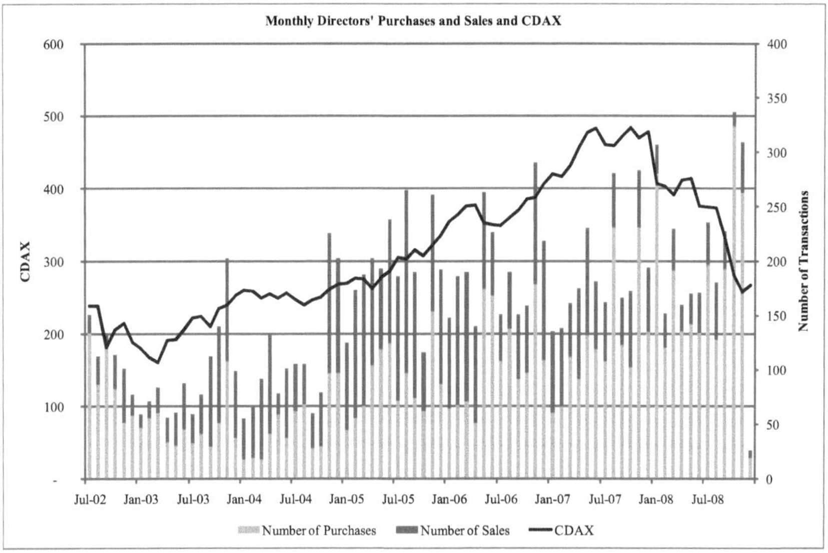

Above figure illustrates the increasing number of monthly directors' dealings since July 2002 jointly with the CDAX index. For most months, the number of purchases surmounts the number of sales. While the figure is certainly not as precise as the empirical study, it still reveals that directors tend to purchase with falling prices and sell after a rise. The next figure illustrates these transactions in million Euro; bars indicate the sum of monthly directors' purchases and sales in million Euro.

Figure 9: Euro Volume Monthly Directors' Dealings & CDAX

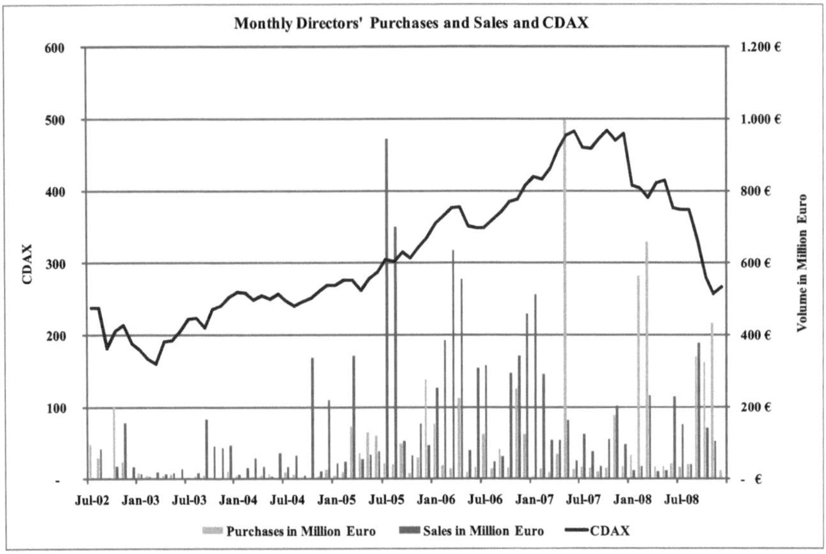

Above figure shows the higher volume in sales following a market rise. On the other hand, purchases seem to increase in volume after a market drop, e.g. November 2002 or March 2005. Certainly, I consider previous two graphs much more as a general indication than conclusive evidence that directors are able to time their transactions. Nevertheless, they allow a first assumption that directors indeed time their transactions respectively can foresee upcoming price movements.

While previous descriptions focused more generally on number and volume of transactions another important question is pending; i.e. who is trading. Each transaction entry in the dataset names the position of the insider. Based on this data, I create five different groups. Group 1 and 2 are members of the executive and the supervisory board. Group 3 are persons in managing position yet no board members, i.e. persons with continuous access to inside information. This may also include external service providers like consultants, lawyers, or accounting firms. Group 4 are closely related persons, i.e. close relatives or other persons living with an insider from one of the previous three groups. Group 5 are legal entities. While it is not always obvious, these legal entities are often private family trusts acting as wealth managers for one the previous insiders. Certainly, this could be any other legal entity. The following table shows the statistics for all five groups. I report only figures for the general sample.

Table 3: Directors' Dealings - Insider Group

This table reports directors' dealings according to insider groups. Panel A reports number of transactions, panel B reports the sum of the volume in million Euro. These figures refer to the final sample.

		Total	2002	2003	2004	2005	2006	2007	2008
Panel A: Number of Directors' Dealings									
Total Group	1	5424	350	677	644	826	945	942	1040
Total Group	2	3427	217	293	421	682	621	578	615
Total Group	3	402	9	0	18	159	114	65	37
Total Group	4	1074	111	138	126	274	179	110	136
Total Group	5	2192	0	0	93	387	453	583	676
Purchases Group	1	3484	302	371	337	395	559	621	899
Purchases Group	2	1951	177	144	127	286	352	371	494
Purchases Group	3	195	0	0	9	76	51	34	25
Purchases Group	4	482	56	62	34	120	58	44	108
Purchases Group	5	1604	0	0	71	185	301	443	604
Sales Group	1	1940	48	306	307	431	386	321	141
Sales Group	2	1476	40	149	294	396	269	207	121
Sales Group	3	207	9	0	9	83	63	31	12
Sales Group	4	592	55	76	92	154	121	66	28
Sales Group	5	588	0	0	22	202	152	140	72
Panel B: Sum Euro Volume									
Total Group	1	2891,3	197,8	231,1	291,4	600,1	506,8	565,0	499,0
Total Group	2	2999,2	350,3	306,8	253,1	519,2	592,1	138,8	839,0
Total Group	3	224,0	0,9	0,0	1,3	55,3	123,2	20,6	22,6
Total Group	4	947,9	178,6	113,5	81,7	408,9	38,4	69,3	57,6
Total Group	5	11196,2	0,0	0,0	372,2	2120,2	3607,5	2544,9	2551,5
Purchases Group	1	552,4	48,1	50,3	53,2	95,4	94,3	107,2	104,0
Purchases Group	2	842,3	260,8	22,9	35,4	54,5	84,3	37,0	347,4
Purchases Group	3	43,4	0,0	0,0	0,3	22,7	14,7	1,1	4,6
Purchases Group	4	481,1	101,1	32,4	4,9	327,3	8,4	1,2	5,9
Purchases Group	5	4923,5	0,0	0,0	16,0	520,8	933,2	1322,6	2130,9
Sales Group	1	2338,8	149,7	180,8	238,2	504,7	412,6	457,8	395,0
Sales Group	2	2156,9	89,5	283,9	217,7	464,7	507,8	101,8	491,6
Sales Group	3	180,6	0,9	0,0	1,0	32,7	108,6	19,6	17,9
Sales Group	4	466,8	77,5	81,1	76,8	81,6	30,0	68,1	51,7
Sales Group	5	6272,7	0,0	0,0	356,2	1599,4	2674,2	1222,3	420,6

Notes: Euro volume is expressed in million Euro

Above table shows the number and Euro volume of directors' dealings sorted for the five different insider groups. Most transactions come from executive and supervisory board members. While executive board members have more transactions, the value of transactions is slightly higher for supervisory board members. Group 3, insiders with continuous access to inside information, have the smallest number of transactions and also the lowest value. Overall, legal entities have the highest Euro volumes for both purchases and sales.

IV.B.2 Return Series and Accounting Data

The empirical short- and long-term analyzes require return series for all firms with directors' dealings. Further, the short-term analysis requires a market index for the abnormal return calculation and the long-term analysis requires matching firms for the buy-and-hold abnormal return calculation. Besides these return data, the analyses require in part accounting data like market and book values. I obtain all return series and financial accounting data from Thomson Datastream. In order to account for dividends and share splits, I use for all firms the Total Return Index.[352] In general, I use daily return series except for the calendar-time portfolio method in the long-term study. This part requires monthly data.

While the CDAX serves as broad market index in the short-term study, I use its constituents to construct matching portfolios in the long-term study. To reduce a potential survivorship-bias in the matching portfolios, I consider all firms listed in the CDAX from 2002 to 2008; however, I restrict the selection in so far that I require firms used to construct a matching portfolio to have available return data over the respective holding period.

IV.B.3 Corporate Actions Data

For the corporate actions study, I use besides previously described directors' dealings and return series data of share repurchases, mergers and acquisitions, and seasoned equity offerings. Data for these three types of corporate actions come from the Thomson One Banker SDC Platinum database. I consider corporate actions for German firms between January 2002 and December 2007. Afterwards, I shortly present these corporate actions. Generally, I divide these corporate actions into two groups; the first group has documented directors' dealings between one year before and three months after the announcement date, the second group has no documented directors' dealings during over this time span.

The first table reports mean and median figures for share repurchases. Panel A reports figures for 41 share repurchases with documented directors' dealings.[353] Generally, the number of purchases is higher than the number of sales; also, purchases occur on average 35 days close to the event than sales. Interestingly, the size of purchases, reported as number of traded shares, is higher than the size of sales. However, the value of sales, as said before, is higher; thus, this suggest insiders may time their trades. Share repurchases between both groups differ insofar as those with documented directors' dealings have a higher average deal value and firms are larger.

352 Item Code is for the total return index is RI.

353 Following Chan, Ikenberry and Lee (2003)., I use in this table "MT" for "mixed trades", i.e. directors' purchases and sales. Due to the small number of corporate actions, I refrain from dividing groups further.

Table 4: Summary Repurchase Sample

This table reports summary statistics on firms repurchasing stock included the analysis. The sample includes repurchase in Germany covering a period from 2002 to 2007. The sample is divided into two groups. Panel A presents results for firms with directors' dealings within one year before and three months after the announcement date of the repurchase. Panel B presents firms without documented directors' dealings during this time period. The first section shows the total number of trades for purchases (P) and sales (S), the mean and median number transactions for each event, followed by the average and median number of days between directors' dealings and the announcement of the repurchase (negative number indicate days before the event), followed by shares traded (in thousands), and finally directors' dealings value in thousand Euro. Section two shows firm size in million Euro. Percent of shares announced shows the percentage the firm intended to repurchase followed by the actual repurchase in million Euro.

	Panel A: MT (N=41)		Panel B: No Insider (N=34)	
	Mean	Median	Mean	Median
Insider Trading				
Number of Purchases	36			
Number of Sales	27			
Number of Trades (P)	8,44	6,50		
Number of Trades (S)	6,56	5,00		
Days to Event (P)	-111,77	-116,33		
Days to Event (S)	-146,93	-148,00		
Size of Trade (P)	127,15	13,03		
Size of Trade (S)	116,79	11,16		
Value (P)	493,02	88,63		
Value (S)	1851,65	179,38		
Firm Characteristics				
Firm Size	14256,21	2616,58	4004,60	218,55
Percent of Shares announced	11,33	10,00	9,40	10,00
Actual Share Repurchase				
N	39		32	
Value	1300,21	126,60	365,66	24,91

Notes: Size of trade is presented in thousand shares. Value of trade in thousand Euro.
Firm size and Value of Repurchase is presented in million Euro
Data source is Thomson Financial. Deal value was originally presented in US Dollar. Figures are converted into Euro using the event day's exchange rate.

The second table reports these figures for mergers and acquisitions. Overall, this part includes 1,125 deals, whereof 605 have documented directors' dealings.[354] Again, purchases happen on average closer to the announcement date than sales. In contrast to share repurchases, both the number of shares bought and the Euro value of purchases are below the sales figures. Further, the value of sales is substantially higher for the M&A sample than for the repurchases sample. As previously, deals with documented directors' dealings come from substantially larger firms. Deal sizes do not vary substantially between both groups.

354 The study focuses on acquiring firms only due to data availability.

Table 5: Summary M&A Sample

This table present summary statistics on acquiror firms included in the analysis. The sample covers M&A transactions in Germany spanning over a period from 2002 to 2007. The sample is divided into two groups, i.e. one group with directors' dealings 12 months before to 3 months after the announcement date and one without directors' dealings during this time span. Number of Purchases and Sales states the number of M&A events with documented directors' purchases and directors' sales. Number of trades for purchases (P) and sales (S) states the average number of documented directors' dealings for each event, followed by the average and median number of days between directors' dealings and the announcement (negative figures indicate days before the event). Shares traded (in thousands) states the average number of shares traded for each event and finally directors' dealings value in thousand Euro for each event. Firm-size and deal-size are expressed in million Euro. Number of deals indicates the number of deals with available deal-size data.

	Panel A: MT (N=605)		Panel B: No Insider (N=520)	
	Mean	Median	Mean	Median
Insider Trading				
Number of Purchases	512			
Number of Sales	410			
Number of Trades (P)	7,54	5,00		
Number of Trades (S)	6,73	4,00		
Days to Event (P)	-111,92	-107,09		
Days to Event (S)	-129,05	-127,95		
Size of Trade (P)	89,85	9,90		
Size of Trade (S)	173,40	30,26		
Value (P)	479,16	67,00		
Value (S)	3174,30	294,40		
Firm Characteristics				
Firm Size	11594,42	1623,11	6454,52	412,72
Deal Value				
n	154		130	
	932,83	81,29	892,55	49,50

Notes: Size of trade is presented in thousand shares. Value of trade in thousand Euro.
Firm size and Value of Deal is presented in million Euro
Data source is Thomson Financial. Deal value was originally presented in US Dollar. Figures are converted into Euro using the event day's exchange rate.

The final table in this section reports these statistics for seasoned equity offerings. I refer to them throughout the analysis as seasoned equity offerings (SEO) yet the sample includes seasoned and secondary offerings. I account for this difference, i.e. mostly the expected dilution effect of a secondary offering, by including a variable measuring the difference in outstanding shares in the regression analysis. The SEO sample consists of 211 transactions, whereof 113 have documented directors' dealings and 98 have no documented directors' dealings. While in previous two datasets directors' sales occurred further away from the event than purchases did, the opposite is true for directors' sales. Here, purchases occur on average 116 days before the announcement and sales 100 days before the announcement.

Again, the number of shares sold and the average value of sales surmounts the purchase figures.

Firm and deal size do not differ substantially, yet the median figures indicate SEOs with documented directors' dealings are larger.

Table 6: Summary SEO Sample

This table present summary statistics on firms conducting a seasoned offering (SEO) included in the analysis. The sample covers SEOs in Germany spanning over a period from 2002 to 2007. The sample is divided into two groups, i.e. one group with directors' dealings between one year before and three months after the announcement date and one without directors' dealings'. Number of Purchases and Sales states the number of SEO events with documented directors' purchases and directors' sales. Number of trades for purchases (P) and sales (S) states the average number of documented directors' dealings for each event, followed by the average and median number of days between directors' dealings and the announcement of the SEO (negative figures indicate days before the event). Size of trade is the number of shares traded (in thousands) and finally directors' dealings value in thousand Euro for each event. Firm-size and deal-size are expressed in million Euro.

	Panel A: MT (N=113)		Panel B: No Insider (N=98)	
	Mean	Median	Mean	Median
Insider Trading				
Number of Purchases	88			
Number of Sales	83			
Number of Trades (P)	5,47	4,00		
Number of Trades (S)	7,05	5,00		
Days to Event (P)	-115,78	-104,50		
Days to Event (S)	-99,67	-89,50		
Size of Trade (P)	42,33	9,77		
Size of Trade (S)	147,62	26,44		
Value (P)	484,63	54,91		
Value (S)	3176,04	347,01		
Firm Characteristics				
Firm Size	6732,11	1585,06	7084,87	932,08
Deal Value				
n	109		92	
	360,97	150,05	467,26	97,18

Notes: Size of trade is presented in thousand shares. Value of trade in thousand Euro.
Firm size and Value of Deal is presented in million Euro
Data source is Thomson Financial. Deal value was originally presented in US Dollar. Figures are converted into Euro using the event day's exchange rate.

All directors' dealings for the corporate actions study are come from the final directors' dealings sample of the short- and long-term study. I matched directors' dealings and corporate actions based on their SEDOL Code. All return series and accounting data comes from the Thomson Datastream database.

V. Empirical Results

In the first chapters, I discussed the theoretical basis for this thesis, followed by an introduction to the empirical methodologies and datasets used in the empirical study. In this chapter, I report results for the empirical studies. In the next three sub-chapters, I present findings on the short-term analysis, the long-term analysis, and the corporate actions study.

V.A Empirical Results Short-Term Study

This sub chapter reports empirical results for the short-term study. First, I present results for all directors' purchases and sales, followed by results sorted according to firm size quartiles and finally sorted by trading insider group.

V.A.1 Empirical Results Short-Term Study

All short-term study results are based on the market model with an estimation period of 250 days ending 21 days before the transaction date. Panels A and B of Table 7 report daily mean abnormal returns (AR) in percent for 6,054 directors' purchases and 4,268 sales from 20 days before the transaction day. Panels C and D report empirical results for these purchases and sales on the publication day and the following 20 days. Panels E through H report corresponding cumulative abnormal returns (CAR). All results include t-statistics together with an indication of significance according to Student t-test, Wilcoxon signed rank test, and Corrado rank test.

Directors' purchases experience highly significant negative ARs on each of the 20 pre-event days. While ARs from day -20 to -11 vary between -0.09% and -0.13%, ARs over the last 10 days before the transaction range from -0.12% to -0.24%. Over the entire period, these ARs accumulate to -2.74%; the last 10 days before the event account for -1.70% and the first 10 days account for -1.04%. The event day shows a positive AR of 0.13%.

Directors' sales show an almost reversed image. While all but one of the 20 pre-event days have positive ARs, they do not show the same consistent significance pattern as purchases do. Nevertheless, all sales ARs are highly significant according to at least one of the three tests. Like in purchases, ARs over the last 10 days before the event have a higher magnitude. Here, they accumulate to 2.41% while days -20 to -11 accumulate to only 0.98%. The event day has a significant AR of 0.37%. Overall, the pre-event window has a highly significant CAR of 3.39%.

Panels C and D report ARs for directors' purchases and sales on and after the publication day. On the purchase publication day, there is a highly significant positive AR at 0.38%. However, the following 20 days show both positive and negative ARs. While the first 10 days after the publication show more positive ARs and accumulate to a CAR of 0.46%, ARs from days 11 to 20 diminish this CAR; over the entire 20-day post-publication period, CARs accumulate to 0.40%.

ARs following the publication of directors' sales have a much more consistent pattern. While the AR of the publication day is 0.08%, the general drift is negative; none of the 20 days have positive ARs. Over the first 10 days, these ARs accumulate to -1.89%, followed by -1.29%, totaling to highly significant -3.18%. Thus, pre-transaction CARs for sales are almost wiped out.

Table 7: Directors' Dealings Short-Term Results

This table reports mean abnormal returns and cumulative abnormal returns of 6054 directors' purchases and 4268 directors' sales before and on the transaction day as well as on and following the publication day. Panels A and B presents daily MARs from 20 days before to the transaction day. CARs for this period are reported in panels E and F. Panels C and D presents MARs on and 20 days after the publication. CARs for this period are presented in panels G and H. Following each abnormal return corresponding t-statistics are reported. Next to them, significance for the t-test, the Wilcoxon test, and the Corrado test is indicated.

	Panel A: Purchases		Panel B: Sales			Panel C: Purchases		Panel D: Sales	
Day	MAR	t-Stats	MAR	t-Stats	Day	MAR	t-Stats	MAR	t-Stats
-20	-0,1321	-3,4771 *** +++ ‡‡‡	0,0910	1,5314 +++ ‡‡‡	0	0,3819	6,8598 *** +++ ‡‡‡	0,0753	1,2082 +++ ‡‡‡
-19	-0,1517	-3,9037 *** +++ ‡‡‡	-0,0350	-0,6242 +++ ‡‡‡	1	0,1055	2,5162 **	-0,2209	-4,7710 *** +++ ‡‡‡
-18	-0,0700	-1,9177 * +++ ‡‡‡	0,1923	3,2543 *** ‡‡	2	0,1022	2,5544 **	-0,1812	-3,1377 *** +++ ‡‡‡
-17	-0,0909	-2,3907 ** +++ ‡‡‡	0,0865	1,7193 * + ‡‡‡	3	0,0856	2,1830 **	-0,1279	-2,1106 ** +++ ‡‡‡
-16	-0,0816	-2,1632 ** +++ ‡‡‡	0,1064	2,0654 ** +++ ‡‡‡	4	0,0103	0,2606 +++ ‡‡	-0,2494	-5,7250 *** +++ ‡‡‡
-15	-0,1109	-3,0713 *** +++ ‡‡‡	0,0823	1,7676 * +++ ‡‡‡	5	-0,0024	-0,0640 ++	-0,2683	-6,3844 *** +++ ‡‡‡
-14	-0,1276	-3,2291 *** +++ ‡‡‡	0,0707	1,5488 ++ ‡‡‡	6	0,1152	2,8366 ***	-0,0910	-1,8613 * +++ ‡‡‡
-13	-0,0979	-2,6603 *** +++ ‡‡‡	0,1271	2,3579 ** ++ ‡‡‡	7	0,0348	0,9113 ++ ‡	-0,1633	-3,7470 *** +++ ‡‡‡
-12	-0,0860	-2,2335 ** +++ ‡‡‡	0,1838	3,5544 *** ‡‡	8	0,0360	0,9676 ++	-0,1282	-2,9950 *** +++ ‡‡‡
-11	-0,0866	-2,1026 ** +++ ‡‡‡	0,0753	1,5610 + ‡‡‡	9	-0,0298	-0,8205 +++	-0,2436	-5,3970 *** +++ ‡‡‡
-10	-0,1167	-2,7966 *** +++ ‡‡‡	0,1113	2,2648 ** ‡‡	10	0,0014	0,0348 +++ ‡‡	-0,2137	-4,6293 *** +++ ‡‡‡
-9	-0,1940	-4,7395 *** +++ ‡‡‡	0,2173	4,0929 *** ‡‡‡	11	-0,0629	-1,5816 +++ ‡‡‡	-0,2004	-4,6343 *** +++ ‡‡‡
-8	-0,1453	-3,3480 *** +++ ‡‡‡	0,1795	3,4156 *** + ‡‡‡	12	0,0915	2,3330 **	-0,0018	-0,0401 +++ ‡‡‡
-7	-0,2202	-5,5025 *** +++ ‡‡‡	0,1309	2,4636 ** ++ ‡‡‡	13	0,0328	0,8512 +++ ‡‡‡	-0,1347	-3,1868 *** +++ ‡‡‡
-6	-0,1639	-3,9161 *** +++ ‡‡‡	0,2139	4,2006 *** ‡	14	-0,0102	-0,2814 +++ ‡‡‡	-0,1375	-2,8181 *** +++ ‡‡‡
-5	-0,1399	-3,3694 *** +++ ‡‡‡	0,2609	4,4648 ***	15	-0,0791	-2,0743 ** +++ ‡‡‡	-0,1599	-3,9810 *** +++ ‡‡‡
-4	-0,1790	-4,1096 *** +++ ‡‡‡	0,2908	5,3057 ***	16	-0,0280	-0,7424 +++ ‡‡‡	-0,1389	-3,2903 *** +++ ‡‡‡
-3	-0,1210	-2,7333 *** +++ ‡‡‡	0,2412	4,3008 *** ‡	17	0,0028	0,0727 +++ ‡‡‡	-0,0174	-0,3280 +++ ‡‡‡
-2	-0,1825	-3,8462 *** +++ ‡‡‡	0,3643	6,3046 *** +++	18	-0,0566	-1,5263 +++ ‡‡‡	-0,0979	-2,0840 ** +++ ‡‡‡
-1	-0,2385	-4,6793 *** +++ ‡‡‡	0,4011	6,3140 *** +++ ‡‡‡	19	0,0849	2,3508 ** +++ ‡‡	-0,2443	-5,6539 *** +++ ‡‡‡
0	0,1291	2,2543 ** ++ ‡‡	0,3714	4,9812 ***	20	-0,0380	-0,9484 +++ ‡‡‡	-0,1572	-2,7043 *** +++ ‡‡‡
Days	Panel E: Purchases		Panel F: Sales			Panel G: Purchases		Panel H: Sales	
[-20:-1]	-2,7363	-15,4347 *** +++ ‡‡‡	3,3916	13,6105 *** +++ ‡‡‡	[1:5]	0,3013	3,6951 *** +++	-1,0477	-9,0722 *** +++ ‡‡‡
[-20:-10]	-1,0353	-9,1837 *** +++ ‡‡‡	0,9804	6,2724 *** ++ ‡‡‡	[1:10]	0,4589	4,1457 *** ++ ‡‡‡	-1,8874	-12,9192 *** +++ ‡‡‡
[-10:-1]	-1,7010	-12,5598 *** +++ ‡‡‡	2,4112	13,4304 *** +++ ‡‡‡	[11:20]	-0,0629	-0,5813 +++ ‡‡‡	-1,2900	-9,4623 *** +++ ‡‡‡
[-5:-1]	-0,8609	-8,6343 *** +++ ‡‡‡	1,5583	12,0515 *** +++	[1:20]	0,3960	2,6203 *** ‡‡‡	-3,1774	-15,8389 *** +++ ‡‡‡

Notes
***, **, * indicate significance on the 1, 5, and 10% level for the t-test.
+++, ++, + indicate significance on the 1, 5, and 10% level for the Wilcoxon test.
‡‡‡, ‡‡, ‡ indicate significance on the 1, 5, and 10% level for the Corrado test.
Returns are expressed in percent.

The following figures depict CARs before the transaction and after the publication. Especially the build-up of positive abnormal returns before sales and the build-up of negative abnormal returns before purchases are obvious. Sales CARs move straight up and, including the transaction day, get close to the 4% line. Purchases, instead, move straight down and are lowest at -2.74% one day before the transaction.

Figure 10: Short-Term CARs before Transaction

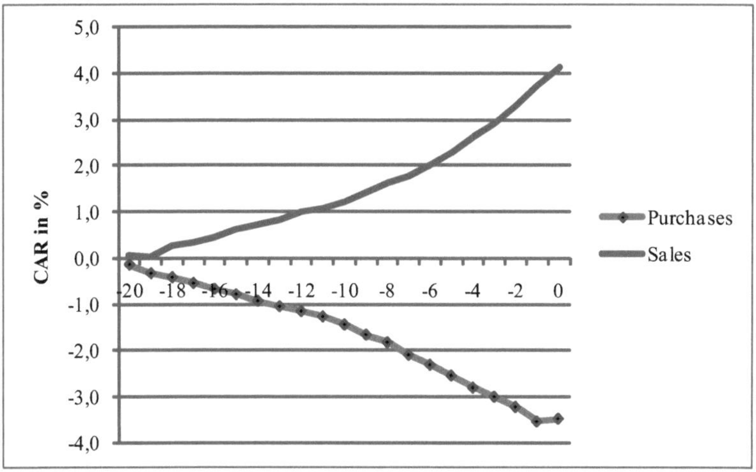

While the pre-event periods shows a clear uptrend for sales and a clear downtrend for purchases, the post-publication period is less distinctive. The following figure depicts post-event CARs including the publication day. Sales show an almost reversed line.

Figure 11: Short-Term CARs after Publication

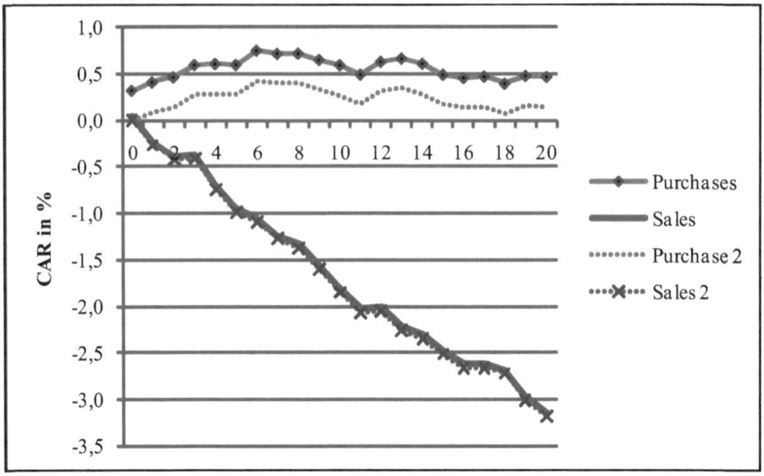

Based on these findings, I suppose that directors are in general able to time their transactions. However, this does by no means indicate that directors exploit inside information. It rather seems that directors follow their firm's share price carefully. These findings show that directors buy at the end of a downtrend and sell following an uptrend. Thus, I conclude that in general, directors have a keen sense for their firm's value and anticipate when the market will correct the firm's value. In particular, directors seem to know when shares are overvalued and thus sell at the peak.

V.A.2 Firm Size Short-Term Results

This sub chapter divides previous results into quartiles based on firm size. Table 9 and Table 9 report empirical findings for purchases and sales before and on the transaction day. Panels A through D represent size quartiles in ascending order.
Previous, unsorted findings showed significant negative ARs before purchases and significant positive ARs before sales. Certainly, it is of great interest to know whether these findings are universally valid or whether they vary for firms of different sizes. In general, the following tables confirm previous results; however, abnormal returns differ among firm size quartiles. The following table reports upper bounds of firm size quartiles in million Euro. Bounds are calculated separately for directors' purchases and sales on the transaction and the publication day.

Table 8: Firm Size Quartiles Short-Term

This table reports breakpoints for firm-size quartiles in million Euro. Breakpoints are calculated separately for purchases and sales on both event dates, i.e. the transaction and the publication day.

	Transaction Day				Publication Day			
Quartiles	1	2	3	4	1	2	3	4
Purchases	27,35	81,13	545,24	82415,38	27,43	81,54	541,69	82735,38
Sales	40,59	186,33	972,88	98395,63	40,375	192,63	976,15	96037

Obviously, firms with directors' sales are generally larger than firms with directors' purchases. I think this effect can in part be explained by the findings of previous subchapters, which indicated that directors sell after a peak and purchase after a trough in share price.

Before all purchase transactions across all firm size quartiles, there are significant negative ARs. Also, as before, the last 10 days before the transaction account for the larger part of the 20-day CAR. However, the significance pattern is not as strong as before. The smallest firms (up to € 27.35m) have negative ARs before a purchase, but they are not as significant as in larger firms. Over the 20-day pre-event period, ARs accumulate to -1.57%. Over the same time, firms in quartiles 2 (up to € 81.13m) and 3 (up to € 545.24m) accumulate -1.89% and -5.12% respectively, while ARs of firms in quartile 4 accumulate -2.36%. On the transaction day, firms in lower quartiles have positive ARs while those in upper quartiles show negative ARs.

Table 9: Firm Size Short-Term Results Purchases before Transaction

This table reports mean abnormal returns and cumulative abnormal returns of 6054 directors' purchases grouped into firm-site quartiles 20 days before and on the transaction day. Panels A through D report daily MARs from 20 days before to the transaction day for quartiles 1 to 4. CARs for these period are reported in panels E through H. Following each abnormal return corresponding t-statistics are reported. Next to them, significance for the t-test, the Wilcoxon test, and the Corrado test is indicated.

	Panel A: Purchases N=1514		Panel B: Purchases N=1513		Panel C: Purchases N=1514		Panel D: Purchases N=1513	
Day	MAR	t-Stats	MAR	t-Stats	MAR	t-Stats	MAR	t-Stats
-20	-0,1747	-1,7795 * +++ ‡	-0,1194	-1,5297 +++ ‡	-0,1182	-1,8247 * +++ ‡‡‡	-0,1159	-2,0618 ** + ‡‡
-19	-0,1373	-1,3205 +	-0,1283	-1,7857 * +++	-0,2400	-3,3437 *** +++ ‡‡‡	-0,1009	-1,8369 * ++ ‡‡‡
-18	0,0315	0,3358	-0,1390	-1,8243 * +++ ‡‡‡	-0,1170	-1,7614 * +++ ‡‡‡	-0,0556	-1,1599 ‡‡
-17	-0,0138	-0,1414	-0,0722	-0,8720 +++ ‡‡	-0,2749	-4,1644 *** +++ ‡‡‡	-0,0028	-0,0564
-16	0,0732	0,7427 +	-0,1666	-2,1807 ** +++ ‡‡	-0,2156	-3,0720 *** +++ ‡‡‡	-0,0173	-0,3648 ‡‡
-15	-0,0298	-0,3254 +	-0,1252	-1,6339 +++ ‡‡‡	-0,2222	-3,3559 *** +++ ‡‡‡	-0,0663	-1,4087 ‡‡
-14	-0,1643	-1,4367 +++ ‡‡	-0,0848	-1,1123 +++ ‡‡	-0,1816	-2,9454 *** +++ ‡‡‡	-0,0797	-1,6637 * +++ ‡‡‡
-13	0,0096	0,0998	0,0197	0,2630 ++	-0,3068	-4,7767 *** +++ ‡‡‡	-0,1141	-2,2340 ** ++ ‡‡‡
-12	0,1950	1,8924 *	-0,0461	-0,5567 +++ ‡	-0,4843	-7,8773 *** +++ ‡‡‡	-0,0085	-0,1762
-11	-0,0407	-0,4190 +++	-0,0040	-0,0397 +++ ‡‡	-0,1514	-2,1011 ** +++ ‡‡‡	-0,1504	-3,0104 *** +++ ‡‡‡
-10	-0,2757	-2,5418 ** +++ ‡‡	0,0007	0,0084 +++ ‡‡	-0,1242	-1,7894 * +++ ‡‡‡	-0,0674	-1,0983
-9	-0,2345	-2,2535 ** +++	-0,1294	-1,4385 +++ ‡‡‡	-0,3352	-5,1214 *** +++ ‡‡‡	-0,0767	-1,2813 ++ ‡‡‡
-8	-0,1884	-1,7090 * ++	-0,1346	-1,4171 +++ ‡‡‡	-0,1061	-1,5452 +++ ‡‡‡	-0,1523	-2,3292 ** +++ ‡‡‡
-7	-0,2816	-2,6783 *** +++	-0,1605	-1,9227 * +++ ‡‡	-0,3175	-4,5372 *** +++ ‡‡‡	-0,1211	-2,3322 ** +++ ‡‡‡
-6	0,0794	0,7023	-0,1461	-1,7499 * +++ ‡‡	-0,3264	-4,8660 *** +++ ‡‡‡	-0,2625	-4,3016 *** +++ ‡‡‡
-5	-0,1726	-1,5189 ++	0,0590	0,6750 ++	-0,3477	-5,2972 *** +++ ‡‡‡	-0,0981	-1,8941 * ++ ‡‡‡
-4	-0,1946	-1,7483 * ++	-0,0666	-0,7012 ++	-0,2701	-3,5366 *** +++ ‡‡‡	-0,1848	-3,3013 *** +++ ‡‡‡
-3	-0,0648	-0,5770 ++	-0,1874	-1,9043 * +++ ‡‡‡	-0,1884	-2,6381 *** +++ ‡‡‡	-0,0433	-0,6895
-2	-0,0102	-0,0785 ++	-0,0697	-0,7755 +++ ‡‡‡	-0,3649	-4,2317 *** +++ ‡‡‡	-0,2854	-4,8344 *** +++ ‡‡‡
-1	0,0209	0,1569 ++	-0,1883	-1,8450 * +++ ‡‡‡	-0,4267	-4,7413 *** +++ ‡‡‡	-0,3599	-4,9747 *** +++ ‡‡‡
0	0,7484	5,2987 *** +++ ‡‡‡	0,3218	3,0866 ***	-0,0592	-0,5368 +++ ‡‡‡	-0,4948	-5,2180 *** +++ ‡‡‡
Days	Panel E: Purchases		Panel F: Purchases		Panel G: Purchases		Panel H: Purchases	
[-20:-1]	-1,5734	-3,5998 *** +++ ‡‡‡	-1,8887	-5,4588 *** +++ ‡‡‡	-5,1193	-15,0272 *** +++ ‡‡‡	-2,3630	-8,8673 *** +++ ‡‡‡
[-20:-10]	-0,2513	-0,9444 +	-0,8660	-3,5078 *** +++ ‡‡‡	-2,3122	-10,7616 *** +++ ‡‡‡	-0,7115	-4,6000 *** +++ ‡‡‡
[-10:-1]	-1,3221	-3,8428 *** +++ ‡‡‡	-1,0227	-3,6425 *** +++ ‡‡‡	-2,8071	-11,8374 *** +++ ‡‡‡	-1,6515	-8,3713 *** +++ ‡‡‡
[-5:-1]	-0,4213	-1,7135 * + ‡‡	-0,4529	-2,1223 ** ++ ‡‡‡	-1,5978	-9,1467 *** +++ ‡‡‡	-0,9715	-6,5481 *** +++ ‡‡‡

Notes
***, **, * indicate significance on the 1, 5, and 10% level for the t-test.
+++, ++, + indicate significance on the 1, 5, and 10% level for the Wilcoxon test.
‡‡‡, ‡‡, ‡ indicate significance on the 1, 5, and 10% level for the Corrado test.
Returns are expressed in percent.

The following table presents the findings for sales. Here, the pattern of positive ARs before directors' sales is present in all quartiles. However, the smallest firms have higher ARs than larger firms. Over a period of 20 days before the sale, ARs accumulate to 7.02%, while firms in quartiles 2, 3 and 4 accumulate only 3.16%, 1.03% and 2.35% respectively. On the transaction day, firms in all four quartiles have significant positive ARs; however, there is no obvious relation to firm size. Firms in quartiles 4 and 2 have the highest event ARs, followed by firms in quartile 1 and finally those in quartile 3.

Though especially the smallest firms show much higher CARs before the transaction than larger firms, the pattern of positive ARs before directors' sales for different firm sizes is similar to that in the unsorted sample in the previous sub chapter.

Table 10: Firm Size Short-Term Results Sales before Transaction

This table reports mean abnormal returns and cumulative abnormal returns of 4268 directors' sales grouped into firm-site quartiles 20 days before and on the transaction day. Panels A through D report daily MARs from 20 days before to the transaction day for quartiles 1 to 4. CARs for these period are reported in panels E through H. Following each abnormal return corresponding t-statistics are reported. Next to them, significance for the t-test, the Wilcoxon test, and the Corrado test is indicated.

	Panel A: Sales N=1068		Panel B: Sales N=1067		Panel C: Sales N=1066		Panel D: Sales N=1067	
Day	MAR	t-Stats	MAR	t-Stats	MAR	t-Stats	MAR	t-Stats
-20	-0,0276	-0,1807 +	0,1634	1,1678 ++ ‡‡‡	0,1460	1,4262 ‡‡	0,0825	1,4637 ‡
-19	0,0248	0,1684	-0,1435	-1,0332 +++ ‡‡‡	-0,0675	-0,8092 ++ ‡‡‡	0,0460	0,9389 ‡‡
-18	0,2163	1,4130	0,3740	2,5951 ***	0,0361	0,3959 ‡‡	0,1426	2,4761 **
-17	0,1237	0,8380 ‡	0,1883	2,0403 **	0,0211	0,2442 ‡‡	0,0127	0,2451 ‡‡
-16	0,3346	2,2564 **	0,1134	1,1362 ++ ‡‡	-0,1059	-1,2495 ++ ‡‡‡	0,0830	1,4596
-15	0,1245	0,9742 ++	0,1295	1,4401 ‡‡	-0,0320	-0,3929 ++ ‡‡‡	0,1070	1,7729 * ‡‡
-14	0,1659	1,2819	0,0123	0,1462 ++ ‡‡‡	-0,0318	-0,3865 ‡‡‡	0,1363	2,5862 ***
-13	0,2205	1,3788	0,2845	2,6660 *** ‡‡	0,0144	0,1835 ‡‡‡	-0,0112	-0,1952 ‡‡
-12	0,3774	2,6418 ***	-0,0140	-0,1715 ++ ‡‡‡	0,1464	1,8731 *	0,2253	2,3124 ** ‡‡
-11	0,3192	2,1591 **	-0,0644	-0,7614 ‡‡	0,0054	0,0723 ‡‡	0,0408	0,7897
-10	0,2414	1,6770 *	0,1415	1,6623 *	0,0054	0,0644 + ‡‡‡	0,0567	0,9364
-9	0,3691	2,4775 **	0,0635	0,7043 ++ ‡‡‡	0,1762	2,1532 **	0,2604	2,9010 *** ‡‡
-8	0,4562	2,9840 ***	-0,0545	-0,6271 +++ ‡‡‡	0,1306	1,3455 ‡‡	0,1853	3,0440 ***
-7	0,3439	2,2511 ** ‡	0,0534	0,5153 ++ ‡‡‡	0,0549	0,6184 ‡‡‡	0,0710	1,2701 ‡
-6	0,6369	4,2013 *** ‡‡	0,1374	1,4500 ‡	0,0395	0,5019 ‡‡‡	0,0414	0,7409
-5	0,4392	2,5241 **	0,4168	3,3361 ***	0,0154	0,2038 + ‡‡‡	0,1717	3,2002 *** +++
-4	0,6530	3,9220 *** + ‡‡‡	0,4050	4,1168 *** +	0,0339	0,3998 + ‡‡‡	0,0706	1,2478
-3	0,5846	3,4139 ***	0,0695	0,7532 ‡‡	0,1755	1,9154 * ‡‡	0,1350	2,1489 **
-2	0,9073	5,1018 *** +++ ‡‡‡	0,3251	3,3628 *** ++	0,0779	0,8793	0,1461	2,2572 **
-1	0,5093	2,5337 **	0,5620	5,3348 *** +++ ‡‡‡	0,1901	2,0475 **	0,3428	5,1963 *** +++ ‡‡‡
0	0,3954	2,0774 **	0,5119	3,6810 *** +	0,0786	0,8748 ‡‡	0,4992	3,1458 *** ++
Days	Panel E: Sales		Panel F: Sales		Panel G: Sales		Panel H: Sales	
[-20:-1]	7,0201	10,3684 *** +++	3,1630	6,6602 *** +++ ‡‡‡	1,0318	2,1531 ** ++ ‡‡‡	2,3459	9,4565 *** +++ ‡‡‡
[-20:-10]	1,8793	4,6947 *** +++	1,0435	3,3754 *** ‡‡‡	0,1322	0,4090 ‡‡‡	0,8651	5,0566 *** +++ ‡‡‡
[-10:-1]	5,1409	9,5447 *** +++ ‡‡‡	2,1195	6,7149 *** +++ ‡‡‡	0,8995	3,1229 *** +++ ‡‡‡	1,4808	8,1576 *** +++
[-5:-1]	3,0934	7,8212 *** +++ ‡‡‡	1,7783	7,8672 *** +++	0,4929	2,5436 ** ++ ‡‡‡	0,8661	6,3474 *** +++

Notes
***, **, * indicate significance on the 1, 5, and 10% level for the t-test.
+++, ++, + indicate significance on the 1, 5, and 10% level for the Wilcoxon test.
‡‡‡, ‡‡, ‡ indicate significance on the 1, 5, and 10% level for the Corrado test.
Returns are expressed in percent.

These findings certainly raise the question whether pre-transaction CARs are followed by inverse post-publication CARs when sorting for firm size. The following two tables report these post-publication results.
While the unsorted sample has a similar pattern in its pre-transaction ARs for both purchases and sales as when divided into firm size quartiles, post-publication ARs differ. Firms in quartile 1 have a highly significant publication day AR at 1.22%. Larger firms have either only slightly significant ARs or insignificant ARs. Furthermore, smallest and largest firms continue their uptrend while firms in quartiles 2 and 3 have negative CARs over a 20-day post-publication period. Over the first 10 days following the publication of purchases, firms in quartile 1 accumulate a CAR of 1.18%, compared to 0.53%, -0.24% and 0.36% in higher quartiles. Over the entire period, CARs accumulate to 1.98%, -0.28%, -0.58% and 0.46%. Thus, firm size post-publication patterns vary from the pattern of the unsorted sample.

Table 11: Firm Size Short-Term Purchase Results after Publication

This table reports mean abnormal returns and cumulative abnormal returns of 6054 directors' purchases grouped into firm-site quartiles on the publication day as well as 20 days following the publication day. Panels A through D report daily MARs for the publication day and subsequent 20 days for quartiles 1 to 4. CARs for these period are reported in panels E through H. Following each abnormal return corresponding t-statistics are reported. Next to them, significance for the t-test, the Wilcoxon test, and the Corrado test is indicated.

	Panel A: Purchases N=1514		Panel B: Purchases N=1513		Panel C: Purchases N=1514		Panel D: Purchases 1513	
Day	MAR	t-Stats	MAR	t-Stats	MAR	t-Stats	MAR	t-Stats
0	1,2179	7,1516 *** +++ ‡‡‡	0,3606	3,5993 *** ++ ‡‡‡	-0,0286	-0,4092 ++ ‡‡‡	-0,0224	-0,3161
1	0,1605	1,4563 + ‡‡‡	0,4150	4,7574 *** ‡‡‡	-0,0556	-0,7588 +++ ‡‡‡	-0,0978	-1,8137 * +++ ‡‡‡
2	0,2035	1,9945 ** ‡‡‡	0,0661	0,7604 ++ ‡	-0,0138	-0,2083 + ‡‡	0,1533	2,6895 ***
3	0,1297	1,3045 ‡‡	0,0482	0,6009 +	-0,0422	-0,5501 +++ ‡‡‡	0,2068	4,2503 *** +++ ‡‡‡
4	0,0989	0,9833	0,0840	1,0601	-0,1291	-1,7140 * +++ ‡‡‡	-0,0123	-0,2215
5	0,0466	0,4674 ‡‡	-0,0300	-0,3975 ++ ‡	-0,0557	-0,8457 +++ ‡‡	0,0293	0,5267
6	0,3054	3,0001 *** ‡‡	0,2085	2,4568 ** ‡	0,0179	0,2443 ++ ‡‡‡	-0,0708	-1,2066 + ‡‡‡
7	0,0435	0,4743	-0,0052	-0,0695	0,0594	0,8857 ++ ‡‡	0,0413	0,5913
8	0,2710	2,7982 *** ‡‡‡	-0,1811	-2,4569 ** +++ ‡‡‡	-0,0112	-0,1665	0,0654	1,2368
9	-0,0651	-0,7269	-0,0327	-0,4123 ++	-0,0337	-0,5059 ++ ‡	0,0122	0,2477
10	-0,0113	-0,1064 ++	-0,0429	-0,5527 ++	0,0235	0,3257 + ‡‡	0,0362	0,6221
11	-0,0453	-0,4251 ++	-0,1626	-2,1380 ** +++ ‡‡‡	-0,1443	-2,1157 ** +++ ‡‡‡	0,1007	1,7097 *
12	0,0671	0,6483 ‡‡‡	0,0217	0,2977	0,2305	3,1247 ***	0,0468	0,8343
13	0,1504	1,4480	-0,0899	-1,2062 +++ ‡	-0,0081	-0,1137 +++ ‡‡‡	0,0787	1,6126
14	0,0283	0,3120	0,0913	1,0776 +++ ‡‡	-0,1393	-2,3630 ** +++ ‡‡‡	-0,0211	-0,4481
15	0,0046	0,0466 ++	-0,1087	-1,3668 +++ ‡‡	-0,1158	-1,8522 * +++ ‡‡‡	-0,0967	-1,7142 * ++ ‡‡‡
16	-0,0409	-0,4332	-0,0699	-0,8248 +++ ‡‡‡	0,0911	1,4036 + ‡‡	-0,0923	-1,8826 * +++ ‡‡‡
17	0,1233	1,2592 ‡‡	0,0090	0,1103 ++	-0,1787	-2,8012 *** +++ ‡‡‡	0,0575	1,0642
18	-0,0088	-0,0897 +	-0,1965	-2,7333 *** +++ ‡‡‡	0,0236	0,3614 ++ ‡‡‡	-0,0448	-0,8401 ‡‡
19	0,3414	3,6095 *** ‡‡‡	-0,0215	-0,2919 +++ ‡‡	-0,0676	-1,0887 +++ ‡‡‡	0,0872	1,7198 *
20	0,1780	1,7380 * ‡‡	-0,2792	-3,6682 *** +++ ‡‡‡	-0,0337	-0,4377 +++ ‡‡‡	-0,0173	-0,2952 ++ ‡‡‡
Days	Panel E: Purchases		Panel F: Purchases		Panel G: Purchases		Panel H: Purchases	
[1:5]	0,6391	3,0899 *** +++ ‡‡	0,5833	3,7487 *** +++	-0,2965	-1,9142 * + ‡‡‡	0,2792	2,2777 ** ++
[1:10]	1,1827	4,3475 *** +++ ‡‡‡	0,5301	2,4360 ** ‡	-0,2406	-1,1152 ‡‡‡	0,3635	2,1904 ** + ‡‡‡
[11:20]	0,7980	2,9588 *** ‡‡‡	-0,8064	-3,8733 *** +++ ‡‡‡	-0,3423	-1,6085 ++ ‡‡‡	0,0987	0,6223 ‡‡‡
[1:20]	1,9807	5,3375 *** +++ ‡‡‡	-0,2764	-0,9473 ++ ‡‡‡	-0,5829	-1,8611 * ‡‡‡	0,4622	2,2547 ** ‡‡‡

Notes
***, **, * indicate significance on the 1, 5, and 10% level for the t-test.
+++, ++, + indicate significance on the 1, 5, and 10% level for the Wilcoxon test.
‡‡‡, ‡‡, ‡ indicate significance on the 1, 5, and 10% level for the Corrado test.
Returns are expressed in percent.

The next table shows whether post-publication ARs of sales differ in the same like those of purchases differ from the unsorted sample. As in the unsorted sample, only firms in quartiles 1 (0.05%) and 2 (0.28%) have positive ARs on the publication day. Firms in upper quartiles have negative ARs at -0.02% and -0.01%. However, post-publication ARs and ARs in the unsorted sample generally do not have opposite signs. ARs in the upper three quartiles are negative on most of the 20 days following the publication. Overall, CARs decrease in magnitude with increasing firm size. Quartiles 1 and 2 differ about 1% with 20-day CARs of -4.80% and -3.80%; however, CARs in quartiles 3 and 4 go down to -2.91% and -1.19% respectively.

Table 12: Firm Size Short-Term Sales Results after Publication

This table reports mean abnormal returns and cumulative abnormal returns of 4268 directors' sales grouped into firm-site quartiles on the publication day as well as 20 days following the publication day. Panels A through D report daily MARs for the publication day and subsequent 20 days for quartiles 1 to 4. CARs for these period are reported in panels E through H. Following each abnormal return corresponding t-statistics are reported. Next to them, significance for the t-test, the Wilcoxon test, and the Corrado test is indicated.

	Panel A: Sales N=1068		Panel B: Sales N=1067		Panel C: Sales N=1066		Panel D: Sales N=1067	
Day	MAR	t-Stats	MAR	t-Stats	MAR	t-Stats	MAR	t-Stats
0	0,0501	0,3017 +++ ‡‡	0,2803	1,9450 *	-0,0239	-0,2258 +++ ‡‡‡	-0,0055	-0,1064 + ‡‡‡
1	-0,5102	-3,6839 *** +++ ‡‡‡	-0,2934	-3,3256 *** +++ ‡‡‡	-0,1181	-1,6349 ++ ‡‡‡	0,0385	0,8678
2	-0,3632	-1,8239 * +++ ‡‡‡	-0,2799	-3,4222 *** +++ ‡‡‡	0,0276	0,3992 ‡‡	-0,1092	-2,3417 ** +++ ‡‡‡
3	-0,0417	-0,2000 +++ ‡	-0,0943	-1,1335 ++ ‡‡‡	-0,2858	-3,6663 *** +++ ‡‡‡	-0,0899	-1,8504 * +++ ‡‡‡
4	-0,5651	-4,6168 *** +++ ‡‡‡	-0,2504	-2,8517 *** +++ ‡‡‡	-0,0571	-0,8148 + ‡‡‡	-0,1247	-2,4358 ** +++ ‡‡‡
5	-0,5162	-4,3572 *** +++ ‡‡‡	-0,2725	-3,5234 *** +++ ‡‡‡	-0,2224	-2,8624 *** +++ ‡‡‡	-0,0619	-1,3457 ++ ‡‡‡
6	0,1873	1,2620 +++ ‡	-0,2854	-3,4221 *** +++ ‡‡‡	-0,1618	-2,0396 ** +++ ‡‡‡	-0,1039	-1,9324 * ++ ‡‡‡
7	-0,6001	-4,8508 *** +++ ‡‡‡	-0,0647	-0,8318 +++ ‡‡‡	0,0524	0,6581 ++ ‡‡‡	-0,0405	-0,8201 +++ ‡‡‡
8	-0,1285	-1,0819 +++ ‡‡	-0,1195	-1,4784 +++ ‡‡‡	-0,0945	-1,2368 +++ ‡‡‡	-0,1704	-3,1874 *** +++ ‡‡‡
9	-0,2244	-1,7234 * +++	-0,1155	-1,3426 +++ ‡‡‡	-0,3533	-4,9629 *** +++ ‡‡‡	-0,2814	-5,0073 *** +++ ‡‡‡
10	-0,1972	-1,7034 * +++ ‡‡‡	-0,3567	-3,3255 *** +++ ‡‡‡	-0,4073	-5,1966 *** +++ ‡‡‡	0,1069	1,9845 **
11	-0,3076	-2,6169 *** +++ ‡‡‡	-0,2379	-2,7921 *** +++ ‡‡‡	-0,1783	-2,2844 ** +++ ‡‡‡	-0,0776	-1,4841 ++ ‡‡‡
12	0,0597	0,4845 +++	-0,1116	-1,2116 +++ ‡‡‡	0,0142	0,1921 ‡‡	0,0306	0,5508
13	-0,3617	-3,3909 *** +++ ‡‡‡	-0,1774	-1,9704 ** +++ ‡‡‡	0,0003	0,0045 ‡‡	0,0002	0,0044
14	-0,0408	-0,2673 +++ ‡‡‡	-0,2839	-3,2797 *** +++ ‡‡‡	-0,2451	-3,5256 *** +++ ‡‡‡	0,0199	0,4068 ‡‡
15	-0,3183	-2,9626 *** +++ ‡‡‡	-0,2186	-2,7306 *** +++ ‡‡‡	-0,0227	-0,3169 ‡‡	-0,0799	-1,5422 ++ ‡‡‡
16	-0,2825	-2,3920 ** +++ ‡‡‡	-0,1450	-1,7800 * +++ ‡‡‡	-0,1342	-1,7793 * +++ ‡‡‡	0,0064	0,1355 ‡‡‡
17	0,0515	0,4414 +++ ‡‡	-0,0637	-0,7304 +++ ‡‡‡	-0,2099	-2,6203 *** +++ ‡‡‡	0,1527	1,1634
18	0,0209	0,2024 +++	-0,0444	-0,5178 ‡	-0,2681	-3,1716 *** +++ ‡‡‡	-0,0999	-0,9935 +++ ‡‡‡
19	-0,4983	-4,3443 *** +++ ‡‡‡	-0,1625	-2,0580 ** +++ ‡‡‡	-0,0877	-1,1073 +++ ‡‡‡	-0,2287	-3,5573 *** +++ ‡‡‡
20	-0,1649	-0,8471 +++ ‡‡‡	-0,2246	-2,5190 ** +++ ‡‡‡	-0,1627	-2,1819 ** +++ ‡‡‡	-0,0767	-1,4706 ‡‡‡
Days	Panel E: Sales		Panel F: Sales		Panel G: Sales		Panel H: Sales	
[1:5]	-1,9963	-5,3645 *** +++ ‡‡‡	-1,1906	-6,2964 *** +++ ‡‡‡	-0,6558	-4,0061 *** +++ ‡‡‡	-0,3472	-3,3143 *** +++ ‡‡‡
[1:10]	-2,9592	-6,8800 *** +++ ‡‡‡	-2,1324	-7,2944 *** +++ ‡‡‡	-1,6204	-7,5688 *** +++ ‡‡‡	-0,8366	-5,5045 *** +++ ‡‡‡
[11:20]	-1,8420	-4,7741 *** +++ ‡‡‡	-1,6696	-6,4338 *** +++ ‡‡‡	-1,2942	-5,8317 *** +++ ‡‡‡	-0,3529	-2,0109 ** +++ ‡‡‡
[1:20]	-4,8012	-8,3043 *** +++ ‡‡‡	-3,8019	-10,0738 *** +++ ‡‡‡	-2,9145	-9,4073 *** +++ ‡‡‡	-1,1895	-4,6691 *** +++ ‡‡‡

Notes
***, **, * indicate significance on the 1, 5, and 10% level for the t-test.
+++, ++, + indicate significance on the 1, 5, and 10% level for the Wilcoxon test.
‡‡‡, ‡‡, ‡ indicate significance on the 1, 5, and 10% level for the Corrado test.
Returns are expressed in percent.

Finally, these result based on firm size quartiles confirm previous results from the unsorted sample. In addition, they further refine conclusions drawn from the last sub chapter. Previous findings implied that directors generally have a good understanding of their firm's value and thus they purchase when they feel their firm is undervalued or sell when they consider it overvalued. Results based on firm size quartiles allow for a more detailed conclusion. Directors' purchases in quartiles 1 and 2 are preceded by smaller CARs than those in quartiles 3 and 4. Even though post-publication CARs barely lessen these losses, I conclude once more from these results that directors know their firm's value precisely; however, smaller firms seem to rebound faster than larger firms. The same applies to directors' sales. Here, especially directors in the smallest firms sell after a strong upward movement just before a share price correction.

V.A.3 Insider Group Short-Term Results

The short-term study closes with the analysis of pre-transaction and post-publication abnormal returns sorted according to the trading insider group. For this purpose, I differentiate between five groups, consisting of members of the executive board (group 1), members of the supervisory board (group 2), other management personnel or persons with access to inside information (group 3), closely related persons such as personal relatives (group 4), and finally legal entities (group 5), which are often related to one of the previous groups and acting as wealth management vehicles.

As in the previous sub chapter, results are presented in four tables. Two tables present pre-transaction ARs and CARs for purchases and sales, followed by two more tables presenting post-publication ARs and CARs. For each insider group mentioned above, the tables show daily results in panels A through E and corresponding cumulative abnormal returns in panels F through J.

The major part of all purchases (N=2,816) is executed by members of the executive board, followed by members of the supervisory board (N=1,575), and then legal entities (N=1,098). Groups 4 and 3 have much smaller numbers, i.e. 404 and 161 purchases respectively. As before, the question is whether the same return pattern as in the general sample can be found when sorting according to insider group. Since the major part of transactions comes from board members, one can assume that at least ARs from these two groups should have a similar pattern. The following table proves this assumption. Group 1 shows a highly significant pattern of negative ARs before and on the transaction day. The very same is true for the second group, although magnitudes are lower and ARs are above zero in two cases. A similar pattern is only found for legal entities (group 5), which seems extremely remarkable as these entities are most often associated to board members. Groups 3 and 4 have patterns of positive and negative ARs before purchases, which are hardly significant. On average, CARs in group 1 reach 3.81% over the 20-day pre-transaction period, followed by group 5 with 2.37% and supervisory board members with 2.09%. Group 3 still shows 0.59% while group 4 has 0.32%. Hence, like the firm size analysis, these results should add to findings from the unsorted sample as figures show dramatic differences between insider groups.

Table 13: Insider Group Short-Term Purchases Results before Transaction

This table reports daily mean and cumulative abnormal returns for directors' purchases for five different insider groups before and on the transaction day. Results for groups 1 to 5 are reported in panels A to E. Groups 1 and 2 consist of members of the executive and the supervisory board. Groups 2 and 3 are persons with continuous access to inside information and closely related persons. Group 5 is made up of legal entities, most often trusts or other wealth management entities associated to an insider. Panels A through E report daily MARs, panels F through J corresponding CARs. Following each abnormal return corresponding t-statistics are reported. Next to them, significance for the t-test, the Wilcoxon test, and the Corrado test is indicated.

	Panel A: Purchases N=2816		Panel B: Purchases N=1575		Panel C: Purchases N=161		Panel D: Purchases N=404		Panel E: Purchases N=1098	
Day	MAR	t-Stats	MAR	t-Stats	MAR	t-Stats	MAR	t-Stats	MAR	t-Stats
-20	-0,1473	-2,5380 ** +++ ‡‡‡	-0,0982	-1,1802 +++ ‡‡‡	0,1453	1,0445	-0,1641	-1,1355	-0,1706	-2,6211 *** +++ ‡‡‡
-19	-0,2512	-4,0911 *** +++ ‡‡‡	0,0434	0,5462	0,0640	0,4153	0,0670	0,4959	-0,2883	-4,0679 *** +++ ‡‡‡
-18	-0,0786	-1,3702 +++ ‡‡‡	-0,1489	-2,0027 ** +++ ‡‡‡	0,1442	0,9546	0,1693	1,3616	-0,0543	-0,7749 +
-17	-0,0905	-1,5300 +++	-0,0798	-1,1326 ++	-0,0726	-0,4596	0,1302	0,8391	-0,1920	-2,3054 ** +++ ‡‡‡
-16	-0,1979	-3,6001 *** +++ ‡‡‡	-0,0788	-1,0305 +++ ‡‡	-0,1482	-0,8598	0,3146	1,9051 *	0,0766	0,9186
-15	-0,1048	-1,9265 * +++ ‡‡‡	-0,1674	-2,3836 ** +++ ‡‡‡	0,1115	0,7229	0,0645	0,4745	-0,1425	-1,7048 * +++ ‡‡‡
-14	-0,1015	-1,6817 * +++ ‡‡‡	-0,0728	-0,8623 +++ ‡‡‡	-0,2633	-1,4804 ‡	-0,2596	-1,8132 * ++ ‡‡	-0,2049	-2,7815 *** +++ ‡‡‡
-13	-0,1590	-2,9027 *** +++ ‡‡‡	-0,1117	-1,5136 +++ ‡‡	-0,0190	-0,0951	-0,0139	-0,0971	0,0360	0,4425
-12	-0,1381	-2,4344 ** +++ ‡‡‡	-0,0906	-1,1653 +++ ‡‡‡	-0,3217	-1,4484	0,1429	1,0414	0,0044	0,0493 ++ ‡‡
-11	-0,1921	-2,9249 *** +++ ‡‡‡	0,0423	0,5375 +	-0,3626	-1,9544 *	-0,0184	-0,1347	0,0143	0,1694 ++ ‡‡‡
-10	-0,2065	-3,3371 *** +++ ‡‡‡	-0,1185	-1,4764 ++ ‡	0,0016	0,0064	0,1564	0,9204	-0,0014	-0,0145 ++ ‡‡
-9	-0,1810	-2,7997 *** +++ ‡‡‡	-0,1871	-2,3077 ** +++ ‡‡	-0,1138	-0,6430 + ‡	-0,2445	-1,6722 * + ‡	-0,2303	-2,8861 *** +++ ‡‡‡
-8	-0,1961	-3,0429 *** +++ ‡‡‡	-0,0839	-1,0359 + ‡	-0,3147	-1,4289 ++ ‡‡	0,1722	0,7513	-0,1954	-2,1419 ** +++ ‡‡‡
-7	-0,2302	-3,9072 *** +++ ‡‡‡	-0,2963	-3,9226 *** +++ ‡‡‡	-0,3324	-1,8082 * ‡	0,2347	1,0524	-0,2361	-2,9076 *** +++ ‡‡‡
-6	-0,2429	-3,8031 *** +++ ‡‡‡	-0,0306	-0,3451 + ‡	-0,0497	-0,2794	-0,0780	-0,5099	-0,2009	-2,5166 ** +++ ‡‡‡
-5	-0,1676	-2,6442 *** +++ ‡‡‡	-0,1372	-1,6021 +++ ‡‡‡	0,3415	1,5284	-0,0191	-0,1496	-0,1878	-2,1531 ** +++ ‡‡‡
-4	-0,3120	-4,5806 *** +++ ‡‡‡	-0,0914	-1,0710 +++ ‡‡‡	0,1075	0,5902	0,0102	0,0666	-0,0754	-0,8294 +++ ‡‡‡
-3	-0,1974	-2,8706 *** +++ ‡‡‡	-0,0664	-0,7945 ++ ‡‡	0,3513	1,6408	-0,0112	-0,0649	-0,1128	-1,1866 ++ ‡‡
-2	-0,1942	-2,7759 *** +++ ‡‡‡	-0,1984	-1,8451 * +++ ‡‡‡	0,2493	1,0967	-0,1653	-1,1084 +++ ‡‡	-0,1995	-2,1801 ** +++ ‡‡‡
-1	-0,4163	-5,6461 *** +++ ‡‡‡	-0,1156	-1,0424 +++ ‡‡‡	-0,1115	-0,4914	-0,1644	-0,7387 + ‡‡	-0,0044	-0,0442
0	-0,0917	-1,0971 +++ ‡‡‡	0,2882	2,3716 **	-0,2625	-1,3332	0,4341	1,8989 *	0,4127	3,3402 ***

Days	Panel F: Purchases		Panel G: Purchases		Panel H: Purchases		Panel I: Purchases		Panel J: Purchases	
[-20:-1]	-3,8052	-14,1628 *** +++ ‡‡‡	-2,0879	-6,0015 *** +++ ‡‡‡	-0,5933	-0,7404 ‡‡‡	0,3237	0,4184 + ‡‡	-2,3653	-6,5533 *** +++ ‡‡‡
[-20:-10]	-1,4609	-8,2960 *** +++ ‡‡‡	-0,7625	-3,6793 *** +++ ‡‡‡	-0,7225	-1,5218 ‡‡‡	0,4326	0,8723	-0,9213	-3,9337 *** +++ ‡‡‡
[-10:-1]	-2,3443	-11,5848 *** +++ ‡‡‡	-1,3254	-4,8080 *** +++ ‡‡‡	0,1292	0,2120 ‡	-0,1089	-0,1845 + ‡‡	-1,4440	-5,2878 *** +++ ‡‡‡
[-5:-1]	-1,2876	-8,7915 *** +++ ‡‡‡	-0,6091	-2,7985 *** +++ ‡‡‡	0,9382	1,8850 * +	-0,3497	-0,9160 ‡‡	-0,5799	-2,9857 *** +++ ‡‡‡

Notes
***, **, * indicate significance on the 1, 5, and 10% level for the t-test.
+++, ++, + indicate significance on the 1, 5, and 10% level for the Wilcoxon test.
‡‡‡, ‡‡, ‡ indicate significance on the 1, 5, and 10% level for the Corrado test.
Returns are expressed in percent.

The next table reports pre-transaction results for directors' sales. Again, groups 1 and 2 contribute the major part of all sales (1,751 and 1,328). Generally, all groups experience only few negative ARs before transaction and all show positive ARs on transaction day except for group 3 (-0.0018%). While members of the executive board (panel A) have only low ARs of 0.13%, event day ARs that are well above 0.50% can be reported for groups 2, 4 and 5. Over the 20-day pre-event period, CARs in groups 1 and 2 are 3.41% and 3.44% respectively. These figures are very close to the 20-day pre-transaction CAR of 3.39% for the unsorted sample. Group 5 has the lowest pre-transaction CAR of 2.06%, followed by group 3 with a CAR of 2.52%. Group 4 has the highest CARs at 4.75%. However, while group 3 accumulates -0.43% between day -20 and -11 and 2.95% over the last ten days before the transaction, group 4 accumulates 1.80% and 2.92% respectively.

Table 14: Insider Group Short-Term Sales Results before Transaction

This table reports daily mean and cumulative abnormal returns for directors' sales for five different insider groups before and on the transaction day. Results for groups 1 to 5 are reported in panels A to E. Groups 1 and 2 consist of members of the executive and the supervisory board. Groups 2 and 3 are persons with continuous access to inside information and closely related persons. Group 5 is made up of legal entities, most often trusts or other wealth management entities associated to an insider. Panels A through E report daily MARs, panels F through J corresponding CARs. Following each abnormal return corresponding t-statistics are reported. Next to them, significance for the t-test, the Wilcoxon test, and the Corrado test is indicated.

	Panel A: Sales N=1751		Panel B: Sales N=1328		Panel C: Sales N=203		Panel D: Sales N=526		Panel E: Sales N=460	
Day	MAR	t-Stats	MAR	t-Stats	MAR	t-Stats	MAR	t-Stats	MAR	t-Stats
-20	0,1052	0,9966 +++ ‡‡‡	0,0018	0,0163 ‡‡	0,1409	1,1845	0,2222	1,8677 *	0,1229	0,9254
-19	0,0694	0,7521 +++ ‡‡‡	-0,0462	-0,4315 ++ ‡‡‡	-0,1617	-1,1280	-0,3779	-2,4966 ** + ‡‡	0,0478	0,3588
-18	0,2193	2,1918 ** +++ ‡‡‡	0,0940	0,8535	-0,0195	-0,1127	0,2567	1,9243 *	0,3929	2,4712 **
-17	0,0687	0,8608 + ‡‡‡	0,0810	0,8233	0,0235	0,1539	0,0379	0,3220 ‡‡	0,2533	1,6969 *
-16	0,0653	0,7345 +++ ‡‡‡	0,1740	2,0179 **	-0,1480	-0,8628	0,1455	1,1192	0,1354	0,8675
-15	0,1152	1,6858 * ‡‡‡	0,0322	0,3612 ++ ‡‡	0,1073	0,6119	0,3358	2,4304 **	-0,1989	-1,3524 +++ ‡‡‡
-14	0,0418	0,6267 +++ ‡‡‡	0,0864	0,9577 ‡	-0,0276	-0,1595	0,1895	1,3251	0,0430	0,3554
-13	0,1916	2,1517 ** ‡‡	0,0129	0,1340 +++ ‡‡‡	-0,2746	-1,7728 *	0,5289	3,2854 ***	-0,0713	-0,5205
-12	0,3672	4,4850 ***	0,0259	0,2724 ‡‡	-0,1767	-1,3346 + ‡	0,2751	1,7662 *	-0,0036	-0,0242
-11	-0,0154	-0,2028 +++ ‡‡‡	0,0736	0,7902	0,1016	0,9227	0,1857	1,5201	0,2878	1,9339 *
-10	0,1105	1,5201 ‡	0,1872	1,8296 *	0,1434	1,0350	-0,0157	-0,1307	0,0260	0,1779
-9	0,2315	2,9036 *** ‡‡‡	0,1709	1,6877 * ‡	0,1439	1,0836	0,3243	2,4951 **	0,2075	1,0405
-8	0,2059	2,6801 *** ‡‡‡	0,3332	3,0524 ***	-0,2436	-1,5129 +++ ‡‡‡	-0,0284	-0,2166	0,0595	0,3765
-7	0,2219	2,6200 *** ‡‡‡	0,1948	1,8876 * ‡‡	-0,0349	-0,2046	-0,1297	-0,9586 ‡‡‡	-0,0291	-0,2030
-6	0,1500	1,9730 ** ‡‡	0,3078	3,0630 ***	0,2917	1,9483 * +	0,2543	1,6902 *	0,1058	0,7223
-5	0,2035	2,4678 **	0,2230	1,8670 *	0,3809	2,8236 *** +	0,4676	3,2845 ***	0,2993	1,3875
-4	0,2288	2,7657 ***	0,3151	2,8387 ***	0,6966	4,1570 *** +++ ‡‡‡	0,5221	3,3302 *** +	0,0128	0,0935
-3	0,1464	1,7966 * ‡‡‡	0,2617	2,2753 **	0,3815	1,9981 ** ++ ‡	0,5552	3,4895 ***	0,1222	0,7887
-2	0,4188	5,0704 *** +	0,4116	3,3843 ***	0,5118	2,9890 *** +++ ‡‡‡	0,3934	2,7699 ***	-0,0782	-0,4312
-1	0,2605	2,5499 **	0,4990	3,9297 *** +++ ‡‡‡	0,6787	3,3230 *** ++ ‡	0,5802	4,0527 *** +++ ‡‡‡	0,3269	1,9954 **
0	0,1261	1,3285 ‡‡‡	0,5578	3,3520 ***	-0,0018	-0,0103	0,6701	3,5570 *** +++ ‡‡‡	0,5895	2,3330 **
Days	Panel F: Sales		Panel G: Sales		Panel H: Sales		Panel I: Sales		Panel J: Sales	
[-20:-1]	3,4059	8,4365 *** +++ ‡‡‡	3,4401	7,2405 *** +++ ‡‡‡	2,5152	3,8663 *** +++	4,7227	6,8749 *** +++	2,0618	3,2679 *** +++ ‡‡‡
[-20:-10]	1,2282	4,6484 *** ‡‡‡	0,5357	1,9072 * ‡‡‡	-0,4347	-0,8853 ‡‡	1,7995	4,5728 *** +++ ‡‡	1,0092	2,3714 ** ‡‡
[-10:-1]	2,1777	7,6941 *** +++ ‡‡‡	2,9044	8,3904 *** +++	2,9499	6,3233 *** +++ ‡‡‡	2,9232	5,8102 *** +++	1,0526	2,1620 ** ++ ‡‡‡
[-5:-1]	1,2580	6,3872 *** +++ ‡‡	1,7104	6,6440 *** +++	2,6495	7,4305 *** +++ ‡‡‡	2,5185	7,2961 *** +++ ‡‡‡	0,6829	1,8286 * +

Notes
***, **, * indicate significance on the 1, 5, and 10% level for the t-test.
+++, ++, + indicate significance on the 1, 5, and 10% level for the Wilcoxon test.
‡‡‡, ‡‡, ‡ indicate significance on the 1, 5, and 10% level for the Corrado test.
Returns are expressed in percent.

For the period of 20 days, unsorted post-publication results of directors' purchases showed both positive and negative ARs with an overall CAR of 0.40%. The following table presents post-publication results. Once again, although all groups experience ARs of mixed signs, they vary greatly in magnitude. Closely related persons (panel D) show a post-publication CAR of 1.45%, followed by supervisory board members with a CAR of 1.26%. In contrast, CARs in groups 1, 3 and 5 are substantially lower at -0.07%, 0.31% and 0.03% respectively.

Table 15: Insider Group Short-Term Purchases Results after Publication

This table reports daily mean and cumulative abnormal returns for directors' purchases for five different insider groups on and after the publication day. Results for groups 1 to 5 are reported in panels A to E. Groups 1 and 2 consist of members of the executive and the supervisory board. Groups 2 and 3 are persons with continuous access to inside information and closely related persons. Group 5 is made up of legal entities, most often trusts or other wealth management entities associated to an insider. Panels A through E report daily MARs, panels F through J corresponding CARs. Following each abnormal return corresponding t-statistics are reported. Next to them, significance for the t-test, the Wilcoxon test, and the Corrado test is indicated.

	Panel A: Purchases N=2816		Panel B: Purchases N=1575		Panel C: Purchases N=161		Panel D: Purchases N=404		Panel E: Purchases N=1098	
Day	MAR	t-Stats	MAR	t-Stats	MAR	t-Stats	MAR	t-Stats	MAR	t-Stats
0	0,1583	1,8239 * ++	0,6036	5,6281 *** +++ ‡‡‡	0,0639	0,3708	0,5546	2,1968 **	0,6206	5,7731 *** +++ ‡‡‡
1	-0,0233	-0,3624 +++ ‡‡	0,3165	3,7497 *** + ‡‡	0,4989	2,7592 ***	0,0849	0,5571	0,0830	0,9421
2	0,1238	2,0704 **	0,0824	1,0639	0,1272	0,6318	0,1029	0,6676	0,0716	0,7636 +
3	0,0420	0,6723	0,0696	0,9519	0,2078	1,0343	0,2562	2,0583 ** +++ ‡‡‡	0,1396	1,6542 *
4	0,1224	1,9648 ** +	-0,0614	-0,7833 + ‡‡	-0,2194	-1,3548 + ‡	-0,2987	-1,9259 * + ‡	-0,0268	-0,3518
5	-0,0215	-0,3633 +++ ‡	-0,1026	-1,3535 +	0,2778	1,6747 * +++ ‡‡	0,3485	2,3299 ** +++ ‡‡‡	0,0198	0,2692
6	-0,0250	-0,3897 +++ ‡‡‡	0,3136	3,8690 ***	0,0133	0,0860	0,3183	2,0664 ** + ‡‡	0,1306	1,7007 *
7	0,0728	1,3272	0,0398	0,5160 + ‡	-0,0051	-0,0316	-0,2822	-1,4550 + ‡	0,0525	0,6488
8	-0,0576	-1,0869 +++	0,1328	1,7219 *	-0,2568	-1,9281 * + ‡	0,2667	1,5843 ‡	0,0954	1,1221
9	-0,0729	-1,3636 +++ ‡	0,0038	0,0534	0,0573	0,4690	-0,1819	-1,3692	0,0754	0,8374
10	0,0012	0,0197 +	0,0123	0,1614 +	0,0138	0,0988	0,2713	1,1348	-0,1148	-1,4294 ++ ‡‡
11	-0,1832	-3,2189 *** +++ ‡‡‡	0,0975	1,1835	0,1851	0,8654	0,0835	0,4244	-0,0747	-0,9235
12	0,0664	1,1247	0,2125	2,6142 ***	0,0405	0,2211	-0,0346	-0,2329	0,0364	0,4497
13	0,0391	0,6750 ++	0,0710	0,8658	-0,2089	-1,3630	0,3499	2,2655 **	-0,1195	-1,6181 +++ ‡‡‡
14	-0,0182	-0,3348 +++ ‡‡	0,0946	1,2235 ++ ‡‡	0,0206	0,1905	-0,2482	-1,9400 * ++ ‡‡	-0,0571	-0,7425 +
15	-0,0777	-1,3753 +++ ‡‡‡	-0,0915	-1,1549 +++ ‡‡	-0,4817	-2,9834 *** +++ ‡‡‡	-0,0225	-0,1768	-0,0269	-0,3085 ++ ‡‡
16	-0,0287	-0,4805 +++ ‡‡‡	0,0183	0,2525 ++ ‡‡	0,2030	1,1408	-0,2244	-1,6367	-0,0541	-0,7191
17	0,0194	0,3378 ++	-0,0902	-1,2511 ++ ‡‡	-0,0839	-0,4994	0,2202	1,2452	0,0262	0,3172 +++ ‡‡
18	-0,1252	-2,2017 ** +++ ‡‡‡	0,0662	0,9161	0,2197	1,4446	0,2067	1,3018	-0,1943	-2,5340 ** +++ ‡‡‡
19	0,1427	2,5860 *** +	0,0384	0,5477	-0,2279	-1,4263 ++ ‡‡	0,1804	1,1798	0,0140	0,1839 ++ ‡‡
20	-0,0648	-1,1259 +++ ‡‡‡	0,0385	0,4671 +++ ‡‡‡	-0,0749	-0,2920 ‡	0,0579	0,3880	-0,1089	-1,1660 +++ ‡‡‡
Days	Panel F: Purchases		Panel G: Purchases		Panel H: Purchases		Panel I: Purchases		Panel J: Purchases	
[1:5]	0,2434	1,9414 * +	0,3046	1,9368 * +	0,8923	2,3699 ** ++	0,4938	1,4073	0,2873	1,7133 * +
[1:10]	0,1620	0,9612 ‡‡‡	0,8070	3,8121 *** ++	0,7147	1,6584 * +	0,8860	1,7734 *	0,5263	2,2349 ** ++ ‡
[11:20]	-0,2302	-1,4423 +++ ‡‡‡	0,4552	2,1220 ** ‡‡‡	-0,4083	-0,8222 ++ ‡‡‡	0,5688	1,2083	-0,5588	-2,3222 ** +++ ‡‡‡
[1:20]	-0,0682	-0,2982 ‡‡‡	1,2622	4,4069 *** ++ ‡‡‡	0,3063	0,4390 ‡‡‡	1,4548	2,1568 ** ++	-0,0325	-0,0989 ‡‡‡

Notes
***, **, * indicate significance on the 1, 5, and 10% level for the t-test.
+++, ++, + indicate significance on the 1, 5, and 10% level for the Wilcoxon test.
‡‡‡, ‡‡, ‡ indicate significance on the 1, 5, and 10% level for the Corrado test.
Returns are expressed in percent.

While post-publication ARs of directors' purchases showed a mixed pattern, results for sales have a similar pattern across all five insider groups. ARs from group

1 are continuously negative except for day 18 after the publication. Almost all ARs from this group are highly significant under all three tests. Overall, the 20-day post-publication CAR of executive board members is -3.88%. Over the 20-day post-publication period, ARs from group 2 accumulate 2.71%, followed by group 4 CAR at 2.35%. Legal entities are closest to group 1; their post-publication CAR is 3.41%.

Table 16: Insider Group Short-Term Sales Results after Publication

This table reports daily mean and cumulative abnormal returns for directors' sales for five different insider groupson and after the publication day. Results for groups 1 to 5 are reported in panels A to E. Groups 1 and 2 consist of members of the executive and the supervisory board. Groups 2 and 3 are persons with continuous access to inside information and closely related persons. Group 5 is made up of legal entities, most often trusts or other wealth management entities associated to an insider. Panels A through E report daily MARs, panels F through J corresponding CARs. Following each abnormal return corresponding t-statistics are reported. Next to them, significance for the t-test, the Wilcoxon test, and the Corrado test is indicated.

	Panel A: Sales N=1751		Panel B: Sales N=1328		Panel C: Sales N=203		Panel D: Sales N=526		Panel E: Sales N=460	
Day	MAR	t-Stats	MAR	t-Stats	MAR	t-Stats	MAR	t-Stats	MAR	t-Stats
0	-0,2403	-2,8874 *** +++ ‡‡‡	0,2515	2,0496 ** + ‡‡	-0,1161	-1,0373	0,6136	2,9171 ***	0,2373	1,0952
1	-0,2658	-3,8858 *** +++ ‡‡‡	-0,2486	-2,8734 *** +++ ‡‡‡	0,1025	0,7916	-0,1784	-1,2579 + ‡	-0,1610	-1,0229 ++ ‡‡‡
2	-0,2747	-3,8294 *** +++ ‡‡‡	-0,0167	-0,1294 +++ ‡‡‡	-0,1202	-0,9515 ‡	-0,4303	-2,4835 ** ++	-0,0424	-0,2414
3	-0,2128	-3,3531 *** +++ ‡‡‡	-0,0693	-0,4324 +++ ‡‡‡	-0,3301	-2,7282 *** +++ ‡‡‡	0,0895	0,6975	-0,1333	-0,9624 ++ ‡‡
4	-0,2735	-4,3123 *** +++ ‡‡‡	-0,2318	-2,8717 *** +++ ‡‡‡	-0,1016	-0,7301	-0,2541	-1,8482 * ++ ‡‡	-0,2679	-1,7919 * ++ ‡‡
5	-0,3471	-5,5910 *** +++ ‡‡‡	-0,2195	-2,7863 *** +++ ‡‡‡	-0,4300	-2,7913 ***	-0,0716	-0,5873	-0,2628	-1,8428 * +++ ‡‡‡
6	-0,0225	-0,2821 +++ ‡‡‡	-0,1928	-2,0626 ** +++ ‡‡‡	-0,0590	-0,4627	-0,0953	-0,7536 +++ ‡‡‡	-0,0671	-0,5224 +
7	-0,2719	-4,2107 *** +++ ‡‡‡	-0,1378	-1,6171 +++ ‡‡‡	-0,2164	-1,7852 * +++ ‡‡‡	0,0586	0,5041 + ‡‡	-0,0534	-0,3613 ++ ‡‡‡
8	-0,1559	-2,3662 ** +++ ‡‡‡	-0,0291	-0,3667 ++ ‡‡‡	0,0514	0,3640 ++ ‡‡	-0,2938	-2,4428 ** +++ ‡‡‡	-0,1989	-1,4201 ++ ‡‡
9	-0,3047	-3,9810 *** +++ ‡‡‡	-0,1158	-1,5198 +++ ‡‡‡	-0,1081	-0,6030	-0,2372	-2,2122 ** +++ ‡‡‡	-0,4474	-3,1035 *** +++ ‡‡‡
10	-0,2721	-4,3987 *** +++ ‡‡‡	-0,1997	-2,4519 ** +++ ‡‡‡	0,1095	0,8248	-0,0742	-0,5617 +++ ‡‡‡	-0,3340	-1,5501
11	-0,1678	-2,7065 *** +++ ‡‡‡	-0,2838	-3,6078 *** +++ ‡‡‡	0,2246	1,2021	-0,1275	-0,9448 +++ ‡‡‡	-0,3548	-2,3398 ** +++ ‡‡‡
12	-0,1152	-1,7036 * +++ ‡‡‡	-0,0034	-0,0411 ++	0,1298	1,1557	0,3969	3,0510 ***	-0,0795	-0,4872 ++ ‡‡
13	-0,0297	-0,4484 +++ ‡‡‡	-0,2816	-3,6200 *** +++ ‡‡‡	0,2498	1,5435	-0,0806	-0,7029	-0,3416	-2,6020 *** +++ ‡‡‡
14	-0,2129	-3,7112 *** +++ ‡‡‡	0,0467	0,4026 +++ ‡‡‡	0,0255	0,1902	-0,2817	-2,7717 *** ++ ‡	-0,2897	-1,7288 * +++ ‡‡‡
15	-0,2450	-4,1197 *** +++ ‡‡‡	-0,1799	-2,5556 ** +++ ‡‡‡	-0,1008	-0,7858	0,0624	0,4404	-0,0586	-0,4515 ++ ‡
16	-0,2243	-3,5059 *** +++ ‡‡‡	-0,1877	-2,4095 ** +++ ‡‡‡	-0,2918	-1,7588 * ++ ‡‡‡	0,0817	0,7073	0,1425	0,9971
17	-0,0880	-1,3710 +++ ‡‡‡	-0,0048	-0,0378 +++ ‡‡‡	-0,0213	-0,1221	0,0949	0,7222	0,0885	0,6060
18	0,0172	0,2798 +++ ‡‡‡	-0,1197	-1,1845 +++ ‡‡‡	-0,3922	-2,2443 ** ++ ‡‡	-0,3154	-2,7752 *** +++ ‡‡‡	-0,0941	-0,5696 + ‡‡
19	-0,3124	-4,7511 *** +++ ‡‡‡	-0,2013	-2,4910 ** +++ ‡‡‡	-0,5965	-3,9815 *** +++ ‡‡‡	-0,1937	-1,6359 ++ ‡‡	-0,0118	-0,0815 + ‡‡
20	-0,1048	-1,2628 +++ ‡‡‡	-0,0324	-0,2453 +++ ‡‡‡	0,0894	0,6024 ‡	-0,4957	-3,8513 *** +++ ‡‡‡	-0,4392	-3,1305 *** +++ ‡‡‡
Days	Panel F: Sales		Panel G: Sales		Panel H: Sales		Panel I: Sales		Panel J: Sales	
[1:5]	-1,3738	-9,5648 *** +++ ‡‡‡	-0,7860	-3,0634 *** +++ ‡‡‡	-0,8793	-2,9142 *** +++	-0,8450	-2,7214 *** +++	-0,8675	-2,1957 ** ++ ‡‡‡
[1:10]	-2,4010	-11,4355 *** +++ ‡‡‡	-1,4611	-5,0715 *** +++ ‡‡‡	-1,1019	-2,6210 *** +++ ‡‡‡	-1,4868	-3,7310 *** +++ ‡‡‡	-1,9682	-3,8445 *** +++ ‡‡‡
[11:20]	-1,4829	-7,5544 *** +++ ‡‡‡	-1,2477	-4,4742 *** +++ ‡‡‡	-0,6836	-1,4853 ‡‡‡	-0,8587	-2,3729 ** +++ ‡‡‡	-1,4383	-3,3794 *** +++ ‡‡‡
[1:20]	-3,8839	-14,0723 *** +++ ‡‡‡	-2,7088	-6,4321 *** +++ ‡‡‡	-1,7855	-3,0306 *** ++ ‡‡‡	-2,3455	-4,0962 *** +++ ‡‡‡	-3,4066	-5,5270 *** +++ ‡‡‡

Notes
***, **, * indicate significance on the 1, 5, and 10% level for the t-test.
+++, ++, + indicate significance on the 1, 5, and 10% level for the Wilcoxon test.
‡‡‡, ‡‡, ‡ indicate significance on the 1, 5, and 10% level for the Corrado test.
Returns are expressed in percent.

Finally, analyzing directors' purchases and sales from the trading person's perspective complements previous results in two ways. First, it confirms findings from the general sample. Second, it reveals in more detail which group of insiders can judge more precisely whether their firm is under- or overvalued and thus purchase or sell stock. Findings from the insider position analysis showed that purchases by executive board members are preceded by an average 20-day CAR of -3.81%; however, post-publication CARs do not show an immediate recovery of the share price. Remaining groups experience negative CARs before purchases, too, but with lower magnitudes. My conclusion drawn from these results is that in general, directors time their trades, and especially executive board members can assess the value of their firm. Since post-publication CARs neither rebound immediately nor move to a level that is even higher than before the transaction, I find no evidence for purchasing on significant inside information. Directors' sales CARs leave a slightly different impression. Here, all groups experience significant positive pre-transaction CARs. While the sales of executive and supervisory board members are preceded by 20-day CARs of around 3.41% and 3.44%, post-publication CARs amount to about -3.88% and 2.71%. Legal entities gain prior sales CARs of only 2.06%, yet their post-publication CARs are almost similar to those of executive board members. Both other insider groups, management personnel and closely related persons, gain 2.52% and 4.72% although their post-publication CARs are only -1.79% and -2.35%. I suppose that these two groups also follow their firm's share price development but they cannot judge as precisely as groups 1, 2 and 5 whether a short-term upward movement of prices is temporary or whether the firm value will remain on a higher level. Overall, I conclude that executive board members are best in assessing their firm's share price, which should be due to the nature of their position. Nevertheless, there is no obvious evidence that this group exploits inside information but rather a strong indication that executive board members really know their firm's value.

V.A.4 Summary of the Short-Term Analysis

The short-term analysis of directors' dealings before the transaction and after the publication brought up several interesting aspects. Using 20-day pre-transaction and 20-day post-publication event windows, results from the unsorted sample showed that directors purchase stock following a price decline (measured CAR -2.74%) and sell stock following a price increase (measured CAR 3.39%). While the post-publication period of purchases did not show significant improvements, CARs following sales diminished almost the entire pre-transaction increase (CAR measured -3.18%). In terms of firm size quartiles, pre-transaction CARs before purchases were higher in larger firms while sales showed highest CARs in the smallest firms. However, sales post-publication CARs in the smallest firms also had the highest negative magnitude and decreased with increasing firm size. The third and final pillar of the short-term analysis consisted of the insider position analysis. Here, executive board members proved to be best in terms of timing their purchases and sales. Overall, I conclude from the short-term study that directors are able to time their transactions in a way that they profit from temporary over- and undervaluation of their firms. Furthermore, comparing pre-transaction and post-publication CARs of executive board members' sales with other insider groups, I conclude that they know best when their firm is temporarily overvalued as positive pre-transaction CARs are followed by negative post-publication CARs of similar magnitude.

V.B Empirical Results Long-Term Study

This sub chapter presents the empirical results of the long-term study. At first, I report BHARs following the publication of directors' purchases and sales over holding periods ranging from 3 to 24. Afterwards, I report BHARs for firm size quartiles and for the five insider groups. Finally, I conclude the long-term study with the calculation of calendar-time returns.

V.B.1 Long-Term Buy-and-Hold Abnormal Returns

This sub chapter presents the empirical results of the long-term study. In line with the short-term study, the results for directors' purchases and sales are presented first. Buy-and-hold abnormal returns (BHAR) are calculated from the publication day onwards for periods of 3, 6, 9, 12, 18 and 24 months. The following table reports the empirical results for purchases and sales following their publication. The number of transactions is reported for each holding period and separately for purchases and sales. Panel A reports the results of purchases and sales with further publications during the respective holding period. Panel B reports only results for purchases and sales without further publications during the respective holding period. Thus, the number of transactions decreases substantially. T-skew states the t-statistics of the skewness-adjusted t-test, followed by significance indicators for the skewness-adjusted and the regular t-test as well as the Wilcoxon test. While the short-term study benchmarked event firms against their expected return, the long-term study uses the previously described buy-and-hold method, which employs reference portfolios from constructed firms in the same size decile. However, since especially the long-term study seems to be valuable for outside investors employing a mimicking strategy, I include the subsequent tables with event firms benchmarked against the CDAX index in the appendix as a reference.
After a three-month holding period, purchases show a highly significant BHAR of 3.15% compared to 0.15% following sales. Purchase BHARs increase constantly over holding periods from 3 to 12 months to 3.26% after 6, 4.94% after 9, and finally 9.10% after 12 months. Over a period of 18 months, BHARs go down to 8.49%, followed by 6.11% over the last reported holding period of 24 months. Sales BHARs show a slightly positive trend with 0.65% after 6 and 1.68% after 9 months. Over the 12-month holding period, sales BHARs are only at 0.47%, followed by -3.19% and 10.83% after 18 and 24 months respectively. Panel B shows BHARs for directors' dealings without any further transaction during the holding period. While the three-month holding period figures for purchases and sales do not differ substantially from those in panel A, subsequent holding periods for purchases show higher BHARs. Over the six-month holding period, BHARs climb

to 7.16%, followed by 9.78%, 18.20%, 23.21% and 25.33% over the 9-, 12-, 18-, and 24-month holding period respectively. On the other hand, BHARs after sales do not vary as much as purchases. After 12 months, BHARs are at -2.84%, followed by -6.05% and -10.05%.

Table 17: Directors' Dealings Long-Term Results

This table reports Buy-And-Hold abnormal returns of directors' dealings after their publication. BHAR are calculated for 3, 6, 9, 12, 18, and 24 months; values are stated in percent. Equally-weighted matching portfolios are constructed with firms in the same firm size decile among CDAX constituents. Panel A presents results with overlapping publications, panel B without overlapping publications.

Panel A	Purchases				Sales			
Months	N	BHAR	T-skew		N	BHAR	T-skew	
3	6.307	3,15	12,42	*** +++ ‡‡‡	4.488	0,15	0,45	‡‡‡
6	5.773	3,26	7,97	*** +++	4.357	0,65	1,34	‡‡‡
9	5.138	4,94	8,01	*** +++	4.234	1,68	2,41	** ++ ‡‡‡
12	4.663	9,10	9,31	*** +++	4.070	0,47	0,53	‡‡‡
18	4.039	8,49	4,74	*** +++ ‡‡‡	3.653	-3,19	-2,49	** +++ ‡‡‡
24	3.351	6,11	2,48	** ++ ‡‡‡	3.199	-10,83	-5,78	*** +++ ‡‡‡

Panel B	Purchases				Sales			
Months	N	BHAR	T-skew		N	BHAR	T-skew	
3	589	4,01	4,00	*** +++ ‡‡	548	0,45	0,42	‡
6	515	7,16	4,45	*** +++ ‡	499	1,45	0,89	‡
9	446	9,78	4,11	*** +++	461	-0,13	-0,03	‡‡‡
12	404	18,20	4,03	*** +++	417	-2,84	-0,98	‡‡‡
18	324	23,21	3,14	*** ++	346	-6,05	-1,30	‡‡‡
24	248	25,33	1,78	* ‡‡	297	-10,05	-1,49	+ ‡‡‡

Notes ***, **, * indicate significance on the 1, 5, and 10 percent level for the bootstrapped skewness-adjusted t-test.
+++, ++, + indicate significance on the 1, 5, and 10 percent level for the t-test.
‡‡‡, ‡‡, ‡ indicate significance on the 1, 5, and 10 percent level for the Wilcoxon test.
Depending on the date of the publication, return series were not available for the entire sample.

Based on these findings, I arrive at the very same conclusion again: directors are able to time their transactions. Short-term results showed that directors sell stock on a temporary peak; long-term results confirm this conclusion as BHARs following sales neither move up nor down substantially over a period of 12 months following the publication or a period of 9 months when accounting for overlapping transactions. Furthermore, the short-term study showed that directors purchase after a price decline. Long-term BHARs confirm previous conclusions about directors' knowledge on their firm's value. While short-term post-publication CARs did not necessarily indicate directors' profit immediately, long-term BHARs show a positive trend for at least 12 months. Findings based on the CDAX (tables presented in the appendix) show very similar results with even higher positive BHARs after purchases when accounting for overlapping transactions.

V.B.2 Firm Size Long-Term Results

This sub chapter presents long-term BHARs following directors' dealings publication with firms sorted into firm size quartiles. To account for changing sample sizes with increasing holding time, quartiles are recalculated for each holding period. The following table reports BHARs for purchases in panels A and B as well as BHARs for non-overlapping purchases in panels C and D. Again, the same table with event firms benchmarked against the CDAX index is available in the appendix.
The following table reports upper bounds of firm size quartiles; here, I calculate these bounds separately for purchases and sales as well as for each holding period as samples decrease with longer holding periods. Panel A shows upper bounds for overlapping transactions, panel B reports results for non-overlapping transactions.

Table 18: Firm Size Quartiles Long-Term

This tabel reports firm size quartiles' upper bounds for long-term BHARs. Bounds are calculated for each holding period, separately for purchases and sales. Panel A reports bounds for overlapping publications, panel B for non-overlapping publications. All figures are expressd in million Euro.

Panel A	Purchases				Sales			
Months	1	2	3	4	1	2	3	4
3	29	87	535	82.735	39	181	939	96.037
6	29	88	555	82.735	39	177	911	96.037
9	28	87	534	82.735	39	177	915	96.037
12	27	83	507	71.035	38	176	902	93.189
18	26	81	490	70.480	36	161	818	81.466
24	26	86	540	70.480	34	139	762	68.346

Panel B	Purchases				Sales			
Months	1	2	3	4	1	2	3	4
3	24	80	497	78.987	28	90	538	88.129
6	24	81	497	78.987	28	90	482	59.453
9	23	79	499	78.987	27	85	474	59.453
12	24	80	494	64.437	26	84	467	59.453
18	23	80	480	64.437	26	77	383	59.453
24	22	69	398	64.437	25	80	415	59.453

Firms in the lower two quartiles show highly significant BHARs of 4.66% and 3.99% over the three-month holding period. Firms in upper quartiles gain only 2.55% and 1.42% within the same time. With increasing holding time, the smallest firms show constantly increasing BHARs with 7.46% (6 months), 11.02% (9 months) and 21.46% (12 months). Firms in quartile 2 also show increasing positive BHARs for these holding periods, with 4.67%, 8.33% and 11.07%. However, while firms in quartile 1 still show increasing BHARs over the 18-month holding period, quartile 2 firms do not. BHARs in the third firm size quartile are significantly positive at 2.55% over three months, although the following holding periods show constantly decreasing BHARs, starting at -0.02% over the 6-month period to ultimately -15.99% after 24 months. The short-term study revealed similar results over the 20-day post-publication period where firms in quartile 3 accumulated ARs to a -0.68% CAR, which was lowest across all quartiles. The largest firms have a similar BHAR pattern over the six reported holding periods as firms in quartile 2 but with a lower magnitude. Over the three-month holding period, these firms gain 1.42% and increase their BHARs to 4.54% over the 12-month period. Afterwards, they drop to 2.53% and move back to 5.12% over the 24-month period. Comparing these results to purchase BHARs without further publication during the holding period (panel C), we find rapidly increasing BHARs for the smallest firms while firms in quartiles 2 and 3 slowly build up positive BHARs of 5.23% and 8.02% over the 12-month holding period. Over 18 and 24 months, BHARs decline again in quartile 2. Largest firms have varying BHARs with a peak at 2.74% over the 6-month holding period and a trough at -2.60% over the 18-month period. None of these BHARs is highly significant.

BHARs following sales are reported in panel B. After a negative BHAR of -2.68%, firms in quartile 1 show increasing values of up to 7.89% over the 12-month holding period but drop to 0.25% over the 24-month holding period. Non-overlapping sales (panel D) show positive BHARs for these firms during the first three holding periods, followed by substantially negative BHARs from 12 months onwards. Firms in quartile 2 and 4 start with positive BHARs of 0.11% and 1.06%. These BHARs are followed by increasingly negative BHARs of up to -22.85 and 11.31%. Directors' sales of firms in quartile 3 do not show negative BHARs over the first five holding periods; however, after 24 months these firms have a significant negative BHAR of 9.44%, which is almost similar to the largest firms. Interestingly, when removing overlapping publications, firms in quartile 2 and 3 have increasingly negative BHARs from the 9-month holding period onwards while those in quartile 4 do not.

Table 19: Directors' Dealings Long-Term Results Firm Size

This table reports Buy-And-Hold abnormal returns of directors' dealings after their publication divided into four quartiles based on firm size. BHAR are calculated for 3, 6, 9, 12, 18, and 24 months; values are stated in percent. Equally-weighted matching portfolios are constructed with firms in the same firm size decile among CDAX constituents. Panels A and B present results for purchases and sales including overlapping transactions, panels C and D present results for purchases and sales without overlapping transactions.

Panel A	Quartile 1 Purchases				Quartile 2 Purchases				Quartile 3 Purchases				Quartile 4 Purchases			
Months	N	BHAR	T-skew		N	BHAR	T-skew		N	BHAR	T-skew		N	BHAR	T-skew	
3	1.579	4,66	7,12	*** +++ ‡‡‡	1.575	3,99	7,74	*** +++ ‡‡‡	1.576	2,55	5,37	*** +++ ‡‡‡	1.577	1,42	3,99	*** +++ ‡‡‡
6	1.443	7,46	6,38	*** +++ ‡	1.444	4,67	6,31	*** +++ ‡‡‡	1.448	-0,02	-0,02	‡‡‡	1.438	0,95	1,67	* +
9	1.285	11,02	6,01	*** +++	1.284	8,33	7,62	*** +++ ‡‡‡	1.287	-1,51	-1,49	‡‡‡	1.282	1,93	2,37	** ++
12	1.169	21,46	6,00	*** +++	1.164	11,07	7,64	*** +++ ‡‡	1.164	-0,73	-0,51	‡‡‡	1.166	4,54	4,36	*** +++
18	1.010	29,84	4,64	*** +++ ‡‡‡	1.010	5,98	2,58	** ++ ‡‡‡	1.009	-4,39	-2,21	** ++ ‡‡‡	1.010	2,53	2,01	* ++
24	847	25,88	3,14	*** ++ ‡‡‡	829	9,24	2,75	*** ++ ‡‡‡	837	-15,99	-5,16	*** +++ ‡‡‡	838	5,12	2,75	*** +++

Panel B	Quartile 1 Sales				Quartile 2 Sales				Quartile 3 Sales				Quartile 4 Sales			
Months	N	BHAR	T-skew		N	BHAR	T-skew		N	BHAR	T-skew		N	BHAR	T-skew	
3	1.122	-2,68	-2,53	** +++ ‡‡‡	1.122	0,11	0,20		1.122	2,10	3,69	*** +++	1.122	1,06	3,00	*** +++ ‡‡‡
6	1.089	1,11	0,81	‡‡‡	1.090	-1,23	-1,38	‡‡‡	1.089	3,37	3,70	*** +++	1.089	-0,64	-1,21	‡‡‡
9	1.060	5,41	2,61	** ++ ‡‡‡	1.059	-1,07	-0,94	‡‡‡	1.057	4,22	3,35	*** +++	1.058	-1,81	-2,57	** +++ ‡‡‡
12	1.019	7,89	2,95	*** +++ ‡‡‡	1.016	-5,27	-4,08	*** +++ ‡‡‡	1.019	2,34	1,57	‡	1.016	-3,13	-3,54	*** +++ ‡‡‡
18	914	1,64	0,49	‡‡‡	914	-8,16	-3,15	*** +++ ‡‡‡	915	1,10	0,53	‡‡‡	910	-7,35	-5,18	*** +++ ‡‡‡
24	801	0,25	0,07	‡‡‡	799	-22,85	-6,63	*** +++ ‡‡‡	801	-9,44	-3,18	*** +++ ‡‡‡	798	-11,31	-5,97	*** +++ ‡‡‡

Panel C	Quartile 1 Purchases				Quartile 2 Purchases				Quartile 3 Purchases				Quartile 4 Purchases			
Months	N	BHAR	T-skew		N	BHAR	T-skew		N	BHAR	T-skew		N	BHAR	T-skew	
3	147	6,26	2,27	** ++	148	3,64	1,70	*	147	3,81	2,32	** ++ ‡	147	2,32	1,97	* +
6	129	16,90	3,51	*** +++	129	4,72	1,49		128	4,26	1,74	* +	129	2,74	1,40	
9	112	26,88	3,50	*** ++	111	5,10	1,19		112	7,28	2,11	** +	111	-0,27	-0,11	
12	101	59,55	3,52	*** ++ ‡	101	5,23	0,98		101	8,02	1,82	* +	101	0,01	0,03	
18	81	86,34	3,23	*** ++	81	-1,08	-0,07	‡	81	10,20	1,45		81	-2,60	-0,61	
24	62	112,50	2,09	**	62	-5,16	-0,38		62	-3,46	-0,36		62	-2,55	-0,39	

Panel D	Quartile 1 Sales				Quartile 2 Sales				Quartile 3 Sales				Quartile 4 Sales			
Months	N	BHAR	T-skew		N	BHAR	T-skew		N	BHAR	T-skew		N	BHAR	T-skew	
3	137	1,39	0,41		137	-0,90	-0,59		137	-0,69	-0,45		137	2,00	1,59	
6	125	5,27	1,12		125	-0,34	-0,09		124	0,26	0,11		125	0,58	0,30	
9	115	2,71	0,42	‡	116	-1,84	-0,48	‡	115	-3,22	-0,88	‡	115	1,86	0,59	
12	104	-3,42	-0,39	‡‡	105	-5,04	-1,06	‡‡	104	-6,29	-1,37		104	3,41	0,86	
18	87	-9,25	-0,67	‡‡	86	-11,59	-1,62	+ ‡‡‡	87	-5,67	-0,61		86	2,33	0,42	
24	74	-8,49	-0,38	‡‡‡	75	-11,43	-1,21	‡‡	74	-19,84	-1,75	* + ‡‡‡	74	-0,43	-0,04	

Notes: ***, **, * indicate significance on the 1, 5, and 10 percent level for the bootstrapped skewness-adjusted t-test.
+++, ++, + indicate significance on the 1, 5, and 10 percent level for the t-test.
‡‡‡, ‡‡, ‡ indicate significance on the 1, 5, and 10 percent level for the Wilcoxon test.
Depending on the date of the publication, return series were not available for the entire sample.

Finally, these results confirm the findings of the short-term analysis. Furthermore, outside investors gain valuable information about the relation between long-term performance and directors' dealings. Purchases of smallest firms continue their positive development, which was already present in the 20-day post-publication CAR in the short-term study. Results for non-overlapping purchases and sales are only of minor importance for outside investors who employ a mimicking strategy[355]. Nevertheless, I suggest from these findings that especially directors in the smallest firms are aware of their firm's prosperous outlook and invest accordingly. However, I cannot transfer this conclusion to larger firms. While quartiles 2 and 4 show positive BHARs over all holding periods, results are not as distinctive. In addition, firms in quartile 3 have a negative development.

Findings for sales confirm the short-term results. Here, I conclude that especially directors in the smallest firms sell shares on a temporary peak without bad news in sight. Directors from firms in the upper three quartiles seem to be aware of their firm's poor future performance. However, I think it is almost impossible to link these directors' sales to specific inside information, which would deem them as illegal insider transactions. Nevertheless, I consider them as important yet diffuse signals to the market.

V.B.3 Insider Group Long-Term Results

As in the short-term study, long-term BHARs are also calculated for the five different insider groups. The structure of the table is similar to previous tables, i.e. panels A and B report results for purchases and sales for all transactions, panels C and D only for non-overlapping transactions.

Over the three-month holding period, directors' purchases show significant positive BHARs across all five insider groups. While executive and supervisory board members earn 3.03% and 3.67% respectively, closely related persons and legal entities earn only 3.16% and 2.69%. Other management personnel (group 3) have BHARs at 3.59%, 5.26%, and 10.11% over the 3-, 6- and 12-month holding period respectively. Over longer holding periods, executive board members do not show substantial increases; BHARs have a peak at 6.00% after 12 months. However, after one year, insiders belonging to groups 2 and 4 have significant increases and reach 17.17% and 18.98% respectively. Supervisory board members peak at 22.49% after 18 months. Focusing on non-overlapping transactions, these figures are even higher although the sample size decreases substantially for all groups. Legal entities have low positive BHARs over the first four holding periods and significant negative BHARs of 7.65% and 13.21% over 18 and 24 months respectively.

Results for sales show increasingly negative BHARs for executive board members starting at 0.18% over the three-month holding period, moving down to 5.93% over one year and finally to 19.27% over the 24-month holding period. Panel D, which reports non-overlapping sales transactions, shows low positive BHARs for holding periods of up to six months but an even lower 24-month BHAR at 21.25% for group 1. Group 4 has positive BHARs over all holding periods in both cases, i.e. with and without overlapping transactions. Groups 2 and 5 have both positive and negative BHARs. However, this pattern changes when accounting for overlapping transactions. In that case, supervisory board members have increas-

355 An outside investor who employs a mimicking strategy cannot know ex-ante whether or not there will be any further directors' dealings during the holding period.

ingly negative BHARs of at most 17.83% while legal entities have positive but insignificant BHARs. Insiders from group 3 have slightly negative BHARs over the first three holding periods, followed by two insignificantly positive BHARs over 12 and 18 months and finally a highly significant BHAR at 16.00% over the 24-month holding period.

Table 20: Directors' Dealings Long-Term Results Insider Group

This table reports Buy-And-Hold abnormal returns of directors' dealings after their publication divided into five groups based on the trading person's insider category. BHAR are calculated for 3, 6, 9, 18, and 24 months; values are stated in percent. Equally-weighted matching portfolios are constructed with firms in the same firm size decile among CDAX constituents. Panels A and B present results purchases and sales including overlapping transactions, panels C and D present results for purchases and sales without overlapping transactions.

Panel A	Group 1 Purchases				Group 2 Purchases				Group 3 Purchases				Group 4 Purchases				Group 5 Purchases			
Months	N	BHAR	T-skew	Sig.	N	BHAR	T-skew	Sig.	N	BHAR	T-skew	Sig.	N	BHAR	T-skew	Sig.	N	BHAR	T-skew	Sig.
3	2.886	3,03	7,72	*** +++ ‡‡‡	1.649	3,67	7,01	*** +++ ‡‡‡	178	3,59	3,47	*** +++ ‡‡	390	3,16	3,82	*** +++ ‡‡‡	1.204	2,69	4,84	*** +++
6	2.687	2,45	3,79	*** +++ ‡‡	1.512	5,31	6,48	*** +++ ‡‡‡	173	5,26	2,91	*** +++ ‡‡‡	372	5,62	4,47	*** +++ ‡‡‡	1.029	1,21	1,45	
9	2.442	3,66	3,81	*** +++ ‡‡	1.314	6,82	5,02	*** +++	160	10,11	3,92	*** +++ ‡‡‡	343	13,02	6,30	*** +++ ‡‡‡	879	1,60	1,35	
12	2.231	6,00	4,81	*** +++ ‡	1.210	17,17	5,46	*** +++	143	12,84	3,79	*** +++ ‡‡‡	327	18,98	7,25	*** +++ ‡‡‡	752	0,27	0,19	
18	1.964	3,99	2,26	** ++ ‡‡‡	1.079	22,49	3,81	*** +++ ‡‡‡	134	6,87	1,58		306	18,09	5,61	*** +++ ‡‡‡	556	-7,65	-3,15	*** +++
24	1.663	4,46	1,62	‡‡‡	925	14,85	2,13	** + ‡‡‡	114	-4,91	-0,99		279	17,12	4,22	*** +++ ‡‡	370	-13,21	-2,74	*** +++
Panel B	**Group 1 Sales**				**Group 2 Sales**				**Group 3 Sales**				**Group 4 Sales**				**Group 5 Sales**			
Months	N	BHAR	T-skew	Sig.	N	BHAR	T-skew	Sig.	N	BHAR	T-skew	Sig.	N	BHAR	T-skew	Sig.	N	BHAR	T-skew	Sig.
3	1.827	-0,18	-0,32	‡‡	1.368	-0,56	-0,96	‡‡‡	204	-1,16	-1,00	‡‡	558	2,58	2,76	*** +++	531	1,05	1,02	
6	1.772	-0,64	-0,82	‡‡‡	1.325	0,24	0,26	‡‡‡	199	-2,12	-1,60	‡‡	551	4,13	3,23	*** +++	510	3,54	2,28	** ++
9	1.715	-2,99	-2,92	*** +++ ‡‡‡	1.289	4,94	3,37	*** +++ ‡‡	194	-0,60	-0,28	‡	543	7,60	4,53	*** +++ ‡‡‡	493	3,82	1,79	* +
12	1.640	-5,93	-4,65	*** +++ ‡‡‡	1.246	5,22	2,80	*** ++ ‡‡‡	190	1,65	0,67		530	5,83	2,77	*** ++	464	3,72	1,43	
18	1.483	-10,23	-4,70	*** +++ ‡‡‡	1.133	-0,49	-0,20	‡‡‡	169	0,40	0,12		489	10,66	3,02	*** +++ ‡	379	-3,14	-0,82	
24	1.295	-19,27	-5,73	*** +++ ‡‡‡	1.011	-8,76	-2,71	** +++ ‡‡‡	148	-16,00	-4,21	*** +++ ‡‡‡	443	2,89	0,63	‡‡‡	302	0,85	0,16	
Panel C	**Group 1 Purchases**				**Group 2 Purchases**				**Group 3 Purchases**				**Group 4 Purchases**				**Group 5 Purchases**			
Months	N	BHAR	T-skew	Sig.	N	BHAR	T-skew	Sig.	N	BHAR	T-skew	Sig.	N	BHAR	T-skew	Sig.	N	BHAR	T-skew	Sig.
3	297	4,37	2,74	*** ++	170	4,90	2,95	*** +++ ‡‡	13	-1,14	-0,32		38	3,86	1,36		71	1,38	0,55	
6	260	6,07	2,75	*** ++	148	9,97	2,94	*** ++	11	-3,64	-0,62		37	8,09	1,63		59	6,34	1,43	
9	226	8,53	2,42	** +	128	12,10	2,53	** ++					32	14,27	1,76	*	51	9,38	1,47	
12	204	11,02	2,46	** +	115	37,36	2,68	** +					32	18,74	1,94	*	47	4,97	0,73	
18	166	15,31	2,11	**	89	43,74	1,90	*					29	36,07	1,65		34	3,75	0,35	
24	123	30,98	1,62		72	37,93	1,18						20	4,25	0,21		27	-7,97	-0,46	
Panel D	**Group 1 Sales**				**Group 2 Sales**				**Group 3 Sales**				**Group 4 Sales**				**Group 5 Sales**			
Months	N	BHAR	T-skew	Sig.	N	BHAR	T-skew	Sig.	N	BHAR	T-skew	Sig.	N	BHAR	T-skew	Sig.	N	BHAR	T-skew	Sig.
3	267	0,16	0,16	‡‡	145	-1,66	-1,06		17	3,52	0,65		59	2,35	0,84		60	4,09	1,13	
6	240	1,70	0,69	‡‡	133	-1,86	-0,65		15	-2,22	-0,37		55	2,12	0,48		56	8,52	1,59	
9	224	-0,60	-0,13	‡‡‡	120	-5,97	-1,26	‡‡‡	14	1,91	0,22		52	0,72	0,13		51	14,27	1,85	*
12	205	-5,15	-1,19	‡‡‡	103	-11,14	-1,78	* ++ ‡‡‡	13	6,71	0,64		51	5,10	0,75		45	14,90	1,71	*
18	171	-9,60	-1,30	‡‡‡	91	-16,64	-2,34	** +++ ‡‡‡	10	12,48	0,87		40	11,51	0,79		34	13,99	1,12	
24	143	-21,25	-2,07	** ++ ‡‡‡	78	-17,83	-2,14	** ++ ‡‡‡					35	14,89	0,73		32	29,54	1,35	

Notes ***, **, * indicate significance on the 1, 5, and 10 percent level for the bootstrapped skewness-adjusted t-test.

From these findings, I conclude that purchases by executive board members show positive long-term developments even though these BHARs are not very high. However, groups 2 and 4 have substantial gains over all holding periods, which may imply that their close relationship to the highest management level provides them with important insights into the firm's business outlook. It would certainly be inappropriate to presume trading on significant information. The driving force might rather be personal confidence in the firm's prospects. On the other hand, I conjecture that management without board positions, represented in group 3, purchases on significant inside information since their BHARs are increasing over the first 12 months but drop afterwards. I assume from this pattern that they purchase on information with a significant short- to medium-term impact on the business. Overall, I conclude that directors purchase stock on positive outlooks and especially executive board members sell shares before price declines.

V.B.4 Cross-Sectional Regression Long-Term BHAR

Based on previous findings, I employ a cross-sectional ordinary least squares (OLS) regression to find possible drivers for these results and to further define my findings. For this purpose, I use each period's BHAR as dependent variable the following set of independent variables:

Purchase-sale dummy becomes 1 for purchases and 0 for sales.

Log firm size is the logarithm of the firm's market capitalization in million Euro.

Log trade as % of market cap is the Euro value of the purchase or sale divided by the firm market capitalization on the publication day in Euro.

Board member dummy is 1 for transactions by members of the executive board and 0 otherwise.

Other insider dummy is 1 for transactions by a person with continuous access to inside information but who is neither a member of the executive nor the supervisory board.

Board purchase dummy is 1 for purchases by members of the executive or supervisory board and 0 otherwise.

Other insider purchase dummy is 1 for purchases by a person with continuous access to inside information but who is neither a member of the executive nor the supervisory board.

I employ the last two variables in a second regression model in exchange for the purchase-sales dummy, the board member dummy and the other insider dummy. While variables in the first model cover the overall trading effects of these insider groups, variables in the second model concentrate on purchases by these three insider groups. As these three insider groups are probably closer to the firm than the other two groups, I assume their purchases are important signals. The following four tables report results for both models for all publications as well as non-overlapping publications.

Table V-15 reports regression results for BHARs with overlapping transactions; results for non-overlapping transactions are presented afterwards. The first row for each variable reports coefficients, the second line reports t-statistics with White (1980) heteroskedasticity adjustment. Obviously, the most important driver for long-term buy-and-hold abnormal returns is the purchase-sale dummy. Over all holding periods, this variable shows increasing loadings with significant t-statistics. Furthermore, the purchase-sale dummy has, as expected, a positive sign. Increasing firm sizes come along with smaller BHARs, although the effect is less pronounced than assumed. The relative size of the trade seems to be important with longer holding periods; here, coefficient increase with longer holding periods. Board members show positive and negative coefficients across different holding periods while the other insider dummy has positive coefficients from the six-month holding period onwards.

Table 21: BHAR Cross-Sectional Regression

This table reports results for the cross-sectional regression for overlapping transactions. Purchase-Sale dummy is 1 for purchases and 0 otherwise. Log firm size is logarithm of firm size in million Euro on the publication day. Log Trade as % of market cap is the value of the transaction in Euro in relation to the market capitalization on the publication day in Euro. Board Member dummy is 1 when a member of the executive or the supervisory board trades and 0 otherwise. Other insider dummy is 1 if a person with continuous access to inside information trades otherwise 0.

	Holding Period					
	3	6	9	12	18	24
N	10.795	10.130	9.372	8.733	7.692	6.550
Variable						
Intercept	0,012	0,060	0,129	0,174	0,206	0,230
	1,229	**4,350**	**6,297**	**5,412**	**3,948**	**3,531**
Purchase-Sale Dummy	0,029	0,027	0,036	0,093	0,127	0,211
	6,329	**3,847**	**3,355**	**5,572**	**4,850**	**6,336**
Log Firm size	-0,001	-0,005	-0,009	-0,014	-0,019	0,001
	-1,112	**-2,508**	**-2,890**	**-2,848**	**-2,386**	0,064
Log Trade as % of Market Cap	0,000	0,003	0,007	0,014	0,020	0,044
	-0,201	**1,655**	**2,724**	**3,681**	**3,881**	**6,894**
Board Dummy	-0,006	-0,008	-0,018	0,004	0,010	-0,015
	-1,237	-1,102	**-1,645**	0,245	0,409	-0,456
Other Insider Dummy	-0,007	0,008	0,039	0,101	0,127	0,027
	-0,705	0,562	**1,840**	**3,255**	**2,775**	0,535
R^2	0,005	0,004	0,006	0,009	0,007	0,011

I hardly find significant coefficients for the non-overlapping transactions. However, the coefficient of the purchase-sale dummy increases substantially with longer holding periods. Furthermore, firm size also shows increasing coefficients.

Table 22: BHAR Cross-Sectional Regression - Non-Overlapping

This table reports results for the cross-sectional regression for non-overlapping transactions. Purchase-Sale dummy is 1 for purchases and 0 otherwise. Log firm size is logarithm of firm size in million Euro on the publication day. Trade as % of market cap is the value of the transaction in Euro in relation to the market capitalization on the publication day in Euro. Board Member dummy is 1 when a member of the executive or the supervisory board trades and 0 otherwise. Other insider dummy is 1 if a person with continuous access to inside information trades otherwise 0.

	Holding Period					
	3	6	9	12	18	24
N	1.137	1.014	907	821	670	545
Variable						
Intercept	0,038	0,118	0,167	0,188	0,264	0,381
	1,074	**2,398**	**2,494**	**2,072**	**1,802**	1,386
Purchase-Sale Dummy	0,039	0,055	0,099	0,199	0,267	0,269
	2,182	**2,137**	**2,711**	**3,177**	**2,673**	1,619
Log Firm size	-0,003	-0,019	-0,026	-0,048	-0,078	-0,153
	-0,374	**-1,763**	-1,556	**-1,746**	**-1,812**	**-1,722**
Log Trade as % of Market Cap	0,003	-0,001	-0,001	-0,008	-0,022	-0,058
	0,728	-0,192	-0,085	-0,538	-0,992	-1,618
Board Dummy	-0,004	-0,023	-0,058	-0,046	-0,109	-0,130
	-0,214	-0,726	-1,319	-0,781	-1,055	-0,856
Other Insider Dummy	0,002	-0,070	-0,063	-0,013	-0,094	-0,256
	0,056	-1,308	-0,843	-0,132	-0,589	-1,336
R^2	0,006	0,015	0,019	0,020	0,021	0,020

The following two tables report regression results for the second model, where I include two interaction variables instead of the purchase-sale, board and other insider dummies. Board and other insider purchase dummies are 1 when either group conducts a purchase, otherwise they are 0. Again, firm size shows negative coefficients that are slightly higher than in the previous model. While the trade size variable showed rather small coefficients previously, they increased substantially in this model from the nine-month holding period onwards. However, the focus in the second model is certainly on the last two variables, representing the purchases by board members and other corporate insiders with continuous access to inside information. The board member dummy has significant coefficients over all holding periods; while their value is 0.023 for the 3-month BHAR, it increases to 0.077 over a period of 12 months and finally reaches 0.161 for the 24-month holding period. The other insider interaction variable has significant coefficients for all but the 18-month holding period. In contrast to the board member variable, coefficients start at 0.048 for the 3-month BHAR, followed by 0.077 and 0.107 for the 12-month BHAR.

Table 23: BHAR Cross-Sectional Regression – Interaction

This table reports results for the cross-sectional regression for overlapping transactions. Log firm size is logarithm of firm size in million Euro on the publication day. Log Trade as % of market cap is the value of the transaction in Euro in relation to the market capitalization on the publication day in Euro. Board Member dummy is 1 when a member of the executive or the supervisory board purchases and 0 otherwise. Other insider dummy is 1 if a person with continuous access to inside information purchases otherwise 0.

	Holding Period					
	3	6	9	12	18	24
N	10.795	10.130	9.372	8.733	7.692	6.550
Variable						
Intercept	0,017	0,048	0,096	0,137	0,143	0,062
	2,280	**4,481**	**5,871**	**4,806**	**2,977**	1,083
Log Firm size	-0,001	-0,007	-0,014	-0,023	-0,033	-0,029
	-1,321	**-4,217**	**-5,322**	**-4,691**	**-3,701**	**-2,851**
Log Trade as % of Market Cap	-0,017	-0,014	0,007	0,064	0,118	0,012
	-1,386	-0,963	0,297	**2,214**	**2,717**	0,244
Board Purchase Dummy	0,023	0,022	0,020	0,077	0,120	0,161
	5,153	**3,081**	**1,811**	**4,157**	**3,952**	**4,308**
Other Insider Purchase Dummy	0,046	0,070	0,101	0,107	0,061	0,109
	2,929	**3,049**	**2,875**	**2,191**	0,996	**1,742**
R^2	0,003	0,004	0,005	0,007	0,007	0,006

The last table in this sub chapter reports regression results for the second model with BHARs of non-overlapping publication as the dependent variable. While the overall number of significant coefficients drops and none of all six holding periods produce significant coefficients for the other insider purchase dummy, the board member purchase dummy is once again significant for all holding periods. Furthermore, coefficients are substantially higher than in the previous table. The other insider purchase dummy has negative coefficients; however, since there are only a few cases in the non-overlapping sample over holding periods of 3 to 18 months and none for 24 months, their informational value is certainly limited.

Table 24: BHAR Cross-Sectional Regression – Interaction

This table reports results for the cross-sectional regression for non-overlapping transactions. Purchase-Sale dummy is 1 for purchases and 0 otherwise. Log firm size is logarithm of firm size in million Euro on the publication day. Trade as % of market cap is the value of the transaction in Euro in relation to the market capitalization on the publication day in Euro. Board Member dummy is 1 when a member of the executive or the supervisory board purchases and 0 otherwise. Other insider dummy is 1 if a person with continuous access to inside information purchases otherwise 0.

	Holding Period					
	3	6	9	12	18	24
N	1.137	1.014	907	821	670	545
Variable						
Intercept	0,033	0,112	0,142	0,192	0,261	0,393
	0,919	**2,380**	**2,158**	**1,828**	1,562	1,199
Log Firm size	-0,005	-0,018	-0,026	-0,042	-0,061	-0,104
	-0,957	**-2,324**	**-2,318**	**-2,062**	**-1,868**	-1,545
Log Trade as % of Market Cap	0,039	-0,018	0,046	0,131	0,224	0,192
	0,730	-0,280	0,538	1,259	1,556	1,051
Board Purchase Dummy	0,039	0,051	0,084	0,216	0,284	0,424
	2,297	**1,836**	**1,965**	**2,554**	**2,148**	**1,763**
Other Insider Purchase Dummy	-0,057	-0,036	-0,097	-0,144	-0,312	-0,265
	-0,887	-0,421	-0,851	-0,947	-1,481	-1,275
R^2	0,007	0,013	0,015	0,019	0,019	0,020

From these results, I conclude that the most important driver for long-term BHARs is whether a purchase or a sale is published. Furthermore, these findings confirm the conclusions drawn from the long-term study. Increasing firm size produces a generally lower BHAR. Also, board members and other management personnel are associated with positive BHARs. Therefore, I conclude that outsiders can profit if they follow the publication of directors' dealings very closely. Especially large purchases in small firms seem worth watching carefully. Furthermore, I consider purchases by board members and other management personnel as important signals. With an increasing number of directors' dealings in the future, this analysis can certainly deliver even better and more accurate results and thus offer the possibility for future research.

V.B.5 Calendar-Time Portfolios

This sub-chapter serves as a robustness-check for previous results and completes the long-term study. For this purpose, I employ the calendar-time portfolio method for all holding periods from 3 to 24 months and subsequently report results. At first, I present calendar-time raw returns, followed by adjusted monthly calendar-time returns. As previously stated, I adjust monthly calendar-time returns using the MSCI Standard index for Germany.[356] Finally, I employ the Fama-French

356 I specifically use the MSCI Standard index to adjust monthly raw returns, as this index, together with other size and style indices from MSCI Barra, is used for the Fama-French

Three-Factor model to analyze calendar-time raw returns. Generally, regression results should yield similar outcomes to the adjusted calendar-time portfolios.

Overall, I calculate three different sets of calendar-time portfolios. However, I will only discuss the first set in this sub-chapter and add the remaining two sets in the annex as comparison. The three sets differ in the way the account for monthly purchases and sales. The first set, presented below, considers firms for the purchase portfolio only when they had pure history of directors' purchases and no directors' sales over the holding period and vice versa for the sale portfolio. Consequently, this set is free of interference between purchases and sales. Naturally, this constraint leads to a smaller number of firms included in monthly purchase and sale portfolios. The second set considers monthly directors' purchases and sales without constraint. Thus, one firm with both, directors' purchases and sales in one month is added to the purchase as well as the sale portfolio. The third and final set of calendar-time portfolios is based on netted monthly directors' purchases and sales; that is the Euro volume of monthly directors' purchases and sales are netted resulting in either a net purchase month or a net sale month. All three sets are based on the same data as used for the BHAR approach, which includes directors' dealings from 2002 to 2008. However, it seem noteworthy to mention, that while the BHAR methodology calculates returns from a purchase or sell event onward and therefore does not require data prior the event, the calendar-time approach adds firms to the appropriate portfolio when they had an event in K previous months, specified by the holding period. Accordingly, with increasing holding periods the calendar-time approach accounts for fewer events; in particular, events in the first months drop out. Therefore, calculated returns of the BHAR and calendar-time approach may deviate substantially from each other with increasing holding periods.

The first table shows calendar-time raw returns for purchase events in panel A and for sale events in panel B. As afore mentioned, this set accounts only for non-overlapping purchase and sale events, i.e. they either only have directors' purchases or sales in the respective holding period. For each holding period, I report both panels the mean and median number of firms included in the portfolios.

Panel A reports positive raw returns over all holding periods, however they constantly decrease. While returns for 3, 6, and 9 months are highly significant, the 12-month calendar-time return is only significant under the Wilcoxon test, the remaining periods are insignificant. Returns for sales peak for the 6-month holding period at 1.16%, yet this figure is only significant under the Wilcoxon test. Interestingly, for the 12-month holding period, sales have a slightly higher calendar-time return than the corresponding purchase figure.

Three-Factor model.

Table 25: Calendar-Time Raw Returns

This table presents raw mean monthly calendar-time returns for 3 to 24 months holding periods. N represents the number of firms included in portfolios. Firms are included in purchases or sales portfolios if they had a purchase and no sale transaction or a sale and no purchase transaction within the respective time-frame. Panel A presents results for purchases panel B presents results for sales. All raw returns are presented in percent.

	Panel A: Purchase Months				Panel B: Sale Months			
Months	N	MMAR	T-skew		N	MMAR	T-skew	
3	452	1.7785	2.2888	** ++ ‡‡‡	378	0.5439	0.7098	
6	437	1.5668	2.0293	* ++ ‡‡	369	1.1695	1.5811	‡‡
9	422	1.4377	1.8961	* + ‡‡	354	1.0950	1.6195	‡‡
12	398	1.0105	1.3665	‡	336	1.0391	1.4706	‡
18	344	0.4236	0.5822		299	0.2617	0.3667	
24	295	0.5380	0.6934		253	0.2887	0.3774	

Notes ***, **, * indicate significance on the 1, 5, and 10 percent level for the bootstrapped skewness-adjusted t-test.
+++, ++, + indicate significance on the 1, 5, and 10 percent level for the t-test.
‡‡‡, ‡‡, ‡ indicate significance on the 1, 5, and 10 percent level for the Wilcoxon test.

Adjusting above returns with the MSCI Standard index for Germany, all monthly calendar-time returns, except the 3-month purchase return, are insignificant. However, the return pattern does not change in comparison to raw returns. Comparing calendar-time returns to previously reported BHAR returns, differences are obvious especially for sales. Scaling these monthly calendar-time returns to the respective holding period, purchases yield 4.67% compared to 4.01% for the non-overlapping BHAR results.

Table 26: Calendar-Time Adjusted Returns

This table presents adjusted mean monthly calendar-time returns for 3 to 24 months holding periods. N represents the number of firms included in portfolios. Firms are included in purchases or sales portfolios if they had a purchase or sales transaction within the respective time-frame. Returns are adjusted by the MSCI Core index Germany. Panel A presents results for purchases panel B presents results for sales. All adjusted returns are presented in percent.

	Panel A: Purchase Months				Panel B: Sale Months		
Months	N	MMAR	T-skew		N	MMAR	T-skew
3	452	1.5576	1.7979	* +	378	0.3230	0.3764
6	437	1.3896	1.6707		369	0.9923	1.2591
9	422	0.9786	1.2451		354	0.6358	0.8523
12	398	0.9048	1.1781		336	0.9335	1.1679
18	344	0.6415	0.8407		299	0.4797	0.6522
24	295	0.7815	0.9613		253	0.5322	0.6748

Notes ***, **, * indicate significance on the 1, 5, and 10 percent level for the bootstrapped skewness-adjusted t-test.
+++, ++, + indicate significance on the 1, 5, and 10 percent level for the t-test.
‡‡‡, ‡‡, ‡ indicate significance on the 1, 5, and 10 percent level for the Wilcoxon test.

Another important issue is certainly the different risk-adjustment. While the BHAR returns are adjusted by corresponding size portfolios, calendar-time returns are adjusted by a benchmark index. Although, results should not vary substantially as CDAX-adjusted BHARs suggest.[357]

As above stated, I use as a second risk-adjustment the Fama-French Three-Factor model. The idea of this three-factor regression model is to control returns of the calendar-time portfolio method for market, size, and book-to-market factors and test, whether the abnormal returns deviate from 0. The intercept measures in this model the excess return and can be compared to above adjusted returns. The next table reports regression outcomes. Panel A shows results for purchase portfolios, panel B for sale portfolios.

While alphas for 3- and 6-month holding periods are almost identical to adjusted returns above, the three-factor model yields higher excess returns for the 9-month horizon than adjusted returns. Also, the three-factor model shows significant excess returns for these three holding periods, while adjusted returns indicate significance only for the first period. Returns in all holding periods show a significant exposure to the market factor. The size factor is significant for the 3-month holding period only, the value factor in the 6-, 18-, and 24-month periods. Generally, results from the Fama-French Three-Factor model for purchases yield comparable returns to adjusted raw returns in panel A above.

357 CDAX-adjusted BHARs are reported in the appendix.

Table 27: Fama-French Three-Factor Regression

This table presents results from the Fama-French three factor regression for the mean monthly calendar-time raw returns for 3 to 24 months holding periods with purchases and no sales or sales and no purchases within the respective time-frame. Results for purchases are reported in panel A, for sales in panel B. Each panel shows alphas and coefficients in the first line for each holding period, White heteroscedasticity-adjusted t-statistics are presented in the second line. RM is represented by the MSCI Core index Germany, RF is represented by German federal securites with 1 year maturity (Bundeswertpapiere) , SML and HML are based on the MSCI Global Large & Small Cap as well as MSCI Global Value & Growth Indices for Germany.

	Panel A: Three-Factor Model Purchases					
Holding Period	α	RM_t-RF_t	SMB_t	HML_t	R^2	adj. R^2
3	0.0157	0.2339	0.4974	0.1430	0.1564	0.1203
	2.2963	**2.6127**	**1.8986**	0.8821		
6	0.0138	0.2214	0.3379	0.3559	0.1708	0.1336
	2.0318	**2.3008**	1.3264	**1.8022**		
9	0.0119	0.2712	0.3295	0.2595	0.1951	0.1574
	1.8375	**2.9033**	1.3139	1.3596		
12	0.0085	0.2336	0.3485	0.2705	0.2054	0.1664
	1.3785	**2.2462**	1.3871	1.4730		
18	0.0036	0.2346	0.2756	0.2634	0.2033	0.1598
	0.6039	**2.1460**	1.2180	**1.6993**		
24	0.0057	0.2379	0.2763	0.3007	0.2378	0.1911
	0.8929	**2.3411**	1.1305	**1.9863**		

	Panel B: Three-Factor Model Sales					
Holding Period	α	RM_t-RF_t	SMB_t	HML_t	R^2	adj. R^2
3	0.0025	0.2579	0.5234	-0.0153	0.1298	0.0925
	0.3395	**2.3451**	**1.6724**	-0.0841		
6	0.0092	0.2830	0.2995	0.1827	0.1445	0.1062
	1.3935	**2.6617**	1.1038	0.8956		
9	0.0081	0.2745	0.2276	0.1797	0.1691	0.1302
	1.3853	**3.2094**	1.0341	1.0865		
12	0.0085	0.1870	0.1949	0.1957	0.1003	0.0561
	1.3311	**1.7771**	0.8033	1.1727		
18	0.0022	0.2895	0.1800	0.3148	0.2140	0.1711
	0.3593	**2.4442**	0.7757	**1.9835**		
24	0.0029	0.2603	0.0693	0.3934	0.2113	0.1630
	0.4601	**1.8300**	0.2839	**2.2025**		

Panel B reports results from the Fama-French Three-Factor regression for sales. Here, none of the alpha is significant. Overall, they are comparable to the adjusted returns in the foregoing table. Again, the market factor is significant in all holding periods while the size factor is only significant for the 3-month holding period as in purchases. The value factor is only significant for the 18- and 24-month holding periods.

Overall, I conclude from these findings that calendar-time portfolio verify especially previous results for purchases, while outcomes on sales are more ambiguous. Though, I attribute these deviations to above described differences in available events for longer holding periods. Interesting is certainly the aspect that the size factor is especially for the 3-month holding period significant. Previously reported BHARs for firms in the first size quartile have also higher returns than larger firms following purchases; non-overlapping sales for this group showed also a positive yet insignificant BHAR for the 3-month holding period. Over longer holding periods, the value factor seems to gain importance besides the market.

V.B.6 Summary Long-Term Study

Finally, I conclude that my findings in this long-term study further emphasize my conclusions from the short-term study. Directors are not only able to time their transactions and thus profit from short-term price movements; they also purchase stock with a prosperous business and market outlook ahead. The analysis confirmed the expected firm size effect, i.e. the smallest firms generally have higher returns and proved the signaling effect of purchases by board members and corporate insiders in the regression analysis. In conclusion, I want to stress once again that these findings do not constitute illicit transactions; in fact, I assume that managers can judge very precisely whether their firm is under- or overvalued and that they generally have a sound understanding of the future of their business and of the general economic situation. Finally, outside investor can achieve long-term gains when following directors' purchases; both, the BHAR and the calendar-time portfolio method proofed this profitable mimicking strategy.

V.C Empirical Results Corporate Actions and Directors' Dealings Study

This final sub-chapter analyzes directors' dealings in conjunction with major corporate events. While the preceding sub-chapters concentrated on the short- and long-term performance of directors' dealings in a rather isolated setting, I will now shed light on this topic from a different angle.
A vast variety of smaller and larger events takes place within inside corporate organizations as part of the daily business routine. Most of these events are not at all noticed by the outside world. I assume that directors convey information on these events to the market through purchases and sales in their firm's stock. However, there are also larger events for firms where explicit information is released. To study such events together with directors' dealings, I focus on three typical corporate actions, in particular share repurchases, mergers and acquisitions (M&A), and seasoned equity offerings (SEO). One can presume all three event types will have a major impact on a firm. While share repurchases usually come with increasing stock prices, M&A[358] and SEO transactions are often associated with decreasing stock prices.[359]

358 I only include acquiring companies in the analysis and not target companies.

359 Current shareholders may be subject to a dilution effect when new shares are issued through a SEO.

The analysis of these events consists of three steps. It seems reasonable to take a closer look at directors' dealings around these events. For this purpose, I account for directors' dealings one year before and three months after the announcement date of each event. The following figure illustrates the set-up for all three event types.

Figure 12: Empirical Model Corporate Actions Study

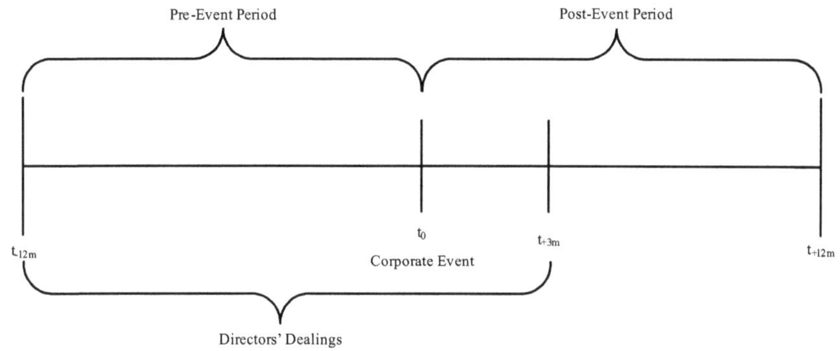

As a first step, I employ previously introduced BHAR methodology to control for abnormal buy-and-hold returns 12 months before and after each event; thereby, I sort results into one group with directors' dealings and one group without directors' dealings. Second, I employ a cross-sectional regression to find possible explanations for post-event BHAR. While the first two steps in the analysis are conducted separately for each event type, I will merge all three event types as a third step in an Ordered-Probit model. The purpose of this last step is to test whether the probability and the number of directors' purchases and sales increases following any of these events.

V.C.1 Share Repurchases

Among the three types of corporate actions, share repurchases have the smallest number of events. Overall, I analyzed analyze 75 share repurchases between 2002 and 2007 in Germany, whereof 41 events have directors' dealings between 12 months before and 3 months after the announcement date and 34 have no documented directors' dealings over this time. As a first step, I calculated buy-and-hold abnormal returns for both groups. One would hypothesize that the group with documented directors' dealings has higher BHARs than the second group without documented directors' dealings. Panels A and B report results for "mixed trades" (MT)[360], i.e. events with both directors' purchases and sales, and "no insider", i.e. events without directors' dealings. Rep and Mat show BHR for repurchase firms and matching firms followed by the BHAR. Firms with directors' dealings have a

360 I adopt this denomination from Chan, Ikenberry, & Lee (2003).

higher BHR during the year before the event (26.29%) than firms without directors' dealings; however, their matching portfolios accumulate a BHR of 27.70%. Firms without documented directors' dealings have substantially lower BHARs as they underperform compared to firms in their matching portfolio by roughly 4.30%. Interestingly, three months before the event, BHARs in both groups turn positive at 1.41% and 3.07%. Following the event, the insider group once again shows higher BHARs with a peak at 7.65% after six months.

Table 28: BHAR Share Repurchases

This table presents buy-and-hold returns (BHR) in percent for 12 and 3 months before the repurchase as well as for 3, 6, and 12 months following the repurchase announcement. Rep shows BHR for repurchase firms, followed by Mat, i.e. returns for matching portfolios. Matching portfolios are build based on similar firm size. BHAR shows buy-and-hold abnormal returns, followed by corresponding t-stats (skewness-adjusted) and significance indicators. Panel A shows BHRs for repurchases with documented directors' dealings and panel B shows results for repurchases without documented directors' dealings.

	Panel A:MT						Panel B: No Insider					
BHR Period	n	Rep	Mat	BHAR	t-Statistics		n	Rep	Mat	BHAR	t-Statistics	
1 Year Prior Repurchase	41	26,29	27,70	-1,41	-0,18		34	9,71	14,00	-4,29	-0,46	
3 Months Prior Repurchase	41	4,24	2,84	1,41	0,53		34	5,31	2,23	3,07	0,81	
3 Months After Repurchase	41	3,91	-1,47	5,38	1,91	*	34	2,60	-2,43	5,03	1,90	*
6 Months After Repurchase	41	7,41	-0,25	7,65	2,35	**	34	1,44	-2,32	3,76	0,98	
1 Year After Repurchase	41	13,13	9,25	3,88	0,94		34	0,71	2,36	-1,65	-0,30	

Notes Returns are expressed in percent.
***,**,* indicate significance at 1, 5, and 10 percent level.

While the sample is probably too small for a generally valid conclusion, it seems obvious that firms with directors' dealings perform substantially better. The data analysis in chapter IV.C.3 already showed that purchases are larger in terms of share bought and occur about 30 days closer to the announcement (111 days) while sales are generally smaller yet higher in transaction value and occur earlier (147 days). Bearing this in mind, I conjecture that directors take advantage of their firm's good performance before the announcement and secure profits well before the announcement; once the event comes closer, they purchase stock again. This hypothesis receives further support by the higher Euro value of directors' sales compared to purchases.

While findings for the insider group explained sales well before the event and subsequent purchase, it seems questionable why directors abstain totally from trading in the second group. I can only presume that they comply with directors' dealings laws more strictly than their trading counterparts.

As a second step, an OLS regression explores now previous findings to find possible factors explaining post-event BHARs. For this purpose, I estimate two models using the 12-month post-event BHAR as a dependent variable and the following independent variables:

- Log firm size is the logarithm of the firm's market capitalization in million Euro on the event day.
- Previous 1-year BHAR, i.e. the firms' BHAR is measured over one year before the event.
- Directors' Dealings Dummy, which becomes 1 when directors' dealings are present and 0 otherwise. It is only used in the first model, as the second model includes only events with directors' dealings.

- Purchases-Sales ratio is the total Euro value of purchases divided by the sum of the total Euro value of purchases and sales; it is only used in the second model with only directors' dealings.
- Market-To-Book ratio and price-earnings ratio variables are the respective ratios on the event day.

The following table reports regression results. Model 1 includes both, events with and without directors' dealings, while model 2 covers only events with directors' dealings. Corresponding correlations are reported in the appendix. Firm size and directors' dealings dummy have high correlation in model 1, and the purchase-sales ratio and the price-earnings ratio in model 2; however, dropping any of these variables did not significantly affect the estimation.

Table 29: Cross-Sectional Regression Repurchases

This table reports results from cross-sectional regressions of the post-event 12-month's buy-and-hold abnormal return from repurchases using various explanatory variables. Log Firm-Volumen is the logarithm of the firm's market capitalization in million Euro on the event day. Previous 1-Year BHAR is the 12-month BHAR reported in previous table. Directors' Dealings Dummy is 1 when diretors' dealings are reported and 0 otherwise; it only applies in model 1. The Purchase-Sales ratio is constructed as Euro value of directors' purchases divided by the sum of the Euro value of directors' sales and purchases; it is only used in model 2, representing solely events with directors' dealings. Market-To-Book as well as Price-Earnings-Ratio are measured on the event day. The first line for each variable represents coefficients, the second line shows White (1980) heteroskedasticity-adjusted t-statistics for each variable. Bold printed t-statistics indicate significance on or above the 10 percent level. Shaded areas indicate excluded variable. Correlations are reported in the appendix.

	Model	
Variable	1	2
N	64	35
Intercept	-0.0598	0.0165
	-0.5804	0.0948
Log Firm-Size	0.0058	-0.0019
	0.3615	-0.1168
Previous 1Yr. BHAR	0.2899	0.4985
	2.7815	**6.0006**
Directors' Dealings Dummy	0.0742	
	0.8558	
Purchase-Sales Ratio		0.1459
		1.4087
Market-To-Book-Ratio	0.0095	0.0139
	0.5173	0.4032
Price-To-Earnings-Ratio	-0.0013	-0.0020
	-1.3744	**-1.7093**
R^2	0.1984	0.4867
adj. R^2	0.1293	0.3982

Notes Shaded areas indicate variables not used in the respective model.

Regression results show clearly that the foregoing BHAR has a significant positive impact in both models; model 2, which includes only events with directors‘ dealings, shows a substantially larger t-value for this factor. The firm-size coefficient, even though insignificant in both models, indicates a negative impact in model 2. For model 1, the directors‘ dealings dummy is insignificant at a positive value. The purchase-sales ratio, used only in model 2, insignificant; however, a t-value of 1.41 indicates at least some influence whether directors purchase or sell stock. Market-To-Book is insignificant for both models. Finally, the coefficient for the price-earnings ratio is negative in both models and significant in model 2. Thus, firms with higher PE-ratios on the event seem to have lower future prospects than those with smaller ratios.

From these findings, I conclude that the most important driver for positive post-event BHARs are positive pre-event BHARs. Thus, firms with high pre-event returns are likely to continue this growth after the repurchase. Especially model 2 shows this fact with highly significant pre-event BHAR. In conjunction with the firm size variable, this seems especially true for smaller firms. Hence, outside investors following these corporate actions may focus on small caps‘ historic returns. I consider the sample to be too small to conclude that firms without directors’ dealings are a worse investment than firms with directors’ dealings yet it seems worth looking out for directors‘ dealings purchasing activity prior a repurchase. However, it seems reasonable to conjecture directors‘ dealings are in close conjunction to firm performance.

V.C.2 Mergers and Acquisitions

Following share repurchases, I will now analyze directors’ dealings around M&A events. The sample size for M&A is substantially larger than for the other two event types. Out of 1,125 M&A events, there are 605 events with documented directors’ dealings and 520 without.

The following table reports buy-and-hold abnormal returns. Panel A reports BHARs for acquiring firms with documented directors’ dealings and panel B for those without. While previously repurchasing firms did not outperform their matching portfolios over the one-year pre-event period, firms in this analysis do. Firms with documented directors’ dealings have a highly significant BHAR of 26.41% over the 12-month pre-event period, which is substantially higher than the BHAR of the second sample at 12.66%. I find significant positive pre-event BHARs for both samples; post-event, all measured returns are insignificant and below 1% except for the 12-month figure of the first sample, which is 1.76%.

Table 30: BHAR M&A

This table presents buy-and-hold returns (BHR) in percent for 12 and 3 months before an acquisition as well as for 3, 6, and 12 months following an acquisition. AC shows BHR for acquirer firms, followed by Mat, i.e. returns for matching portfolios. Matching portfolios are build based on similar firm size. BHAR shows buy-and-hold abnormal returns, followed by corresponding t-stats (skewness adjusted) and significance indicators. Panels A reports results for acquirer firms with documented directors' dealings, panel B reports results for firms without documented directors' dealings.

	Panel A: Directors' Dealings						Panel B: Without Directors' Dealings					
BHR Period	n	AC	Mat	BHAR	t-Statistics		n	AC	Mat	BHAR	t-Statistics	
1 Year Prior M&A	605	54,23	27,82	26,41	3,89	***	520	31,03	18,37	12,66	4,76	***
3 Months Prior M&A	605	7,41	5,34	2,07	2,47	***	520	8,08	4,12	3,96	4,52	***
3 Months After M&A	605	4,28	4,18	0,10	0,15		520	2,31	1,78	0,53	0,57	
6 Months After M&A	605	7,43	7,53	-0,11	-0,08		520	3,49	3,45	0,04	0,04	
1 Year After M&A	605	17,49	15,76	1,73	0,80		520	12,09	11,75	0,34	0,17	

Notes: Returns are expressed in percent.
***,**,* indicate significance at 1, 5, and 10 percent level.

These findings reflect the general perception of low or negative returns for acquiring firms once a deal is announced. Preceding BHAR results confirm my conclusions drawn from previous repurchase analyses. Directors sell well before an announcement and lock in profits. Admittedly, data analysis pointed out an important difference. While repurchases showed high Euro values for sales and larger numbers of shares purchases, M&A data reveals a strong preference for sales overall; both the number of shares sold and the Euro value of sales surmount purchases by far.

The next table reports results for the cross-sectional regression with the 12-month post-event BHAR as the dependent variable. All independent variables are the same as in the repurchase analysis. Overall, I estimate four models. Models 1 and 2 cover events with and without directors‘ dealings. Model 1 includes the previous 1-year BHAR as independent variable, model 2 not. The same applies to models 3 and 4; however they only cover events with directors‘ dealings and feature therefore the purchase-sales ratio as variable instead of the directors‘ dealings dummy. While firm-size played a minor role in repurchases, is positive significant in all four models presented below. Interestingly, the previous 1-year BHAR, included in models 3 and 4, is negative. Thus, while past positive performance indicated positive post-event BHARs for repurchases, the opposite seems true for acquiring firms in M&A transaction, even though this coefficient is insignificant. Model 2 suggests that firms with directors‘ dealings have a positive post-event BHAR. Higher market-to-book values show highly significant negative loadings in all four models, while the price-earnings ratio is positive significant on all models. This suggests the market adjusts its firm valuation following the event, i.e. post-event BHARs are higher for undervalued firms.

Table 31: Cross-Sectional Regression M&A

This table reports results from cross-sectional regressions of the post-event 12-month's buy-and-hold abnormal return from M&A using various explanatory variables. Log Firm-Volumen is the logarithm of the firm's market capitalization in million Euro on the event day. Previous 1-Year BHAR is the 12-month BHAR reported in previous table. Directors' Dealings Dummy is 1 when diretors' dealings are reported and 0 otherwise; it only applies in models 1 and 2. The Purchase-Sales ratio is constructed as Euro value of directors' purchases divided by the sum of the Euro value directors' sales and purchases; it is only used in models 3 and 4, representing solely events with directors' dealings. Market-To-Book as well as Price-Earnings-Ratio are measured on the event day. The first line for each variable represents coefficients, the second line shows White (1980) heteroskedasticity-adjusted t-statistics for each variable. Bold printed t-statistics indicate significance on or above the 10 percent level. Shaded areas indicate excluded variable. Correlations are reported in the appendix.

	Model			
Variable	1	2	3	4
N	886	886	518	518
Intercept	0.1305	0.1142	0.3126	0.2163
	1.6999	**4.0819**	**2.3182**	**4.2826**
Log Firm-Size	0.1491	0.1500	0.1499	0.1559
	3.6516	**3.7061**	**2.2514**	**2.3735**
Previous 1Yr. BHAR	-0.0023		-0.0124	
	-0.2581		-0.9258	
Directors' Dealings Dummy	0.0576	0.0558		
	1.6316	**1.7350**		
Purchase-Sales Ratio			-0.0082	-0.0047
			-0.1575	-0.0882
Market-To-Book-Ratio	-0.0352	-0.0354	-0.0530	-0.0547
	-5.3102	**-5.2421**	**-3.5269**	**-3.4963**
Price-To-Earnings-Ratio	0.0006	0.0006	0.0006	0.0007
	1.8254	**1.7350**	**1.6780**	**2.1810**
adj. R^2	0.0728	0.0737	0.0774	0.0766
R^2	0.0780	0.0779	0.0864	0.0838

Notes Shaded areas indicate variables not used in the respective model.

I conclude from the M&A analysis that directors' dealings maybe an indicator for positive post-event BHARs. However, the regression analysis showed a very strong influence of valuation ratios on post-event BHARs. Finally, I suppose that M&A events are a type of corporate events with vast numbers of unknown variables. Further, it seems unreasonable to consider directors‘ dealings as an important indicator for post-event BHARs as directors most likely violate insider dealing laws when trading close to these events.

V.C.3 Seasoned Equity Offerings

Seasoned equity offerings[361] are the third and last type of corporate actions I analyze in the light of directors' dealings. Sample size is small again with a total of 211 events, 113 of which are with documented directors' dealings and 98 without. As previously, I start with a discussion of long-term BHARs and follow with a cross-sectional OLS regression.

The next table reports BHARs for SEO events between one year before and one year after the announcement date. Panel A reports BHARs for firms with documented directors' dealings and panel B for firms without directors' dealings between one year before and three months after the announcement. Both groups have high 12-month pre-event buy-and-hold returns – firms with directors' dealings have 67% and those without have 44%. Adjusting these BHRs to their respective matching portfolios, the first group has a highly significant BHAR of 24% and the second group has an insignificant BHAR of 12%. Three months before the event, this value drops substantially to 3.3% and 1.6% respectively. Post-event, the second group peaks after three months at 3.1% and then falls to -7.2% over the 12-month holding period. On the other hand, the first group goes down to -1.6% over six months but recovers to 4.3% over the 12-month holding period.

Table 32: SEO BHAR

This table presents buy-and-hold returns (BHR) in percent for 12 and 3 months before an SEO announcement as well as for 3, 6, and 12 months afterwards. SEO shows BHR for SEO firms, followed by Mat, i.e. returns for matching portfolios. Matching portfolios are constructed based on similar firm size. BHAR shows buy-and-hold abnormal returns, followed by corresponding t-stats and significance indicators. Panel A reports results for SEOs with documented directors' dealings and panel B without.

	Panel A: Directors' Dealings						Panel B: Without Directors' Dealings					
BHR Period	n	SEO	Mat	BHAR	t-Statistics		n	SEO	Mat	BHAR	t-Statistics	
1 Year Prior SEO	113	65,66	41,61	24,05	2,40	***	98	44,14	32,34	11,80	1,57	
3 Months Prior SEO	113	12,67	9,38	3,29	1,50		98	10,02	8,39	1,63	0,75	
3 Months After SEO	113	3,92	3,87	0,06	0,08		98	4,55	1,50	3,06	1,86	*
6 Months After SEO	113	5,93	7,54	-1,61	-0,74		98	3,36	4,44	-1,08	-0,42	
1 Year After SEO	113	18,41	14,15	4,27	0,98		98	5,98	13,18	-7,20	-1,77	*

Notes Returns are expressed in percent.
***,**,* indicate significance at 1, 5, and 10 percent level.

High pre-event BHARs can for sure be associated with the timing of the SEO; firms or stockholders certainly want to profit from superior valuations when they announce a SEO. However, considering the data analysis for SEOs, I conclude that directors are aware of a potentially negative impact due to a dilution effect, and thus rather sell shares than purchase them. The data analysis revealed that the average purchase is 0.48 million Euro compared to 3.18 million Euro for sales. The next table reports results for the cross-sectional analysis. I use the same variables as in the repurchase cross-sectional regression.

361 The sample includes secondary offerings without new shares issued and seasoned equity offerings. I will refer to this as seasoned equity offering (SEO). The original SDC database definition for this item is: FOLLOWONS, Number of Follow-On Issues after IPO: Number of follow-on stock offerings that a company has issued. A follow-on offering (a.k.a. secondary offering), is any common stock offering that occurs after a company's Initial Public Offering (IPO).

Table 33: Cross-Sectional Regression SEO

This table reports results from cross-sectional regressions of the post-event 12-month's buy-and-hold abnormal return from SEOs using various explanatory variables. Log Firm-Volumen is the logarithm of the firm's market capitalization in million Euro on the event day. Previous 1-Year BHAR is the 12-month BHAR reported in previous table. Directors' Dealings Dummy is 1 when diretors' dealings are reported and 0 otherwise; it only applies in model 1. The Purchase-Sales ratio is constructed as Euro value of directors' purchases divided by the sum of the Euro value directors' sales and purchases; it is only used in model 2, representing solely events with directors' dealings. Market-To-Book as well as Price-Earnings-Ratio are measured on the event day. The first line for each variable represents coefficients, the second line shows White (1980) heteroskedasticity-adjusted t-statistics for each variable. Bold printed t-statistics indicate significance on or above the 10 percent level. Shaded areas indicate excluded variable. Correlations are reported in the appendix.

	Model	
Variable	1	2
N	152	84
Intercept	0.2189	0.4079
	0.9995	1.0003
Log Firm-Size	-0.0021	-0.0170
	-0.0794	-0.3951
Previous 1Yr. BHAR	0.0473	0.0496
	1.2205	1.0179
Directors' Dealings Dummy	0.0771	
	0.9727	
Purchase-Sales Ratio		0.0758
		0.6410
Market-To-Book-Ratio	-0.0629	-0.0762
	-3.7181	**-3.2871**
Price-To-Earnings-Ratio	0.0002	0.0004
	0.5177	0.5213
adj. R^2	0.0628	0.0905
R^2	0.0939	0.1453

Notes Shaded areas indicate variables not used in the respective model.

Above regression results show for both models insignificant coefficients, except the market-to-book ratio; this is negative and highly significant in both models. Firm-size has a negative impact, while the pre-event 1-year BHAR shows a positive trend. Overall, regression outcomes are less conclusive than the previous two, although it shows that undervalued firms tend to higher post-event BHARs.

V.C.4 Ordered-Probit Analysis of Corporate Actions

Previous analyzes of corporate actions and directors' dealings focused on returns before and after the event. Moving one step further, this sub-chapter joins all three types of corporate action in one analysis. The objective is to find a possible connection between corporate actions, directors' dealings, and other accounting and valuation measures. For this purpose, the following analysis investigates the number of directors' dealings in connection with corporate actions from the previous quarter. The analysis is based on an ordered-probit model, which uses the number of directors' dealings as dependent variable. Independent variables are three dummies for repurchases, M&A, and SEOs; these become 1 if any of these three corporate actions took place in the previous quarter. Further, I use previous quarter's logarithmic market value, market-to-book-value, price-earnings ratio, logarithmic volume, and previous one year BHAR. Altogether, I estimate three ordered-probit models, although I report only results for the first two models afterwards; results for model 3 are reported in the appendix. For models 1 and 2, I code the number of directors' purchases or sales as follows:

- 0 for no transaction,
- 1 for one or two transactions,
- 2 for three or four transactions,
- 3 for five or six transactions,
- 4 for seven or eight transactions,
- 5 for nine or more transactions.

Model 1 investigates purchases, model 2 sales.

Beyond this set-up, it might also be of interest to combine directors' sales and purchases in one model. For this purpose, I use in model 3 the netted number of directors' purchases and sales with the following coding:

- 0 for sales,
- 1 for no transaction,
- 2 for purchases.

While model 1 and 2 analyze purchases and sales separatly, model 3 joins them; since purchases and sales are not directly comparable, it might be difficult to interpret results correctly. Thus, I solely present these results for informational purpose uncommented in the appendix; generally, results and marginal effects reflect outcomes from models 1 and 2, presented afterwards.

Results from the ordered-probit models are presented in the following table. The first line for each variable shows coefficients, the second line z-statistics. Bold printed values indicate significance on the 10%-level or above. Limit points, reported below the estimation outcomes, represent the cut-off points between the categories 0-6 for models 1 and 2. The table's last section reports model statistics.

Table 34: Corporate Actions Ordered-Probit Model

This table reports regression results from the ordered-probit model. Model 1 and model 2 use as dependant variables the number of quarterly purchases and quarterly sales, respectively. These variables are coded with 0 for no transaction, 1 for one to two transactions, 2 for three to four transactions, 3 for five to six transactions, 4 for seven to eight transactions, and 5 for nine or more transactions. The first line for each variable shows coefficients, second line shows z-statistics. Bold printed figures indicate significance on or above th 10%-level. Limit points for the ordered groups is reported for each model below the regression results.

	Model	
Variable	1	2
N	9581	9581
Repurchases	-0.2348	-0.1451
	-1.0396	-0.5566
M&A	-0.0606	0.0527
	-1.2361	1.0141
SEO	0.0778	0.1889
	0.6765	1.5974
Log Market-Value	0.0035	-0.0102
	0.4602	-1.2424
Market-To-Book Value	0.0042	-0.0023
	2.1756	-1.1063
Price-Earnings Ratio	0.0001	0.0001
	0.5523	0.8551
Log Volume	-0.0207	0.0040
	-2.8672	0.4888
Previous 1Yr. BHAR	-0.2866	0.1961
	-5.0154	**3.1397**
Limit Points		
Limit 1	1.0437	1.1928
Limit 2	1.3511	1.4961
Limit 3	1.5672	1.7068
Limit 4	1.7346	1.9072
Limit 5	1.8745	2.0339
Pseudo-R^2	0.0035	0.0016
LR statistic (8 df)	42.9025	15.1382
Probability(LR stat)	0.0000	0.0565

Notes Shaded areas indicate variables not used in the respective model.

At first, it is important to remind that coefficients in above table cannot be directly interpreted as those in an OLS regression, for example. At this point, coefficients offer only a qualitative but no quantitative interpretation how they influence directors' dealings.[362] I report corresponding marginal effects below.

Model 1, using directors' purchases as dependent variable, shows significant coefficients only for market-to-book value, volume, and previous 12-months BHAR. Thus, this indicates that the purchase probability rises with increase in the market-to-book-value, while both, higher volume and higher previous 1-year BHAR, lead to a significant decrease in probability for purchases. The opposite seems true for

362 Cf. Kaiser and Szczesny (2002), p. 367.

these two factors when it comes to sales. Here, analyzed in model 2, both have a positive sign, although only the 1-year BHAR is significant.

For a better understanding of previous results, the next two tables report marginal effects for the first two models. The next table reports these marginal effects for model 1.

Table 35: Marginal Effects Directors' Purchases

This table reports marginal effects for directors' purchases. Marginal effects are shown for each variable and indicate the change in probability of falling into the respective transaction category for a one-percent change in the variable. Second shows z-statistics.

Transaction Category	0	1	2	3	4	5
Repurchases	0.0549	-0.0167	-0.0102	-0.0067	-0.0047	-0.0167
	5.3777	-1.6316	-0.9986	-0.6542	-0.4605	-1.6328
M&A	0.0142	-0.0043	-0.0026	-0.0017	-0.0012	-0.0043
	1.3889	-0.4214	-0.2579	-0.1690	-0.1189	-0.4217
SEO	-0.0182	0.0055	0.0034	0.0022	0.0016	0.0055
	-1.7811	0.5404	0.3307	0.2167	0.1525	0.5408
Log Market-Value	-0.0008	0.0002	0.0002	0.0001	0.0001	0.0002
	-0.0796	0.0241	0.0148	0.0097	0.0068	0.0242
Market-To-Book Value	-0.0010	0.0003	0.0002	0.0001	0.0001	0.0003
	-0.0951	0.0288	0.0177	0.0116	0.0081	0.0289
Price-Earnings Ratio	0.0000	0.0000	0.0000	0.0000	0.0000	0.0000
	-0.0012	0.0004	0.0002	0.0001	0.0001	0.0004
Log Volume	0.0048	-0.0015	-0.0009	-0.0006	-0.0004	-0.0015
	0.4747	-0.1440	-0.0881	-0.0577	-0.0407	-0.1441
Previous 1Yr. BHAR	0.0670	-0.0203	-0.0125	-0.0082	-0.0057	-0.0204
	6.5630	**-1.9912**	-1.2187	-0.7984	-0.5620	**-1.9927**

Notes: Bold print indicates significance on the 10%-level or above.

Above table reports for each variable marginal effects in each transaction category with corresponding z-statistics. For directors' purchases, two corporate actions dummy variables are significant. Repurchases have for category 0 a highly significant positive marginal effect. Thus, if the probability for purchases rises 1%, the probability for no directors' purchases in the subsequent quarter rises 0.55% while probabilities for purchases decrease; however, these decreases are insignificant. The probability for no directors' purchases decreases significantly by 0.18% while marginal effects in transaction categories 1 to 5 have a positive sign. Beyond these variables, only the previous 1-year BHAR has significant marginal effects. Results show that an increasing 1-year BHAR increases significantly the probability for no purchases transactions in the following quarter. Also, the probability for one or two as well as for nine or more purchases decreases significantly by 0.2% in both cases.

The next table reports similar results for model 2, i.e. directors‘ sales. Interestingly, the repurchases show again a significant positive marginal effect in category 0. Thus, the probability for no directors‘ sales increases by 0.25% when the probability for repurchases increases. This suggests that directors tend to hold their positions following such an action and wait in which direction the share price will move.

Table 36: Marginal Effects Directors' Sales

This table reports marginal effects for directors' sales. Marginal effects are shown for each variable and indicate the change in probability of falling into the respective transaction category for a one-percent change in the variable. Second shows z-statistics.

Transaction Category	0	1	2	3	4	5
Repurchases	0.0254	-0.0089	-0.0049	-0.0036	-0.0018	-0.0061
	2.4893	-0.8756	-0.4822	-0.3567	-0.1774	-0.5974
M&A	-0.0092	0.0033	0.0018	0.0013	0.0007	0.0022
	-0.9048	0.3183	0.1753	0.1297	0.0645	0.2171
SEO	-0.0331	0.0116	0.0064	0.0047	0.0024	0.0079
	-3.2406	1.1399	0.6278	0.4644	0.2309	0.7776
Log Market-Value	0.0018	-0.0006	-0.0003	-0.0003	-0.0001	-0.0004
	0.1754	-0.0617	-0.0340	-0.0251	-0.0125	-0.0421
Market-To-Book Value	0.0004	-0.0001	-0.0001	-0.0001	0.0000	-0.0001
	0.0394	-0.0138	-0.0076	-0.0056	-0.0028	-0.0094
Price-Earnings Ratio	0.0000	0.0000	0.0000	0.0000	0.0000	0.0000
	-0.0013	0.0005	0.0003	0.0002	0.0001	0.0003
Log Volume	-0.0007	0.0002	0.0001	0.0001	0.0001	0.0002
	-0.0692	0.0244	0.0134	0.0099	0.0049	0.0166
Previous 1Yr. BHAR	-0.0344	0.0121	0.0067	0.0049	0.0024	0.0082
	-3.3647	1.1835	0.6518	0.4821	0.2398	0.8074

Notes: Bold print indicates significance on the 10%-level or above.

Also, as for directors‘ purchases, the SEO dummy-variable has a significant negative marginal effect in category 0; for sales, it is even higher at 0.33%. However, for directors‘ sales this translates into a significant decrease in probability that directors will not sell. Finally, the previous 1-year BHAR is highly negative significant in category 0, which suggest that with higher past returns directors tend to sell their share and secure profits.

Overall, the ordered-probit analysis adds important information to previous outcomes. It shows that corporate actions do not play a significant for directors when deciding whether to purchase or sell stock. Certainly, it is important to remember that this analysis focused on directors‘ dealings in the quarter following a corporate action. Thus, one has to be aware that transactions close to any of these events may either are suspicious to supervising authorities or prohibited under insider dealing laws. Obviously, when directors perceive such an event‘s prospects either promising or poor and trade on their perception, be it based on facts or solely personal judgment, these transactions are easily considered insider trading. The most important trigger for directors‘ purchases or sales seems to be the firm‘s past performance, i.e. directors purchase when their firm had a low previous 1-year BHAR, and sell after a high previous 1-year BHAR.

V.C.5 Summary Corporate Actions and Directors' Dealings Study

This chapter analyzed corporate actions in connection with directors' dealings. The first part discussed repurchases, M&A, and SEOs individually, while the last part joint all three types of corporate actions in an ordered-probit model. Results for the repurchases showed that the previous 1-year BHAR has a significant impact on post-event performance while other variable had no major influence. Also, the directors' dealings dummy was insignificant. Interestingly, the previous 1-year BHAR was not significant for M&A. Here, firm-size, market-to-book ratio, and price-earnings-ratio were significant in all estimated OLS models. Intuitively, one would presume a highly significant directors' dealings dummy; however, it is only slightly significant in one model. I conjecture the main reason for insignificant directors' dealings dummies in three out of four estimated models is that either directors abstain from trading around M&As, or, when they trade, other factors, e.g. firm size, market-to-book ratio, and price-earnings ratio, outweigh and impact the post-event performance significantly more. Hence, I suppose directors' dealings have only a minor or no signaling effect at all for the post-event performance. The ordered-probit model joined all three types of corporate actions in one analysis. Using the number of quarterly directors' dealings as dependent variable and as independent variables dummies for corporate actions from the previous quarter as well as accounting and valuation measures from the previous quarter, the model seeks to explain which factors influence purchase and sales decision by directors. Findings showed that the main driver for directors' purchases or sales is the previous 1-year BHAR. From these findings I conclude a firm's past performance is the main trigger for directors' dealings while corporate actions only play a minor role. I attribute their low influence on the trading behavior of directors for great parts to the strict supervision by authorities around any corporate action.

VI. Excursus

The previous chapters only considered legitimate transactions by corporate insiders, which are considered as directors' dealings. The findings obtained so far showed that directors generally have a sound understanding of their firm's value and thus purchase or sell shares based on this perception. Moreover, these transactions did not unfavorably affect outside investors. Directors' dealings seemed to rather convey diffuse but important information about a firm's prospects to the market. Certainly, some of these directors' dealings may be driven by significant inside information. Unfortunately, it seems unlikely that these illicit transactions are detected by BaFin as long as they do not show a direct connection to an event affecting the firm.

On the other hand, there are of course violations of insider dealing provisions in Germany, which are uncovered by BaFin. This excursus explores a small sample of three major types of violations, i.e. dealing on inside information, market manipulation and price manipulation. All cases are by courtesy of BaFin and are strictly confidential as some are still under investigation or brought to court. The sample consists of 294 insider transactions, 28 cases of market manipulation and 33 cases of price manipulation.

VI.A Description of Dataset

The dataset provided by BaFin contains illicit insider transactions and can be split up into three separate parts. The largest part consists of purchases and sales by insiders or persons exploiting inside information. Panel A in the following table presents the distribution of transactions over the years 1998 to 2006. While illicit sales exceed purchases in 2001 and 2002, the pattern changed in 2003 when the number of insider purchases was almost twice as high as that of sales.[363] Thus, one can conjecture that illicit purchases come along with a recovering market and vice versa. Panel B presents corresponding firm sizes. Interestingly, illegal purchases seem to occur generally in larger firms while illegal sales show smaller firm sizes on average. In part, this observation is confirmed by cases that were made public by BaFin. These cases show that most frequently, firms with illegal insider sales are in a distressed position and therefore tend to lower market values.

Panel C presents cases of market manipulation. This sample is comparably small with only 28 entries covering the years 2002 to 2006. Panel D presents their corresponding firm sizes, which are quite low. In market manipulation cases, insiders try to move prices to their advantage by disseminating false information. Consequently, this type of fraud is most effective in smaller firms, which tend to react faster and stronger to pieces of information than larger firms.

---

363 One should bear in mind that these transactions were supplied by BaFin as transactions they had identified as being illegal; hence, the real number of insider transactions may be even higher.

Panel E shows cases of price manipulation from 2000 to 2004. Altogether, there are 33 cases of price manipulation. Panel F shows corresponding firm sizes. Insiders conducting price manipulation try to influence securities' prices with round-trip trades, high sell or high buy orders.

Table 37: Statistical Properties Insider Trading

This table presents destriptive statistics of the insider trading sample used in the subsequent analysis. Panel A shows the number of insider trading cases over the entire period covered and in each respective year as aggregate number and subdivided into purchases and sales. Panel B shows average and median firm sizes for transactions from panel A. Panel C presents cases of market manipulation together with their mean and median firm size in panel D. Panel E presents cases of price manipulation together with their mean and median firm size in panel F. Dataset is supplied by BaFin

		Total	1998	1999	2000	2001	2002	2003	2004	2005	2006
Panel A: Insider Tradings											
Total		294	1	1	10	37	75	50	51	47	22
Purchases		166	1	1	3	10	37	32	28	34	20
Sales		128	0	0	7	27	38	18	23	13	2
Panel B: Firm Size - Insider Tradings											
Total	Mean	2159	123	434	1072	616	1143	2170	2440	4698	2784
	Median	47	123	434	92	32	27	56	38	71	235
Purchases	Mean	3223	123	434	411	93	1076	3351	3856	6353	3062
	Median	81	123	434	75	24	76	147	39	132	283
Sales	Mean	780			1356	810	1209	71	716	370	8
	Median	26			95	35	6	10	35	52	8
Panel C: Market Manipulation											
Cases		28	0	0	0	0	1	2	5	12	8
Panel D: Firm Size - Market Manipulation											
Total	Mean	107					9	14	99	192	22
	Median	16					9	14	38	21	3
Panel E: Price Manipulation											
Cases		33	0	0	1	2	10	13	7	0	0
Panel F: Firm Size - Price Manipulation											
Total	Mean	547			47	63	1049	566	4		
	Median	10			47	63	181	11	3		
Notes:	Firm size is expressed in million Euro.										

VI.B Empirical Results

In the following three sub-chapters, I present empirical results on the insider dealing, market manipulation, and price manipulation sample.

VI.B.1 Empirical Results Insider Trading

In contrast to the event study in chapter V.A there is only one single event date for the insider transactions sample. Hence, abnormal returns are measured before, on, and after one single day. The setup of the event study thus follows the traditional design. As in the directors' dealings short-term study, the estimation period is set

to 250 days, followed by an event window of 41 days that is centered on the event date. One fundamental difference to the directors' dealings study is that the event is not the actual day when an insider trades or when his trade is made public; in fact, it is the day when event the event occurs. Even though, the real insider trading takes place only within a few days before the event. Due to the nature of this sample, it is not possible to determine the trading day precisely.
Results are presented in Table 38. Significance is determined as before using a standard t-test, the Corrado test, and the Wilcoxon signed rank test. Panel A shows mean abnormal returns around the purchases, with the event day on day zero. Looking at the abnormal returns from 20 days to one day before the event, it is immediately obvious that all abnormal returns except for six are positive. Compared to the results from the directors' dealings sample, this is highly interesting as almost all abnormal returns were negative prior to the transaction and not positive as in this case. Significant abnormal returns are first observed 18 days before the event. On this day, the abnormal return reaches 0.0027%, which is significant under the Corrado test at the 10% level. Afterwards, days 15 and 7 before the transaction are significant with abnormal returns of 0.88% and 0.52%. On day two and one before the event, ARs climb to 1.00% and 1.22% respectively. On the event day, abnormal returns jump to 10.27% and are significant at the 1% level under all three tests. Clearly, these high abnormal returns are triggered by a firm-specific event, e.g. a news release, earnings announcements or something similar, and not through the trading of the insider himself. As the insider traded before the event, he yields an extraordinary high return on his transaction. Panel C shows the mean cumulative abnormal returns. Over the entire pre-event period of 20 days, abnormal returns cumulate to roughly 5.1%, where the first ten days contribute about 2.2% and the last ten days before the event contribute about 3%. Looking at CAR from day 5 to day 1 before the event, there is an increase to 3.3% percent compared to the CAR covering ten days before the event. The main reason for this is the absence of negative returns over the last five days. Thus, even if the insider traded only five days before the event, he was able to generate enormous profits, assuming that shares are held beyond the event. If an insider holds his shares over the entire event window, he gains an average of 4.7% after the event in addition to his pre-event returns, plus the 10.3% on the event day. Hence, over the entire event window, an insider would achieve a return of 20.03%, which is shown in panel C. Comparing these results to previously abnormal returns after directors' dealings; it seems evident that insiders in this case traded on proprietary information with high relevance to the firm and its share price. Furthermore, this information has a high short-term relevance. However, it is possible that a trade that is defined as directors' dealing is in fact insider trading but this is not captured by the BaFin as no exceptional event took place around the date of the transaction or because the transaction did not reach a certain threshold in BaFin's stock watch program. Such a director's trade is then rather based on information that is impor-

tant to the firm in the long run. It is certainly almost impossible for the legislator to identify these trades.

Panel B presents abnormal returns for transactions identified as insider sales by the BaFin. Here, only four out of 20 days before the event have positive abnormal returns. Day 16 before the event is one of them; it shows a significantly positive AR of 0.81% and is significant under the Corrado test. Negative abnormal returns increase dramatically towards the event. The first AR is significantly negative under all three tests and occurs on day eight before the event; the abnormal return is 1.36%. Over the following days, ARs continue their negative trend, reaching a first low on day four at 2.46%, dropping down to 1.81% on day three and even further to 1.45% on day two, only to increase to 2.83% on the day before the event. Cumulative abnormal returns sum up this picture to an overall pre-event CAR of 15.56%, which can be split into 2.19% from day 20 till day eleven before the event and 13.36%, cumulated during the last ten days before the event (see panel D). Of these -13.36%, one can allocate 9.89% to the final five days before the event. The abnormal return on the event day is extremely high. With 21.97% it is more than twice as high as transactions indicated as purchases. This highly negative abnormal return suggests a serious event in the firm history, such as extremely bad news that was made public on this particular day. In many cases, this news informs the market of a firm's inability to pay and thus indicate a pending bankruptcy. Other possibilities are low earnings announcements or any other event with a serious impact on the firm. One day after the event, negative abnormal returns are still high with -6.65%, followed by -2.55% on day two and -3.26% on day three. Even though the following days are still mostly negative, no significant abnormal returns are observed till day eleven after the event. On this day, an AR of -1.36% is measured. Considering the post-event period, it becomes obvious in panel C that most of the CAR of -20.42% is accumulated during days one till five (-14.48%). Over the first ten days, abnormal returns sum up to 15.85%, followed by 4.57% from day eleven till day 20. The entire event window shows an astonishing CAR of 57.95%, thus expressing the exceptional impact of the event on the firm's stock price.

Table 38: Insider Transactions

This table presents mean abnormal returns of purchase and sale transactions. These transaction are identified by the BaFin as illegal. Day zero indicates the event day, even though trading took place prior this date.

	Panel A: Purchases | N=166					Panel B: Sales | N=128				
Day	MAR	t-Statistics				MAR	t-Statistics			
-20	-0,0233	-0,0767				-0,7406	-1,3779			‡
-19	0,0746	0,2725				0,2009	0,3898			
-18	-0,0027	-0,0083		†		-0,4005	-0,7421			
-17	-0,2175	-0,6552				-0,2309	-0,2819			
-16	0,2770	0,8721				0,8087	1,4486		††	
-15	0,8874	2,0584	**		‡	-0,1074	-0,1619			
-14	0,4913	1,5501				0,2582	0,4209			
-13	0,2341	0,4858				-1,0276	-1,2601			
-12	0,1664	0,3836				-0,5563	-1,2097			
-11	0,2912	0,9407				-0,3963	-0,8701			‡
-10	-0,0949	-0,3042				0,1299	0,2289			
-9	0,1771	0,5986				-0,6252	-1,3247			
-8	0,1641	0,6857				-1,3550	-2,3277	**	†	‡‡‡
-7	-0,5224	-1,1563		††	‡‡	-0,7301	-1,4615			
-6	-0,1157	-0,1811				-0,8936	-1,8053	*		‡‡
-5	0,5554	1,4474				-1,3475	-2,0955	**		‡‡
-4	0,1970	0,4981				-2,4564	-3,2985	***	†	‡‡‡
-3	0,3245	0,9126				-1,8100	-2,4473	**	†††	‡‡‡
-2	1,0032	1,5539		††	‡	-1,4479	-1,7501	*		
-1	1,2170	2,1240	**	†††	‡‡‡	-2,8321	-3,5941	***	†††	‡‡‡
0	10,2697	6,2833	***	†††	‡‡‡	-21,9703	-7,9783	***	†††	‡‡‡
1	2,8343	2,9223		†	‡	-6,6459	-4,1825	***	†††	‡‡‡
2	-0,0724	-0,1597				-2,5488	-2,7624	***	†††	‡‡‡
3	0,4207	1,0006				-3,2577	-3,2002	***	†	‡‡‡
4	-0,5944	-0,6471				-1,4070	-1,3543			
5	0,1165	0,3666				-0,6237	-0,6509			
6	-0,0379	-0,1009				0,2646	0,4128			
7	0,3386	1,2463				-0,4063	-0,5380			
8	-0,3544	-1,1871				-1,1151	-1,0724			
9	-0,1854	-0,4558			‡	0,0747	0,1235			
10	0,1503	0,4385				-0,1888	-0,2947			
11	0,3080	0,9906				-1,3592	-2,0522	**		‡‡
12	0,1808	0,6262				0,3727	0,3354		††	
13	-0,1209	-0,3951			‡‡	-0,3717	-0,6313			
14	0,2611	0,9841				-0,0508	-0,0699			
15	0,6716	2,3478	**			-0,3271	-0,5459			
16	-0,2255	-0,7950				-0,2837	-0,2592			
17	0,6949	1,8322	*	††	‡	-1,0725	-0,9380			
18	-0,2504	-0,9850				-1,1374	-1,5675			‡‡
19	0,1581	0,5919				-1,2446	-2,2225	**		‡‡
20	0,3845	1,0717				0,9061	1,0158			
	Panel C: CARs Purchases					Panel D: CARs Sales				
[-20;-1]	5,0839	2,0592	**		‡‡	-15,5596	-5,3504	***		‡‡‡
[-20;-11]	2,1784	1,6224				-2,1917	-0,9850		†	‡
[-10;-1]	2,9055	1,8152	*		‡‡‡	-13,3679	-5,4798	***	†††	‡‡‡
[-5;-1]	3,2972	3,1840	***		‡‡‡	-9,8938	-5,4654	***	†††	‡‡‡
[1;5]	2,7048	2,0429	**		‡‡	-14,4831	-5,6156	***	†††	‡‡‡
[1;10]	2,6160	1,7104	*		‡‡	-15,8540	-5,5719	***	††	‡‡‡
[11;20]	2,0623	2,2089	**			-4,5682	-1,6711	*		‡‡‡
[1;20]	4,6782	2,6600	***		‡‡‡	-20,4223	-5,4464	***		‡‡‡
[-20;20]	20,0318	5,4180	***		‡‡‡	-57,9521	-9,6634	***	†††	‡‡‡

Notes
***, **, * indicate significance on the 1, 5, and 10 percent level for the t-test.
†††, ††, † indicate significance on the 1, 5, and 10 percent level for the Corrado test.
‡‡‡, ‡‡, ‡ indicate significance on the 1, 5, and 10 percent level for the Wilcoxon test.

The following figure illustrates the daily abnormal returns from the previous table graphically. One can see clearly that the development of abnormal returns in sales is stronger than in purchases.

Figure 13: Insider Transactions – Daily Abnormal Returns

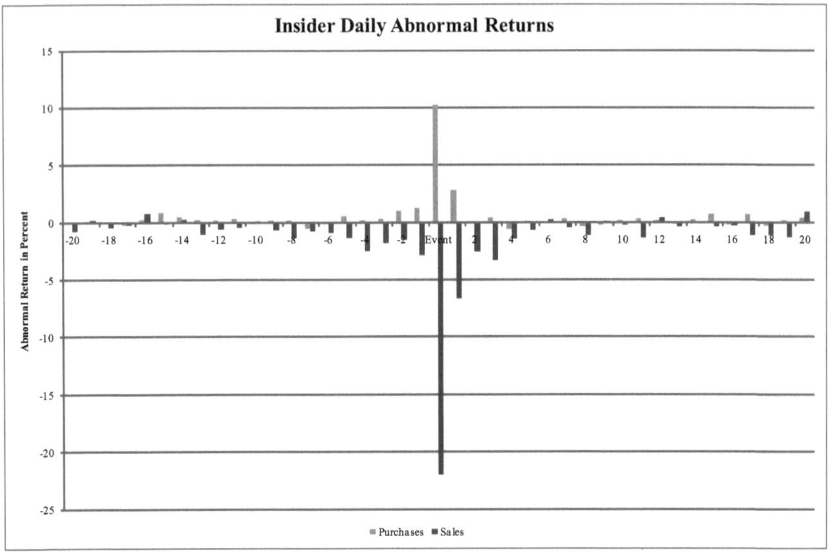

According to the daily abnormal returns in Figure 13, the next figure presents cumulative abnormal returns for purchases and sales. Here, one can see even more precisely how abnormal returns in sales accumulate faster before the event than in purchases.

Figure 14: Cumulative Abnormal Returns

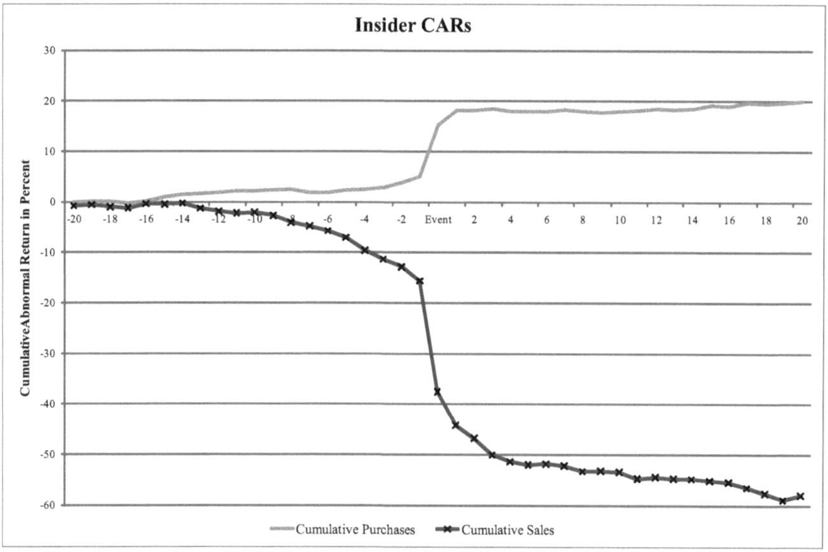

This figure shows clearly how cumulative abnormal returns build up slowly in both purchases and sales. Shortly before the event, they increase and jump to a new level and finally stabilize there.

VI.B.2 Insider Market Manipulation

This sub chapter presents empirical results on insider market manipulation cases. As explained above, this type of market fraud is conducted by misleading, i.e. manipulating, the security market. Most cases of market manipulation are carried out by disseminating false information either directly or indirectly. A direct way would be to spread false, in most cases overstated, earnings information. Also, announcing large business deals can lead to a sudden price increase. Since this information is published by the firm, it is considered direct market manipulation. The second possibility, indirect market manipulation, involves disseminating false information anonymously. Usually, internet discussion groups are the platform of choice for indirect market manipulation. Insiders can hide their identity and spread rumors. Of course, if these rumors are plausible, they can move prices as well. Certainly, this may take a bit longer than disseminating false information directly through the firm, but it makes it much harder to identify those responsible for the false information.

The following table presents the results of the empirical analysis of the market manipulation sample provided by BaFin. The sample I analyzed compromises 28 cases. Panel A shows daily abnormal returns for 41 days, centered on the event date indicated by BaFin. The left hand side presents days -20 to 0 while the right hand side presents abnormal returns for days after the event. Panel B presents corresponding cumulative abnormal returns.

Table 39: Insider Market Manipulation

This table presents mean abnormal returns of market manipulation cases. These transaction are identified by the BaFin as illegal. Day zero indicates the event day given by BaFin, even though manipulative actions may took place before or after this date.

Panel A: Market Manipulation | N=28							
Day	MAR	t-Statistics		Day	MAR	t-Statistics	
-20	-2,5700	-0,9301		1	-9,8873	-2,2614 **	††† ‡‡
-19	1,2579	0,9615		2	-1,2665	-0,7670	
-18	-1,3142	-1,0356		3	-1,5745	-1,1937	
-17	0,4611	0,3181		4	-3,0903	-1,3158	
-16	-1,0502	-1,0506		5	2,3256	1,2735	
-15	2,6157	1,3379		6	0,5254	0,2611	
-14	-0,8841	-0,8214		7	-2,4034	-1,6737	
-13	0,4881	0,2945		8	1,4923	0,9459	†
-12	-0,9601	-0,2153	††† ‡	9	-0,4863	-0,2672	
-11	2,6156	1,3932		10	-1,3588	-1,6625	
-10	-1,3267	-0,9573		11	-1,6804	-2,2341 **	‡
-9	1,9397	1,1138		12	0,5242	0,4927	
-8	-2,3393	-1,4104		13	-1,6211	-1,2440	
-7	1,8877	1,9413 *	††† ‡‡	14	-0,5687	-0,3225	
-6	-0,4400	-0,2319		15	1,0885	0,4190	
-5	1,7706	0,9615	†	16	0,1939	0,1429	
-4	3,4313	1,5219	†† ‡	17	1,7849	0,7420	
-3	5,2958	1,7042 *		18	-1,7496	-1,1450	
-2	1,7858	1,2177	††	19	-2,9064	-1,4456	† ‡
-1	2,2532	0,7492		20	3,7990	1,4113	†
0	1,6834	0,5546	†				
Panel B: CARs Market Manipulation							
[-20;-1]	14,9178	1,1140	†	[1;10]	-15,7238	-1,9158 *	‡
[-20;-11]	0,6599	0,0869		[11;20]	-1,1357	-0,2296	
[-10;-1]	14,2580	1,7290 *	††† ‡	[1;20]	-16,8595	-1,4992	‡
[-5;-1]	14,5366	2,2777 **	††† ‡‡	[-20;20]	-0,2582	-0,0146	
[1;5]	-13,4930	-1,8696 *	‡				

Notes: ***, **, * indicate significance on the 1, 5, and 10 percent level for the t-test. †††, ††, † indicate significance on the 1, 5, and 10 percent level for the Corrado test. ‡‡‡, ‡‡, ‡ indicate significance on the 1, 5, and 10 percent level for the Wilcoxon test.

At first sight, it is obvious that most days do not show significant abnormal returns. However, abnormal returns are high with a peak at 5.29%on day three before the event. Over the 20-day pre-event period, abnormal returns accumulate to 14.92%. Most of this CAR accumulates during the last five days before the event. However, this cumulative abnormal return is only significant on the 10% level under the Corrado test. The first day after the event shows a significant drop; the abnormal return on this day is -9.88% and it is significant under all three tests. The days afterwards show negative abnormal returns as well. All in all, abnormal returns during the first ten days amount to -15.72%, thus diminishing pre-event CAR. Over 20 days after the event, cumulative abnormal returns are -16.86%.

VI.B.3 Insider Price Manipulation

After presenting the empirical results for the market manipulation sample, this sub chapter presents the empirical results for the price manipulation sample. Price manipulation can be conducted in several ways. One example are round-trip trades, which increase the trading volume and thus attract the attention of other market participants. Also, entering several purchase orders in a short period of time may inflate prices.

The following table presents the results of the empirical analysis for 33 cases provided by BaFin. Like the foregoing analysis, this analysis covers 41 days, centered on the event date given by BaFin. Panel A in Table 40 shows daily abnormal returns. The left hand side displays the 20 days before the event until the event day, the right hand side presents the 20 days after the event. Panel B shows corresponding cumulative abnormal returns. Even though daily abnormal returns before the event are often high compared to previously discussed directors' dealings, they are seldom significant. Again, to ensure a certain level of validity, all three statistical tests are used. After 20 days before the event, the cumulative abnormal return is 5.67%, followed by 5.35% on the event day. However, the pre-event CAR does not accumulate to the mentioned level directly; instead, it shows several up-and-down movements. Figure VIII-16 in the appendix shows this movement together with daily abnormal returns. Comparing this graph to the previous one in the appendix, it is obvious that market manipulation shows a pattern where cumulative abnormal returns slowly build up and peak on the event day. In contrast, price manipulation shows an ever changing pattern with a peak on the event day; however, cumulative abnormal returns do not drop as sharply as in the market manipulation sample.

Table 40: Insider Price Manipulation

This table presents mean abnormal returns of price manipulation cases. These transaction are identified by the BaFin as illegal. Day zero indicates the event day given by BaFin, even though price manipulation may took place before or after this date.

Panel A: Price Manipulation | N=33									
Day	MAR	t-Statistics			Day	MAR	t-Statistics		
-20	0,1944	0,1759			1	-1,4765	-0,7009	†	
-19	0,0606	0,0657			2	-1,1281	-0,5896		
-18	-1,1491	-1,8269 *			3	-0,7686	-0,7834		
-17	1,9353	1,2531			4	-0,3451	-0,3536		
-16	1,3623	1,4658			5	0,6613	0,6049		
-15	-1,8832	-1,7514 *			6	-2,1824	-2,3516 **		‡
-14	0,9171	1,1819	†††	‡‡	7	-1,6483	-2,4439 **	††	‡‡‡
-13	-1,3275	-1,4329			8	2,1617	1,5210	††	‡
-12	-1,6984	-1,2852			9	-0,8959	-1,2741		‡
-11	3,0790	1,8364 *	††		10	-1,1034	-0,7047		
-10	3,4958	1,2116			11	1,6573	1,1373		
-9	-0,9074	-1,0799			12	-2,0022	-2,0332 *		
-8	2,0128	1,2559			13	-1,0496	-0,8387		
-7	-0,4007	-0,3998			14	-1,5378	-0,5629		
-6	-0,1729	-0,1752			15	-0,8613	-1,1082		
-5	-4,9418	-1,1784	††	‡‡	16	-1,4941	-0,8459		
-4	0,1576	0,1268			17	2,0498	0,5790		
-3	0,9039	0,6871			18	-0,3370	-0,3315		
-2	1,7723	1,1190			19	0,3273	0,3464		
-1	2,2628	1,2866			20	-0,1218	-0,1092		
0	5,3492	1,6905	††	‡					
Panel B: CARs Price Manipulation									
[-20;-1]	5,6729	0,7198	†		[1;10]	-6,7252	-1,9375 *		‡
[-20;-11]	1,4905	0,3110			[11;20]	-3,3696	-0,8349		
[-10;-1]	4,1823	0,6539			[1;20]	-10,0948	-1,7977 *		‡‡
[-5;-1]	0,1547	0,0283			[-20;20]	0,9272	0,0903		
[1;5]	-3,0570	-1,0153							

Notes: ***, **, * indicate significance on the 1, 5, and 10 percent level for the t-test.
†††, ††, † indicate significance on the 1, 5, and 10 percent level for the Corrado test.
‡‡‡, ‡‡, ‡ indicate significance on the 1, 5, and 10 percent level for the Wilcoxon test.

After the event, abnormal returns experience an overall negative trend. During the first ten days, they accumulate to -6.73%, and after 20 days, they accumulate to 10.09%. Both values are only significant on the 10% level under the t-test, and on the 10% and 5% level under the Wilcoxon test respectively.

Results suggest that insiders conducting price manipulation rather go for short-term reactions while insiders manipulating security markets through false information seek mid- to long-term price improvements. However, cumulative abnormal returns do not ensure superior price improvements over the entire event window. Certainly, since all cases analyzed in this study are identified by BaFin as such cases, it is likely that the public knew about the false signaling immediately after the event and thus prices moved from their artificial level back to their equilibrium. As a consequence, one can conjecture that especially "undetected" market manipulation carried out through indirect news channels can move prices in the favor of an insider.

VI.B.4 Summary Excursus Insider Dealing

In this short excursus, I presented three types of market misconduct. The first, illegal insider dealing is by far closest to directors' dealings. Certainly, presented findings show tremendous differences in return patterns and it is obvious, that significant information is disclosed on the event day. However, this excursus shows also how close directors' dealings and illegal insider trading are. Naturally, directors behave like any investor and sell on bad news or purchase on good news. Though, directors must under such circumstances put outside investors first and abstain from trading or disclose the information. The same is true for market and price manipulation. While in present cases insiders intentionally influenced the price or market, it is obvious that directors can easily influence the markets perceptions for example in interviews without intending to manipulate the market.

VII. Conclusion

The last chapter closed the empirical section of this thesis with an excursus on illegal insider dealing in Germany after presenting empirical results for the short- and long-term study, as well as the corporate actions study. Therewith, I conclude that this thesis achieved the research objectives set out in the introduction.

To achieve these objectives, I laid the legal and economic basics in the first chapters. After decades of unregulated directors' dealings in Germany, the national supervisor set out to implement a regulatory framework and requirements to disclose directors' dealings and combat market misconduct. Based on this theoretical framework, I conducted three empirical studies.

The first empirical study analyzed short-term abnormal returns before directors purchase or sell stock and after the publication of these transactions. Firstly, this part confirmed earlier research on German directors' dealings. Secondly, it added tremendous significance to previous studies due to the substantially higher sample size. Generally, my findings showed that directors exploit short-term under- or over-valuations to purchase or sell stock. Analyzing these results further, I found executive board members have higher CARs than other insiders, suggesting they have the best knowledge on their firm. These findings are in line with Tebroke & Wollin and Rau , who find significant higher CAR for executive board members as well.

The long-term study extended my findings from the short-term study. Again, I find directors can achieve long-term above average returns or avoid losses by selling stock. So far, no other German study has comparable long-term results. However, my findings are in line with international studies like Rozeff & Zaman (1988) and Seyhun (1992) .

Finally, the corporate actions study put directors' dealings in a larger setting. Overall, I did not find a concrete relationship between directors' dealings and corporate actions. Individual analyzes of repurchases, M&A, and SEOs showed no significant difference between firms with and without directors' dealings; OLS regressions showed that other factors, like firm size or market-to-book ratio, have a significant influence on post-event performance. The ordered-probit model showed that the most important trigger for directors' dealings is the previous 1-year BHAR. Higher previous 1-year BHARs increased the probability of directors' sales while lower previous 1-year BHARs increased the probability of directors' purchases. My findings are insofar in line with previous research as insiders tend to sell overvalued stock.[364]

Overall, I conclude directors can time their transactions and exploit temporarily under- or over-valuations. Directors purchase after a decline in prices and sell after a rise. Also, over prolonged holding periods directors proofed to trade profitably. Of course, outsiders are interested whether it's worth following a mimick-

364 Cf. Lee (1997), p. 1463.

ing strategy. I suggest it is worthwhile following directors' dealings closely yet it seems important to consider other factors as well.

Directors' dealings will offer a broad field of future research. With a daily increasing sample of available transactions, future analyzes will be more accurate and it might be easier to link directors' dealings to corporate actions in Germany.

VIII. Appendix

Table 41: Long-Term BHAR - CDAX Benchmark

This table reports Buy-And-Hold abnormal returns of directors' dealings after their publication. BHAR are calculated for 3, 6, 9, 12, 18, and 24 months; values are stated in percent. CDAX index is used as benchmark. Panel A presents results with overlapping publications, panel B without overlapping publications.

Panel A	Purchases				Sales			
Months	N	BHAR	T-skew		N	BHAR	T-skew	
3	6.307	1,78	6,53	*** +++	4.488	-0,59	-1,67	* + ‡‡‡
6	5.773	1,79	4,00	*** +++ ‡‡‡	4.357	-0,38	-0,75	‡‡‡
9	5.138	3,18	4,67	*** +++ ‡‡‡	4.234	0,61	0,84	‡‡‡
12	4.663	6,79	6,14	*** +++ ‡‡‡	4.070	-1,65	-1,73	* + ‡‡‡
18	4.039	7,55	3,96	*** +++ ‡‡‡	3.653	-3,90	-2,95	*** +++ ‡‡‡
24	3.351	8,52	3,42	*** +++ ‡‡‡	3.199	-10,76	-5,64	*** +++ ‡‡‡

Panel B	Purchases				Sales			
Months	N	BHAR	T-skew		N	BHAR	T-skew	
3	589	3,87	3,78	*** +++ ‡	548	0,31	0,30	‡‡
6	515	7,25	4,18	*** +++	499	1,21	0,71	‡‡
9	446	10,91	4,28	*** +++	461	0,08	0,06	‡‡‡
12	404	20,25	4,21	*** +++	417	-3,31	-1,12	‡‡‡
18	324	28,30	3,76	*** +++	346	-3,92	-0,85	‡‡‡
24	248	31,64	2,17	** ‡	297	-6,38	-0,98	‡‡‡

Notes
***, **, * indicate significance on the 1, 5, and 10 percent level for the bootstrapped skewness-adjusted t-test.
+++, ++, + indicate significance on the 1, 5, and 10 percent level for the t-test.
‡‡‡, ‡‡, ‡ indicate significance on the 1, 5, and 10 percent level for the Wilcoxon test.
Depending on the date of the publication, return series were not available for the entire sample.

Table 42: Firm Size Long-Term BHAR - CDAX Benchmark

This table reports Buy-And-Hold abnormal returns of directors' dealings after their publication divided into four quartiles based on firm size. BHAR are calculated for 3, 6, 9, 12, 18, and 24 months; values are stated in percent. CDAX index is used as benchmark. Panels A and B present results for purchases and sales including overlapping transactions, panels C and D present results for purchases and sales without overlapping transactions.

Panel A	Quartile 1 Purchases				Quartile 2 Purchases				Quartile 3 Purchases				Quartile 4 Purchases			
Months	N	BHAR	T-skew		N	BHAR	T-skew		N	BHAR	T-skew		N	BHAR	T-skew	
3	1.579	3,68	5,31	*** +++ ‡	1.575	1,38	2,45	** ++ ‡	1.576	1,46	2,91	*** +++	1.577	0,59	1,60	
6	1.443	7,11	5,58	*** +++	1.444	0,75	0,96	‡‡‡	1.448	-1,32	-1,89	* + ‡‡‡	1.438	0,62	1,09	
9	1.285	12,40	6,44	*** +++	1.284	2,66	2,16	** ++ ‡‡‡	1.287	-4,44	-4,16	*** +++ ‡‡‡	1.282	2,10	2,64	** +++
12	1.169	23,06	6,20	*** +++	1.164	3,71	2,24	** ++ ‡‡‡	1.164	-4,73	-3,13	*** +++ ‡‡‡	1.166	5,05	4,95	*** +++
18	1.010	34,29	5,35	*** +++ ‡‡‡	1.010	-2,03	-0,72	‡‡‡	1.009	-6,69	-3,21	*** +++ ‡‡‡	1.010	4,61	3,63	*** +++
24	847	38,86	4,85	*** +++ ‡‡‡	829	1,25	0,34	‡‡‡	837	-15,85	-5,06	*** +++ ‡‡‡	838	9,40	5,02	*** +++ ‡‡‡

Panel B	Quartile 1 Sales				Quartile 2 Sales				Quartile 3 Sales				Quartile 4 Sales			
Months	N	BHAR	T-skew		N	BHAR	T-skew		N	BHAR	T-skew		N	BHAR	T-skew	
3	1.122	-2,45	-2,21	** ++ ‡‡‡	1.122	-1,76	-2,87	*** +++ ‡‡‡	1.122	1,96	3,30	*** +++	1.122	-0,10	-0,26	
6	1.089	1,06	0,77	‡‡‡	1.090	-4,58	-4,74	*** +++ ‡‡‡	1.089	3,29	3,56	*** +++	1.089	-1,30	-2,43	** ++ ‡‡‡
9	1.060	6,14	2,97	*** +++ ‡‡‡	1.059	-5,71	-4,71	*** +++ ‡‡‡	1.057	3,82	2,99	*** +++	1.058	-1,83	-2,58	** +++ ‡‡‡
12	1.019	6,76	2,45	** ++ ‡‡‡	1.016	-11,65	-8,40	*** +++ ‡‡‡	1.019	1,15	0,75	‡‡‡	1.016	-2,87	-3,24	*** +++ ‡‡‡
18	914	1,19	0,35	‡‡‡	914	-15,46	-5,35	*** +++ ‡‡‡	915	2,33	1,09	‡‡‡	910	-3,66	-2,72	*** +++ ‡‡‡
24	801	-1,81	-0,34	‡‡‡	799	-29,87	-7,46	*** +++ ‡‡‡	801	-6,23	-2,10	** ++ ‡‡‡	798	-5,14	-2,83	*** +++ ‡‡‡

Panel C	Quartile 1 Purchases				Quartile 2 Purchases				Quartile 3 Purchases				Quartile 4 Purchases			
Months	N	BHAR	T-skew		N	BHAR	T-skew		N	BHAR	T-skew		N	BHAR	T-skew	
3	147	8,81	3,21	*** +++ ‡‡	148	1,48	0,67		147	3,41	1,99	* + ‡	147	1,79	1,54	
6	129	20,82	3,95	*** +++	129	1,54	0,48		128	4,12	1,62		129	2,50	1,28	
9	112	34,64	4,22	*** +++ ‡	111	2,52	0,59		112	6,08	1,62		111	0,25	0,11	
12	101	71,36	4,06	*** +++ ‡‡	101	3,03	0,55		101	6,36	1,34		101	0,26	0,11	
18	81	105,22	3,91	*** +++ ‡‡	81	-2,62	-0,21	‡‡	81	10,54	1,41		81	0,07	0,03	
24	62	137,95	2,53	** +	62	-13,72	-1,02	‡	62	-0,97	-0,08		62	3,28	0,54	

Panel D	Quartile 1 Sales				Quartile 2 Sales				Quartile 3 Sales				Quartile 4 Sales			
Months	N	BHAR	T-skew		N	BHAR	T-skew		N	BHAR	T-skew		N	BHAR	T-skew	
3	137	3,27	0,86		137	-2,35	-1,51	‡‡	137	-1,28	-0,79		137	1,61	1,20	
6	125	7,40	1,52		125	-3,55	-1,13	‡‡‡	124	0,20	0,08		125	0,80	0,39	
9	115	7,98	1,18		116	-5,65	-1,49	‡‡‡	115	-4,62	-1,22	‡	115	2,66	0,81	
12	104	0,25	0,07	‡‡	105	-9,44	-1,99	* ++ ‡‡‡	104	-8,26	-1,72	* + ‡‡	104	4,28	1,04	
18	87	0,47	0,10	‡	86	-15,31	-2,13	** ++ ‡‡‡	87	-6,40	-0,68	‡	86	5,54	0,99	
24	74	1,31	0,13	‡‡‡	75	-13,77	-1,46	‡‡	74	-19,75	-1,73	* + ‡‡‡	74	6,78	1,08	

Notes
***, **, * indicate significance on the 1, 5, and 10 percent level for the bootstrapped skewness-adjusted t-test.
+++, ++, + indicate significance on the 1, 5, and 10 percent level for the t-test.
‡‡‡, ‡‡, ‡ indicate significance on the 1, 5, and 10 percent level for the Wilcoxon test.
Depending on the date of the publication, return series were not available for the entire sample.

Table 43: Insider Group Long-Term BHAR - CDAX Benchmark

This table reports Buy-And-Hold abnormal returns of directors' dealings after their publication divided into five groups based on the trading person's insider category. BHAR are calculated for 3, 6, 9, 12, 18, and 24 months; values are stated in percent. CDAX index is used as benchmark. Panels A and B present results for purchases and sales including overlapping transactions, panels C and D present results for purchases and sales without overlapping transactions.

Panel A	Group 1 Purchases			Group 2 Purchases			Group 3 Purchases			Group 4 Purchases			Group 5 Purchases		
Months	N	BHAR	T-skew	N	BHAR	T-skew	N	BHAR	T-skew	N	BHAR	T-skew	N	BHAR	T-skew
3	2.886	1,56	3,76 *** +++	1.649	2,89	5,09 *** +++	178	2,15	1,88 * +	390	2,34	2,71 ** +++ ‡‡‡	1.204	0,53	0,94
6	2.687	1,32	1,95 * + ‡‡‡	1.512	4,75	5,16 *** +++	173	4,74	2,67 ** ++ ‡‡	372	4,52	3,45 *** +++ ‡	1.029	-2,81	-2,89 *** +++ ‡‡‡
9	2.442	3,28	3,22 *** +++ ‡‡‡	1.314	5,61	3,72 *** +++ ‡‡	160	9,13	3,58 *** +++ ‡‡‡	343	12,77	6,37 *** +++ ‡‡‡	879	-5,56	-3,90 *** +++ ‡‡‡
12	2.231	5,73	4,41 *** +++ ‡‡‡	1.210	15,49	4,55 *** +++ ‡	143	12,69	4,12 *** +++ ‡‡‡	327	17,77	6,46 *** +++ ‡‡‡	752	-9,96	-5,18 *** +++ ‡‡‡
18	1.964	5,63	3,05 *** +++ ‡‡‡	1.079	21,60	3,54 *** +++ ‡‡‡	134	6,03	1,44	306	18,70	5,60 *** +++ ‡‡‡	556	-18,70	-6,39 *** +++ ‡‡‡
24	1.663	9,95	3,74 *** +++ ‡‡‡	925	17,75	2,49 ** ++ ‡‡‡	114	-4,76	-1,00	279	17,62	4,20 *** +++ ‡‡‡	370	-23,71	-4,06 *** +++ ‡‡‡

Panel B	Group 1 Sales			Group 2 Sales			Group 3 Sales			Group 4 Sales			Group 5 Sales		
Months	N	BHAR	T-skew	N	BHAR	T-skew	N	BHAR	T-skew	N	BHAR	T-skew	N	BHAR	T-skew
3	1.827	-0,97	-1,59 + ‡‡‡	1.368	-1,00	-1,66 + ‡‡‡	204	-2,16	-1,87 * + ‡‡‡	558	2,57	2,91 *** +++	531	-0,91	-0,81 ‡‡
6	1.772	-1,27	-1,57 ‡‡‡	1.325	-0,79	-0,82 ‡‡‡	199	-2,85	-2,19 ** ++ ‡‡	551	4,05	3,16 *** +++	510	-0,08	-0,03 ‡‡
9	1.715	-3,60	-3,35 *** +++ ‡‡‡	1.289	4,31	2,90 *** +++ ‡‡‡	194	-2,14	-1,05 ‡‡	543	7,16	4,38 *** +++	493	-0,59	-0,23 ‡‡‡
12	1.640	-7,43	-5,55 *** +++ ‡‡‡	1.246	3,31	1,70 * ‡‡‡	190	0,61	0,25	530	4,29	1,95 * + ‡‡	464	-2,23	-0,75 ‡‡‡
18	1.483	-8,61	-3,89 *** +++ ‡‡‡	1.133	-2,78	-1,11 ‡‡‡	169	-0,54	-0,15	489	11,75	3,27 *** +++ ‡	379	-10,51	-2,59 ** +++ ‡‡‡
24	1.295	-14,77	-4,51 *** +++ ‡‡‡	1.011	-11,23	-3,31 *** +++ ‡‡‡	148	-15,45	-4,49 *** +++ ‡‡‡	443	2,87	0,61 ‡‡‡	302	-9,64	-1,39 ‡‡‡

Panel C	Group 1 Purchases			Group 2 Purchases			Group 3 Purchases			Group 4 Purchases			Group 5 Purchases		
Months	N	BHAR	T-skew	N	BHAR	T-skew	N	BHAR	T-skew	N	BHAR	T-skew	N	BHAR	T-skew
3	297	4,29	2,67 ** ++	170	5,23	3,05 *** +++ ‡‡	13	-1,15	-0,31	38	3,20	1,03	71	0,11	0,07
6	260	6,23	2,59 ** ++	148	11,31	3,10 *** ++	11	-5,24	-1,00	37	8,03	1,70 *	59	3,39	0,75
9	226	10,32	2,65 ** ++	128	14,17	2,82 *** ++				32	16,91	2,21 ** + ‡	51	4,44	0,74
12	204	15,01	2,95 *** ++	115	40,08	2,78 *** +				32	21,18	2,24 ** +	47	-2,66	-0,38
18	166	23,95	3,13 *** ++	89	48,78	2,09 **				29	41,21	1,86 +	34	-5,91	-0,41 ‡
24	123	42,87	2,16 **	72	45,76	1,41				20	7,19	0,35	27	-24,46	-1,60 ‡‡

Panel D	Group 1 Sales			Group 2 Sales			Group 3 Sales			Group 4 Sales			Group 5 Sales		
Months	N	BHAR	T-skew	N	BHAR	T-skew	N	BHAR	T-skew	N	BHAR	T-skew	N	BHAR	T-skew
3	267	0,07	0,13 ‡‡	145	-1,71	-1,03	17	4,05	0,81	59	3,19	1,14	60	2,38	0,65
6	240	1,38	0,53 ‡‡	133	-2,16	-0,76 ‡	15	-0,98	-0,19	55	5,20	1,16	56	5,18	0,92
9	224	-0,42	-0,06 ‡‡‡	120	-4,56	-0,91 ‡‡‡	14	1,18	0,15	52	3,33	0,61	51	9,57	1,15
12	205	-4,33	-0,97 ‡‡‡	103	-12,20	-1,99 * +++ ‡‡‡	13	4,84	0,49	51	8,14	1,24	45	6,40	0,68
18	171	-5,38	-0,72 ‡‡‡	91	-16,46	-2,40 ** +++ ‡‡‡	10	11,09	0,84	40	22,48	1,65	34	1,52	0,14
24	143	-14,61	-1,48 + ‡‡‡	78	-15,71	-1,92 * ++ ‡‡‡				35	24,07	1,22	32	20,25	0,90

Notes: ***, **, * indicate significance on the 1, 5, and 10 percent level for the bootstrapped skewness-adjusted t-test.
+++, ++, + indicate significance on the 1, 5, and 10 percent level for the t-test.
‡‡‡, ‡‡, ‡ indicate significance on the 1, 5, and 10 percent level for the Wilcoxon test.
Depending on the date of the publication, return series were not available for the entire sample.

Table 44: Overlapping Calendar-Time Raw Returns

This table presents raw mean monthly calendar-time returns for 3 to 24 months holding periods. N represents the number of firms included in portfolios. Firms are included in purchases or sales portfolios if they had a purchase or sales transaction within the respective time-frame. Panel A presents results for purchases panel B presents results for sales. All raw returns are presented in percent.

	Panel A: Purchase Months				Panel B: Sale Months			
Months	N	MMAR	T-skew		N	MMAR	T-skew	
3	484	1.4752	1.9675	* ++ ‡‡	426	0.5674	0.7785	
6	468	1.3582	1.7856	* + ‡‡	417	1.0473	1.4157	‡‡
9	465	1.1773	1.5902	+ ‡‡	416	0.9006	1.2938	‡‡
12	463	0.6993	0.9782	‡	415	0.6118	0.8750	‡
18	452	0.2705	0.3602		414	0.1944	0.2529	
24	432	0.3141	0.3797		400	0.2445	0.2928	

Notes ***, **, * indicate significance on the 1, 5, and 10 percent level for the bootstrapped skewness-adjusted t-test.
+++, ++, + indicate significance on the 1, 5, and 10 percent level for the t-test.
‡‡‡, ‡‡, ‡ indicate significance on the 1, 5, and 10 percent level for the Wilcoxon test.

Table 45: Overlapping Calendar-Time Adjusted Returns

This table presents adjusted mean monthly calendar-time returns for 3 to 24 months holding periods. N represents the number of firms included in portfolios. Firms are included in purchases or sales portfolios if they had a purchase or sales transaction within the respective time-frame. Returns are adjusted by the MSCI Core index Germany. Panel A presents results for purchases panel B presents results for sales. All adjusted returns are presented in percent.

	Panel A: Purchase Months			Panel B: Sale Months		
Months	N	MMAR	T-skew	N	MMAR	T-skew
3	484	1.2542	1.4815	426	0.3465	0.4131
6	468	1.1810	1.4221	417	0.8701	1.0759
9	465	0.7181	0.9085	416	0.4414	0.5736
12	463	0.5937	0.7722	415	0.5061	0.6553
18	452	0.4885	0.6154	414	0.4123	0.5165
24	432	0.5576	0.6519	400	0.4880	0.5681

Notes ***, **, * indicate significance on the 1, 5, and 10 percent level for the bootstrapped skewness-adjusted t-test.
+++, ++, + indicate significance on the 1, 5, and 10 percent level for the t-test.
‡‡‡, ‡‡, ‡ indicate significance on the 1, 5, and 10 percent level for the Wilcoxon test.

Table 46: Fama-French Three-Factor Regression - Overlapping CTR

This table presents results from the Fama-French three factor regression for the mean monthly calendar-time raw returns for 3 to 24 months holding periods with purchases and sales within the respective time-frame. Results for purchases are reported in panel A, for sales in panel B. Each panel shows alphas and coefficients in the first line for each holding period, White heteroscedasticity-adjusted t-statistics are presented in the second line. RM is represented by the MSCI Core index Germany, RF is represented by German federal securites with 1 year maturity (Bundeswertpapiere) , SML and HML are based on the MSCI Global Large & Small Cap as well as MSCI Global Value & Growth Indices for Germany.

	Panel A: Three-Factor Model Purchases					
Holding Period	α	RM_t-RF_t	SMB_t	HML_t	R^2	adj. R^2
3	0.0126	0.2325	0.4454	0.1462	0.1514	0.1150
	1.9138	**2.5707**	**1.7727**	0.9396		
6	0.0117	0.1998	0.3429	0.3287	0.1617	0.1241
	1.7595	**2.0949**	1.3518	**1.7532**		
9	0.0094	0.2320	0.3001	0.2853	0.1839	0.1456
	1.5050	**2.5708**	1.2622	1.5786		
12	0.0054	0.1955	0.3485	0.2663	0.1984	0.1589
	0.9128	**2.0376**	1.4861	1.5764		
18	0.0020	0.1763	0.3057	0.2678	0.1859	0.1415
	0.3348	**1.6964**	1.3353	**1.7690**		
24	0.0035	0.1919	0.2782	0.3383	0.2166	0.1686
	0.5305	**1.7793**	1.0623	**2.1357**		

	Panel B: Three-Factor Model Sales					
Holding Period	α	RM_t-RF_t	SMB_t	HML_t	R^2	adj. R^2
3	0.0032	0.2385	0.4839	0.0696	0.1436	0.1069
	0.4748	**2.4336**	**1.7450**	0.4500		
6	0.0081	0.2376	0.3683	0.2045	0.1464	0.1082
	1.2191	**2.3691**	1.3344	1.0767		
9	0.0066	0.2193	0.2656	0.2720	0.1819	0.1435
	1.1372	**2.6461**	1.2299	**1.6752**		
12	0.0045	0.1853	0.2964	0.2557	0.1707	0.1299
	0.7587	**1.9333**	1.3397	1.5758		
18	0.0013	0.1753	0.3057	0.2731	0.1822	0.1376
	0.2087	1.6436	1.3008	**1.7212**		
24	0.0028	0.1748	0.2434	0.3673	0.2060	0.1573
	0.4181	1.5405	0.9180	**2.2027**		

Table 47: Netted Calendar-Time Raw Returns

This table presents raw mean monthly calendar-time returns for 3 to 24 months holding periods. N represents the number of firms included in portfolios. Monthly purchases and sales are netted resulting in either purchase or sale months. Panel A presents results for purchases panel B presents results for sales. All raw returns are presented in percent.

	Panel A: Net Purchase Months				Panel B: Net Sale Months			
Months	N	MMAR	T-skew		N	MMAR	T-skew	
3	468	1.6134	2.1126	** ++ ‡‡	410	0.4789	0.6535	
6	449	1.4592	1.9033	* + ‡‡	402	0.9996	1.3662	‡‡
9	446	1.2745	1.7098	* + ‡‡	401	0.8099	1.1561	‡‡
12	444	0.7533	1.0486	‡	400	0.5504	0.7738	‡
18	433	0.2880	0.3820		399	0.1913	0.2466	
24	415	0.3551	0.4292		389	0.2443	0.2900	

Notes ***, **, * indicate significance on the 1, 5, and 10 percent level for the bootstrapped skewness-adjusted t-test.
+++, ++, + indicate significance on the 1, 5, and 10 percent level for the t-test.
‡‡‡, ‡‡, ‡ indicate significance on the 1, 5, and 10 percent level for the Wilcoxon test.

Table 48: Netted Calendar-Time Adjusted Returns

This table presents adjusted mean monthly calendar-time returns for 3 to 24 months holding periods. N represents the number of firms included in portfolios. Monthly purchases and sales are netted resulting in either purchase or sale months. Returns are adjusted by the MSCI Core index Germany. Panel A presents results for purchases panel B presents results for sales. All adjusted returns are presented in

	Panel A: Net Purchase Months			Panel B: Net Sale Months		
Months	N	MMAR	T-skew	N	MMAR	T-skew
3	468	1.1798	1.3827	410	0.0453	0.0684
6	449	1.2819	1.5424	402	0.8224	1.0128
9	446	0.8154	1.0333	401	0.3507	0.4534
12	444	0.6477	0.8448	400	0.4448	0.5691
18	433	0.5060	0.6373	399	0.4093	0.5054
24	415	0.5986	0.6980	389	0.4878	0.5614

Notes ***, **, * indicate significance on the 1, 5, and 10 percent level for the bootstrapped skewness-adjusted t-test.
+++, ++, + indicate significance on the 1, 5, and 10 percent level for the t-test.
‡‡‡, ‡‡, ‡ indicate significance on the 1, 5, and 10 percent level for the Wilcoxon test.

Table 49: Fama-French Three-Factor Regression - Netted CTR

This table presents results from the Fama-French three factor regression for the mean monthly calendar-time raw returns for 3 to 24 months holding periods with netted purchases and sales within the respective time-frame. Results for purchases are reported in panel A, for sales in panel B. Each panel shows alphas and coefficients in the first line for each holding period, White heteroscedasticity-adjusted t-statistics are presented in the second line. RM is represented by the MSCI Core index Germany, RF is represented by German federal securites with 1 year maturity (Bundeswertpapiere) , SML and HML are based on the MSCI Global Large & Small Cap as well as MSCI Global Value & Growth Indices for Germany.

	Panel A: Three-Factor Model Purchases					
Holding Period	α	RM_t-RF_t	SMB_t	HML_t	R^2	adj. R^2
3	0.0141	0.2327	0.4792	0.1605	0.1583	0.1222
	2.0846	**2.5643**	**1.8520**	0.9995		
6	0.0127	0.2058	0.3431	0.3544	0.1683	0.1311
	1.8977	**2.1407**	1.3411	**1.8420**		
9	0.0104	0.2370	0.3154	0.2949	0.1935	0.1557
	1.6594	**2.6332**	1.3308	1.6070		
12	0.0060	0.1994	0.3598	0.2694	0.2057	0.1666
	1.0051	**2.0656**	1.5346	1.5723		
18	0.0023	0.1784	0.3140	0.2813	0.1947	0.1507
	0.3725	**1.7034**	1.3595	**1.8092**		
24	0.0040	0.1920	0.2847	0.3481	0.2221	0.1745
	0.5994	**1.7736**	1.0830	**2.1477**		

	Panel B: Three-Factor Model Sales					
Holding Period	α	RM_t-RF_t	SMB_t	HML_t	R^2	adj. R^2
3	0.0025	0.2043	0.5023	0.1057	0.1404	0.1036
	0.3764	**2.0579**	**1.7940**	0.6565		
6	0.0079	0.2002	0.3508	0.2796	0.1516	0.1136
	1.2230	**2.0618**	1.3054	1.5262		
9	0.0059	0.2051	0.2847	0.3002	0.1904	0.1525
	1.0094	**2.4085**	1.3160	**1.8276**		
12	0.0040	0.1750	0.3111	0.2824	0.1773	0.1369
	0.6621	**1.7974**	1.4045	**1.7431**		
18	0.0013	0.1565	0.3055	0.3092	0.1841	0.1396
	0.2126	1.4472	1.2934	**1.8719**		
24	0.0028	0.1630	0.2446	0.3854	0.2055	0.1569
	0.4199	1.4285	0.9250	**2.2819**		

Table 50: Correlation Matrix - Repurchases

Panel A: Model 1

	Firm-Size	Previous 1-Yr. BHAR	Directors' Dealings Dummy	Market-To-Book Ratio	Pirce-Earnings Ratio
Firm-Size	1.0000	-0.1262	0.3940	0.0602	0.1060
Previous 1-Yr. BHAR	-0.1262	1.0000	0.0328	-0.0156	0.0968
Directors' Dealings Dummy	0.3940	0.0328	1.0000	-0.0685	0.0962
Market-To-Book Ratio	0.0602	-0.0156	-0.0685	1.0000	0.0499
Price-Earnings Ratio	0.1060	0.0968	0.0962	0.0499	1.0000

Panel B: Model 2

	Firm-Size	Previous 1-Yr. BHAR	Purchase-Sales Ratio	Market-To-Book Ratio	Price-Earnings Ratio
Firm-Size	1.0000	-0.1471	-0.1050	-0.1851	0.1514
Previous 1-Yr. BHAR	-0.1471	1.0000	-0.0832	-0.0795	0.0597
Purchase-Sales Ratio	-0.1050	-0.0832	1.0000	-0.0865	0.3454
Market-To-Book Ratio	-0.1851	-0.0795	-0.0865	1.0000	-0.0575
Price-Earnings Ratio	0.1514	0.0597	0.3454	-0.0575	1.0000

Table 51: Correlation Matrix M&A

Panel A: Model 1

	Firm-Size	Previous 1-Yr. BHAR	Directors' Dealings Dummy	Market-To-Book Ratio	Price-Earnings Ratio
Firm-Size	1.0000	-0.1227	0.0140	0.3127	0.1469
Previous 1-Yr. BHAR	-0.1227	1.0000	0.1621	0.0174	-0.0942
Directors' Dealings Dummy	0.0140	0.1621	1.0000	-0.0305	-0.0162
Market-To-Book Ratio	0.3127	0.0174	-0.0305	1.0000	0.1935
Price-Earnings Ratio	0.1469	-0.0942	-0.0162	0.1935	1.0000

Panel B: Model 2

	Firm-Size		Directors' Dealings Dummy	Market-To-Book Ratio	Price-Earnings Ratio
Firm-Size	1.0000		0.0140	0.3127	0.1469
Directors' Dealings Dummy	0.0140		1.0000	-0.0305	-0.0162
Market-To-Book Ratio	0.3127		-0.0305	1.0000	0.1935
Price-Earnings Ratio	0.1469		-0.0162	0.1935	1.0000

Panel C: Model 3

	Firm-Size	Previous 1-Yr. BHAR	Purchase-Sales-Ratio	Market-To-Book Ratio	Price-Earnings Ratio
Firm-Size	1.0000	-0.1588	-0.0005	0.1321	0.0340
Previous 1-Yr. BHAR	-0.1588	1.0000	-0.0337	0.0835	-0.1088
Purchase-Sales-Ratio	-0.0005	-0.0337	1.0000	0.1344	-0.0024
Market-To-Book Ratio	0.1321	0.0835	0.1344	1.0000	0.0624
Price-Earnings Ratio	0.0340	-0.1088	-0.0024	0.0624	1.0000

Panel D: Model 4

	Firm-Size		Purchase-Sales-Ratio	Market-To-Book Ratio	Price-Earnings Ratio
Firm-Size	1.0000		-0.0005	0.1321	0.0340
Purchase-Sales-Ratio	-0.0005		1.0000	0.1344	-0.0024
Market-To-Book Ratio	0.1321		0.1344	1.0000	0.0624
Price-Earnings Ratio	0.0340		-0.0024	0.0624	1.0000

Table 52: Correlation Matrix SEO

Panel A: Model 1					
	Firm-Size	Previous 1-Yr. BHAR	Directors' Dealings Dummy	Market-To-Book Ratio	Pirce-Earnings Ratio
Firm-Size	1.0000	-0.2755	0.1461	0.0764	-0.0643
Previous 1-Yr. BHAR	-0.2755	1.0000	0.0387	0.1053	0.0394
Directors' Dealings Dummy	0.1461	0.0387	1.0000	0.0703	0.0049
Market-To-Book Ratio	0.0764	0.1053	0.0703	1.0000	0.1538
Price-Earnings Ratio	-0.0643	0.0394	0.0049	0.1538	1.0000

Panel B: Model 2					
	Firm-Size	Previous 1-Yr. BHAR	Purchase-Sales Ratio	Market-To-Book Ratio	Price-Earnings Ratio
Firm-Size	1.0000	-0.3363	-0.0449	0.0274	-0.0438
Previous 1-Yr. BHAR	-0.3363	1.0000	-0.0740	0.1120	0.0214
Purchase-Sales Ratio	-0.0449	-0.0740	1.0000	0.0851	-0.1098
Market-To-Book Ratio	0.0274	0.1120	0.0851	1.0000	0.2122
Price-Earnings Ratio	-0.0438	0.0214	-0.1098	0.2122	1.0000

Table 53: Ordered-Probit Model 3

This table reports regression results from the ordered-probit model. Model 3 uses the netted number of quarterly purchases and sales, with 0 for sales, 1 for no transaction, and 2 for purchases. The first line for each variable shows coefficients, second line shows z-statistics. Bold printed figures indicate significance on or above th 10%-level. Limit points for the ordered groups is reported for each model below the regression results.

Variable	Model 3
N	9581
Repurchases	-0.0333
	-0.1859
M&A	-0.0775
	-2.0757
SEO	-0.0997
	-0.9151
Log Market-Value	0.0051
	0.7998
Market-To-Book Value	0.0040
	2.2262
Price-Earnings Ratio	0.0000
	0.4399
Log Volume	-0.0159
	-2.4484
Previous 1Yr. BHAR	-0.2823
	-6.0521
Limit Points	
Limit 1	-1.4068
Limit 2	1.1623
Pseudo-R^2	0.0042
LR statistic (8 df)	51.6181
Probability(LR stat)	0.0000

Notes Shaded areas indicate variables not used in the r

Table 54: Marginal Effects Model 3

This table reports marginal effects for netted directors' purchases and sales. Marginal effects are shown for each variable and indicate the change in probability of falling into the respective transaction category for a one-percent change in the variable. Second shows z-statistics.

Transaction Category	0	1	2
Repurchases	0.0048	0.0021	-0.0069
	0.4736	0.2041	-0.6777
M&A	0.0113	0.0048	-0.0161
	1.1013	0.4746	-1.5759
SEO	0.0145	0.0062	-0.0207
	1.4154	0.6100	**-2.0254**
Log Market-Value	-0.0007	-0.0003	0.0011
	-0.0726	-0.0313	0.1039
Market-To-Book Value	-0.0006	-0.0003	0.0008
	-0.0575	-0.0248	0.0822
Price-Earnings Ratio	0.0000	0.0000	0.0000
	-0.0005	-0.0002	0.0008
Log Volume	0.0023	0.0010	-0.0033
	0.2259	0.0973	-0.3232
Previous 1Yr. BHAR	0.0410	0.0177	-0.0586
	4.0092	**1.7278**	**-5.7370**

Notes: Bold print indicates significance on the 10%-level or above.

Figure 15: Insider Market Manipulation

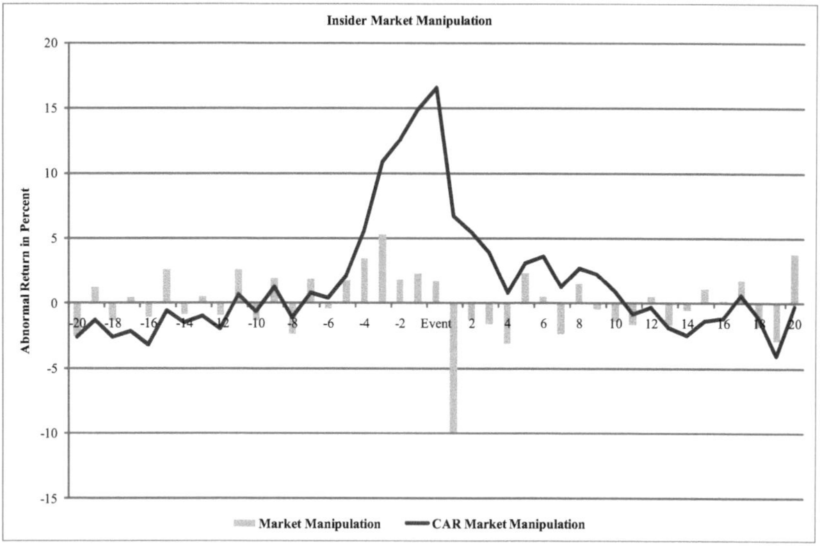

Figure 16: Insider Price Manipulation

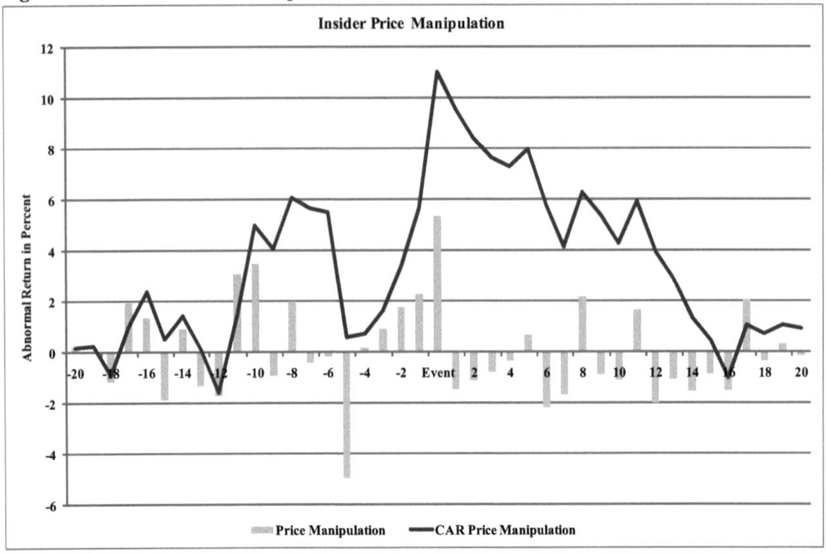

IX. References

Aboody, D., & Lev, B. (2000). Information Asymmetry, R&D, and Insider Gains. *The Journal of Finance, 55*(6), 2747-2766.

Akerlof, G. A. (1970). The Market for "Lemons": Quality Uncertainty and the Market Mechanism. *The Quarterly Journal of Economics, 84*(3), 488-500.

Akhter, S., & Misir, A. (2005). Capital Markets Efficiency: Evidence from the Emerging Capital Market with Particular Reference to Dhaka Stock Exchange. *South Asian Journal of Management, 12*(3), 35.

Alexander, S. S. (1964). Price Movements in Speculative Markets--Trends or Random Walks, Number 2. *IMR; Industrial Management Review (pre-1986), 5*(2), 25.

Ambarish, R., John, K., & Williams, J. (1987). Efficient Signalling with Dividends and Investments. *The Journal of Finance, 42*(2), 321-343.

Amit, R., Brander, J., & Zott, C. (1998). Why do venture capital firms exist? theory and canadian evidence. *Journal of Business Venturing, 13*(6), 441-466.

Anonymous. (1966). Securities Acts. Federal Exchange Act: Insider Purchases Based on Undisclosed Information of Special Significance to Insiders Are Not Violations of Rule 10b-5; Purchases Immediately after Public Announcement Are Not Violations Because There Is Sufficient Public Disclosure at the Moment the Announcement Is Made. Sec v. Texas Gulf Sulphur Co., 258 F. Supp. 262 (S. D. N. Y. 1966). *Harvard Law Review, 80*(2), 468-476.

Anonymous. (1969). Securities Acts. Federal Securities Exchange Act. Stock Purchases by Insiders Possessing Material inside Information, and Misleading Corporate Press Release Unrelated to Securities Transactions by Corporation, Violate SEC Rule 10b-5. SEC v. Texas Gulf Sulphur Co., 401 F.2d 833 (2d Cir. 1968) (en banc), Petitions for cert. filed, 37 U. S. L. W. 3250 (U. S. Jan. 3, 1969) (No. 897), 37 U. S. L. W. 3264 (U. S. Jan. 13, 1969) (No. 937). *Harvard Law Review, 82*(4), 938-951.

Assmann, H.-D. (1994). Das künftige deutsche Insiderrecht (I). *Die Aktiengesellschaft*(5), 196-206.

Bachelier, L. (1900). Théorie de la spéculation. *Annales Scientifiques de L'É.N.S., 3*(17), 21-86.

BaFin. (2005). *Emittentenleitfaden der Bundesanstalt für Finanzdienstleistungsaufsicht*. Retrieved. from http://ww2.bafin.de/schreiben/89_2005/emittentenleitfaden.pdf.

BaFin. (2006). *Jahresbericht 2006*. Retrieved. from http://www.bafin.de.

Bainbridge, S. M. (1999). *Securities law : insider trading*. New York: Foundation Press.

Bainbridge, S. M. (2001). *The Law and Economics of Insider Trading: A Comprehensive Primer*: SSRN.

Ball, R., & Brown, P. (1968). An Empirical Evaluation of Accounting Income Numbers. *Journal of Accounting Research, 6*(2), 159-178.

Betzer, A., & Theissen, E. (2005). Insider Trading and Corporate Governance - The Case of Germany.

Gesetz über die integrierte Finanzdienstleistungsaufsicht, § 25 (2002).

Bhagat, S., & Romano, R. (2001). *Event Studies and the Law - Part I: Technique and Corporate Litigation*: SSRN.

Binder, J.-H. (2001). Die geplante deutsche Allfinanzaufsicht und der britische Prototyp - ein vergleichender Blick auf den deutschen Referentenentwurf. *Zeitschrifr für Wirtschafts- und Bankrecht, 55*(47), 9.

Binder, J. (1998). The Event Study Methodology Since 1969. *Review of Quantitative Finance and Accounting, 11*(2), 111-137.

Bisson, F., & Kunz, A. (2005). Die Kurs- und Marktpreismanipulation nach In-Kraft-Treten des Gsetzes zur Verbesserung des Anlegerschutzes am 28.10.2004 und der Verordnung zur Konkretisierung des Verbots der Marktmanipulation vom 1.3.2005. *Zeitschrift für Bank- und Kapitalmarktrecht*(5), 186-190.

Bowman, R. G. (1983). Understanding and Conducting Event Studies. *Journal of Business Finance & Accounting, 10*(4), 561-584.

Boyle, J. (1992). A Theory of Law and Information: Copyright, Spleens, Blackmail, and Insider Trading. *California Law Review, 80*(6), 1413-1540.

Brealey, R. A., & Myers, S. C. (2000). *Principles of corporate finance* (6th ed.). Boston: Irwin/ McGraw-Hill.

Bromberg, A. R. (1970). Disclosure Programs for Publicly Held Companies: A Practical Guide. *Duke Law Journal, 1970*(6), 1139-1179.

Brown, S. J., & Warner, J. B. (1980). Measuring security price performance. *Journal of Financial Economics, 8*(3), 205-258.

Brudney, V. (1979). Insiders, Outsiders, and Informational Advantages under the Federal Securities Laws. *Harvard Law Review, 93*(2), 322-376.

BT-Drucksache. (14/7033). Entwurf eines Gesetzes über die integrierte Finanzdienstleistungsaufsicht (Vol. 14, pp. 45): Bundesregierung.

Bürgers, T. (2004). Das Anlegerschutzverbesserungsgesetz. *Zeitschrift für Bank- und Kapitalmarktrecht*(11), 424-432.

Carlton, D. W., & Fischel, D. R. (1983). The Regulation of Insider Trading. *Stanford Law Review, 35*(5), 857-895.

CESR. (2002). CESR's Advice on Level 2 Implementing Measures for the proposed Market Abuse Directive.

CESR. (2003). Additional Level 2 Implementing Masures for Market Abuse Directive - Feedback Statement. (CESR/03-213b).

Chan, K., Ikenberry, D., & Lee, I. (2003). Do managers trade consistently? Evidence linking insider trading to actual share repurchase activity. Unpublished Presentation at professional meeting.

Chen, N.-F., Roll, R., & Ross, S. A. (1986). Economic Forces and the Stock Market. *The Journal of Business, 59*(3), 383-403.

Clifford_Chance_LLP. (2005). EU legal and regulatory developments: Market Abuse Directive - Status of implementation in various EU Member States (as at 29th July, 2005). *Derivatives Use, Trading & Regulation, 11*(2), 175-181.

Copeland, T. E., & Galai, D. (1983). Information Effects on the Bid-Ask Spread. *The Journal of Finance, 38*(5), 1457-1469.

Cornell, B., & Sirri, E. R. (1992). The Reaction of Investors and Stock Prices to Insider Trading. *The Journal of Finance, 47*(3), 1031-1059.

Corrado, C. J. (1989). A nonparametric test for abnormal security-price performance in event studies. *Journal of Financial Economics, 23*(2), 385-395.

Damodaran, A., & Liu, C. H. (1993). Insider Trading as a Signal of Private Information. *The Review of Financial Studies, 6*(1), 79-119.

Diekmann, H., & Sustmann, M. (2004). Gesetz zur Verbesserung des Anlegerschutzes (Anlegerschutzverbesserungsgesetz - AnSVG). *Neue Zeitschrift für Gesellschaftsrecht*(20), 929-939.

Dymke, B. M., & Walter, A. (2006). Insider Trading in Germany - Do Corporate Insiders Exploit Inside Information?

Easley, D., & O'Hara, M. (1987). Price, trade size, and information in securities markets. *Journal of Financial Economics, 19*(1), 69-90.

Easterbrook, F. H. (1981). Insider Trading, Secret Agents, Evidentiary Privileges, and the Production of Information. *The Supreme Court Review, 1981*, 309-365.

EU. (2008). Die Geschichte der Europäischen Union. Retrieved 11.01.2008, 2008, from http://europa.eu/abc/history/index_de.htm

European Commission. (1998a). *Financial Services: Building a Framework for Action.* Retrieved 18.01.2008. from http://ec.europa.eu/internal_market/finances/docs/actionplan/index/fs_en.pdf.

European Commission. (1998b). *IP/98/941/Financial services: Commission proposes framework for action*. Retrieved 18.01.2008. from http://europa.eu/rapid/pressReleasesAction.do?reference=IP/98/941&format=HTML&aged=1&language=EN&guiLanguage=en.

European Commission. (1999a). *Financial Services: Implementing the Framework for Financial Markets: Action Plan*. Retrieved 18.01.2008. from http://ec.europa.eu/internal_market/finances/docs/actionplan/index/action_en.pdf.

European Commission. (1999b). *IP/99/327/Financial services: Commission outlines Action Plan for single financial market*. Retrieved 18.01.2008. from http://europa.eu/rapid/pressReleasesAction.do?reference=IP/99/327&format=HTML&aged=1&language=EN&guiLanguage=en.

European Commission. (2004). Commission Directive 2004/72/EC of 29 April 2004 implementing Directive 2003/6/EC of the European Parliament and of the Council as regards accepted market practices, the definition of inside information in relation to derivatives on commodities, the drawing up of lists of insiders, the notification of managers' transactions and the notification of supsicious transactions. *Official Journal*(L 162), 70-75.

European Council. (1989). Council Directive 89/592/EEC of 13 November 1989 coordinating regulations on insider dealing. *Official Journal*(L 334), 30-32.

European Council, & European Parliament. (2003). Directive 2003/6/EC of the European Parliament and of the Council of 28 January 2003 on insider dealing and market manipulation (market abuse). [Directive]. *Official Journal*(L 96).

Fahrmeir, L., Künstler, R., Pigeot, I., & Tutz, G. (2003). *Statistik* (4th ed.). Berlin, Heidelberg, New York: Springer.

Fama, E. F. (1965). The Behavior of Stock-Market Prices. *The Journal of Business, 38*(1), 34-105.

Fama, E. F. (1970). Efficient Capital Markets: A Review of Theory and Empirical Work. *The Journal of Finance, 25*(2), 383-417.

Fama, E. F. (1991). Efficient Capital Markets: II. *The Journal of Finance, 46*(5), 1575-1617.

Fama, E. F., & Blume, M. E. (1966). Filter Rules and Stock-Market Trading. *The Journal of Business, 39*(1), 226-241.

Fama, E. F., Fisher, L., Jensen, M. C., & Roll, R. (1969). The Adjustment of Stock Prices to New Information. *International Economic Review, 10*(1), 1-21.

Fama, E. F., & French, K. R. (1993). Common risk factors in the returns on stocks and bonds. *Journal of Financial Economics, 33*(1), 3-56.

Fergusson, L. (2005, 03.02.2005). Market Abuse - The EU Directive on Insider Dealing and Market Manipulation. *Mondaq Business Briefing*.

Ferrara, R. C., & Crespi, G. S. (1988). Laying ot the Basics: A Close-up View of the Supreme Court Decision in Basic vs. Levinson. *American Business Law Journal, 26*(2), 325.

Ferrarini, G. A. (2004). The European Market Abuse Directive. *Common Market Law Review, 41*(3), 711.

Findlay, M. C., & Williams, E. E. (2000). A fresh look at the efficient market hypothesis: How the intellectual history of finance encouraged a real "fraud-on-the-market". *Journal of Post Keynesian Economics, 23*(2), 181.

Finnerty, J. E. (1976a). Insiders' Activity and Inside Information: A Multivariate Analysis. *Journal of Financial & Quantitative Analysis, 11*(2), 205.

Finnerty, J. E. (1976b). Insiders and Market Efficiency. *Journal of Finance, 31*(4), 1141.

Fuller, K. P. (2003). The impact of informed trading on dividend signaling: a theoretical and empirical examination. *Journal of Corporate Finance, 9*(4), 385-407.

Garfinkel, J. A. (1993). IPO Underpricing, Insider Selling and Subsequent Equity Offerings: Is Underpricing a Signal of Quality? *FM: The Journal of the Financial Management Association, 22*(1), 74-83.

Glosten, L. R., & Milgrom, P. R. (1985). Bid, ask and transaction prices in a specialist market with heterogeneously informed traders. *Journal of Financial Economics, 14*(1), 71-100.

Greene, E. (2005). International Insider Dealing - United States. In M. Stamp & T. Jaggers (Eds.), *International Insider Dealing* (pp. 1-40). Surrey: City & Financial Publishing.

Güth, W., Krahnen, J. P., & Rieck, C. (1997). Financial markets with asymmetric information: A pilot study focusing on insider advantages. *Journal of Economic Psychology, 18*(2-3), 235-257.

Haddock, D., & Macey, J. (1986). A coasian model of insider trading. *Northwestern University Law Review, 80*(Summer), 1449-1470.

Haft, R. J. (1982). The Effect of Insider Trading Rules on the Internal Efficiency of the Large Corporation. *Michigan Law Review, 80*(5), 1051-1071.

Hagemeister, H.-O. (2002). Die neue Bundesanstalt für Finanzdienstleistungsaufsicht. *Zeitschrift für Wirtschafts- und Bankrecht, 56*(35), 8.

Hansen, J. L. (2002). The new Proposal for a European Union Directive on Market Abuse. *University of Pennsylvania Journal of International Economic Law*(23 U. Pa. J. Int'l Econ. L. 241).

Hansen, J. L. (2004). MAD in a Hurry: The Swift and Promising Adoption of the EU Market Abuse Directive. *European Business Law Review, 15*(2), 183-221.

Hayek, F. A. (1945). The Use of Knowledge in Society. *The American Economic Review, 35*(4), 519-530.

Heidorn, T., Meyer, B., & Pietrowiak, A. (2004). Performance-Effekte nach Directors' Dealings in Deutschland, Italien und den Niederlanden. [Working Páper]. *Arbeitsberichte der Hochschule für Bankwirtschaft, 57*, 1-29.

Heiring, W. (2005). *Das neue Anlegerschutzverbesserungsgesetz - AnSVG - Besserer Schutz für private Anleger*. Köln: Bank-Verlag Köln.

Henderson, G. V., Jr. (1990). Problems and Solutions in Conducting Event Studies. *The Journal of Risk and Insurance, 57*(2), 282-306.

Hienzsch, A. (2006). *Das deutsche Insiderhandelsverbot in der Rechtswirklichkeit.* Halle, Wittenberg, Univ., Diss., 2005, Baden-Baden.

Ickler, N. L., Schultz, M., & Yates, P. H. (1982). Recent Decision: Securities - Insider Trading - The Extension of the Duty to disclose Material Inside Information. *Notre Dame Law Review*(58), 132-152.

Ikenberry, D., Lakonishok, J., & Vermaelen, T. (1995). Market underreaction to open market share repurchases. *Journal of Financial Economics, 39*(2-3), 181-208.

Jaffe, J. F. (1974). Special Information and Insider Trading. *The Journal of Business, 47*(3), 410-428.

Jensen, M. C., & Meckling, W. H. (1976). Theory of the firm: Managerial behavior, agency costs and ownership structure. *Journal of Financial Economics, 3*(4), 305-360.

John, K., & Lang, L. H. P. (1991). Insider Trading around Dividend Announcements: Theory and Evidence. *The Journal of Finance, 46*(4), 1361-1389.

John, K., & Mishra, B. (1990). Information Content of Insider Trading Around Corporate Announcements: The Case of Capital Expenditures. *The Journal of Finance, 45*(3), 835-855.

John, K., & Williams, J. (1985). Dividends, Dilution, and Taxes: A Signalling Equilibrium. *The Journal of Finance, 40*(4), 1053-1070.

Johnson, N. J. (1978). Modified t Tests and Confidence Intervals for Asymmetrical Populations. *Journal of the American Statistical Association, 73*(363), 536-544.

Kaiser, U., & Szczesny, A. (2002). Logit- und Probit-Modelle für Kreditrisiken. In M. Schröder (Ed.), *Finanzmarkt-Ökonometrie* (pp. 359-396). Stuttgart: Schäffer - Poeschel.

Klinge, M., Seifert, U., & Stehle, R. (2005). *Abnormal Returns in the Vicinity of Insider Transactions: Unbiased Estimates for Germany*: SSRN.

Kothari, S. P., & Warner, J. B. (1997). Measuring long-horizon security price performance. *Journal of Financial Economics, 43*(3), 301-339.

Kothari, S. P., & Warner, J. B. (2004). The Econometrics of Event Studies. *Journal*. Retrieved from http://ssrn.com/paper=608601

Krawiec, K. (2001). Fairness, Efficiency, and Insider Trading: Deconstructing the Coin of the Realm in the Information Age. *Northwestern University Law Review, 95*(Winter), 443-503.

Kreditausschuss, & BVI. (2004). Stellungnahme des Zentralen Kreditausschusses und des BVI Bundesverband Investment und Assetmanagement e.V. zum Entwurf der Bundesregierung für ein Gesetz zur Verbesserung des Anlegerschutzes (Anlegerschutzverbesserungsgesetz - AnSVG).

Kyle, A. S. (1985). Continuous Auctions and Insider Trading. *Econometrica, 53*(6), 1315-1335.

Lakonishok, J., & Lee, I. (2001). Are insider trades informative? *The Review of Financial Studies, 14*(1), 79.

Lastra, R. (2003). The Governance Structure for Financial Regulation and Supervision in Europe. *10 Colum. J. Eur. L. 49.*

Lee, I. (1997). Do Firms Knowingly Sell Overvalued Equity? *The Journal of Finance, 52*(4), 1439-1466.

Leland, H. E., & Pyle, D. H. (1977). Informational Asymmetries, Financial Structure, and Financial Intermediation. *The Journal of Finance, 32*(2), 371-387.

Levmore, S. (1982). Securities and Secrets: Insider Trading and the Law of Contracts. *Virginia Law Review, 68*(1), 117-160.

Levmore, S. (1984). Efficient Markets and Puzzling Intermediaries. *Virginia Law Review, 70*(4), 645-667.

Lintner, J. (1965). The Valuation of Risk Assets and the Selection of Risky Investments in Stock Portfolios and Capital Budgets. *Review of Economics & Statistics, 47*(1), 13.

Lo, A. W., & MacKinlay, A. C. (1988). Stock Market Prices do not Follow Random Walks: Evidence from a Simple Specification Test. *The Review of Financial Studies, 1*(1), 41-66.

Lo, A. W., & MacKinlay, A. C. (1999). *A non-random walk down Wall Street.* Princeton, N.J.: Princeton University Press.

London_Economics. (2002). *Quantification of the Macro-economic Impact of Integration of EU Financial Markets - November 2002.* London: London Economics.

Lorie, J. H. (1980). Insider Trading: Rule 10b-5, Disclosure, and Corporate Privacy: A Comment. *The Journal of Legal Studies, 9*(4), 819-822.

Lorie, J. H., & Niederhoffer, V. (1968). Predictive and Statistical Properties of Insider Trading. *Journal of Law and Economics, 11*(1), 35-53.

Loughran, T., & Ritter, J. R. (2000). Uniformly least powerful tests of market efficiency. *Journal of Financial Economics, 55*(3), 361-389.

Lyon, J. D., Barber, B. M., & Tsai, C.-L. (1999). Improved Methods for Tests of Long-Run Abnormal Stock Returns. *The Journal of Finance, 54*(1), 165-201.

Macey, J. R. (1991). *Insider trading : economics, politics and policy*. Washington, D.C.

Lanham, Md.: AEI Press ;

University Press of America [distributor].

MacKinlay, A. C. (1997). Event Studies in Economics and Finance. *Journal of Economic Literature, 35*(1), 13-39.

MaKonV. (2005). *Verordnung zur Konkretisierung des Verbotes der Marktmanipulation (Marktmanipulations-Konkretisierungsverordnung - MaKonV)*. Retrieved. from.

Mandelker, G. (1974). Risk and return: The case of merging firms. *Journal of Financial Economics, 1*(4), 303-335.

Manne, H. G. (1966). In Defense of Insider Trading. *Harvard Business Review, 44*(6), 113.

Manove, M. (1989). The Harm From Insider Trading and Informed Speculation. *The Quarterly Journal of Economics, 104*(4), 823-845.

Markowitz, H. (1952). Portfolio Selection. *The Journal of Finance, 7*(1), 77-91.

Meulbroek, L. K. (1992). An Empirical Analysis of Illegal Insider Trading. *The Journal of Finance, 47*(5), 1661-1699.

Mitchell, M. L., & Stafford, E. (2000). Managerial Decisions and Long-Term Stock Price Performance. *Journal of Business, 73*(3), 287.

Mossin, J. (1966). Equilibrium in a Capital Asset Market. *Econometrica, 34*(4), 768-783.

Paefgen, T. C. (1991). Insiderhandel im Spannungsverhältnis zwischen gemeinschaftsrechtlicher Integration und nationalstaatlicher Regulation - e pluribus unum. *Die Aktiengesellschaft*(11).

Perridon, L., & Steiner, M. (1999). *Finanzwirtschaft der Unternehmung* (10 ed.). München: Franz Vahlen.

Peterson, P. P. (1989). Event Studies: A Review of Issues and Methodology. *Quarterly Journal of Business & Economics, 28*(3), 36.

Pham, V. T. L. (2007). Constructing Fama-French Factors from style indexes: Japanses Evidence. *Economics Bulletin, 7*(7), 1-10.

Pluskat, S. (2004). Die durch das Anlegerschutzverbesserungsgesetz geänderte Regelung der Directors' Dealings vor dem Hintergrund der Richtlinie zur Durchführung der Marktmissbrauchsrichtlinie. *Zeitschrift für Bank- und Kapitalmarktrecht*(12), 467-473.

Posner, R. A. (2003). *Economic analysis of law* (6th ed.). New York: Aspen Publishers.

Rau, M. (2004). *Directors' Dealings am deutschen Aktienmarkt*. Zürich: Deutscher Universitäts-Verlag.

Reiling, H. B., & Camargo, M. M. (2004). Texas Gulf Sulphur: The Timmins Ontario Mine. *Harvard Business School Cases*, 1-4.

Reilly, F. K., & Brown, K. C. (2003). *Investment analysis and portfolio management, 7/e* (7th ed.). Cincinnati, OH: South-Western/Thomson Learning.

Reynolds, C., & Rutter, M. (2004). Market abuse - A pan-European approach. *Journal of Financial Regulation and Compliance, 12*(4), 306.

Ritter, J. R. (1991). The Long-Run Performance of Initial Public Offerings. *The Journal of Finance, 46*(1), 3-27.

Robert W. Faff. (2003). Creating Fama and French Factors with Style. *The Financial Review, 38*(2), 311-322.

Ross, S. A. (1976). The arbitrage theory of capital asset pricing. *Journal of Economic Theory, 13*(3), 341-360.

Ross, S. A., Westerfield, R., & Jaffe, J. F. (2002). *Corporate finance* (6th ed.). Boston, Mass.: McGraw-Hill/Irwin.

Rozeff, M. S., & Zaman, M. A. (1988). Market Efficiency and Insider Trading: New Evidence. *Journal of Business, 61*(1), 25-44.

Rozeff, M. S., & Zaman, M. A. (1998). Overreaction and insider trading: Evidence from growth and value portfolios. *Journal of Finance, 53*(2), 701.

SA. (1933). *Securities Act of 1933*. Retrieved 2007/08/20. from http://www.sec.gov/about/laws/sa33.pdf.

Schoen, K. (1999). Insider Trading: The "Possession versus Use" Debate. *University of Pennsylvania Law Review, 148*(1), 239-284.

Scott, K. E. (1980). Insider Trading: Rule 10b-5, Disclosure and Corporate Privacy. *The Journal of Legal Studies, 9*(4), 801-818.

SEA. (1934). *Securities Exchange Act of 1934*. Retrieved 2007/08/20. from http://www.sec.gov/about/laws/sea34.pdf.

Securities and Exchange Commission, Plaintiff-Appellant, v. Texas Gulf Sulphur Co., a Texas Corporation, Charles F. Fogarty, Richard D. Mollison, Walter Holyk, Kenneth H. Darke, Francis G. Coates, Claude O. Stephens, John A. Murray, Earl L. Huntington, and Harold B. Kline, Defendants-Appellees. Securities and Exchange Commission, Plaintiff-Appellee, v. David M. Crawford and Richard H. Clayton, Defendants-Appellants (United States Court of Appeals for the Second Circuit 1968).

Securities and Exchange Commission, Plaintiff-Appellee, v. Anthony Materia, Defendant-Appellant, 745 F.2d 197 84-6043 (United States Court of Appeals for the Second Circuit 1984).

Serra, A. P. S. (2002). *Event Study Tests: A Brief Survey*: SSRN.

Seyhun, H. N. (1986). Insiders' profits, costs of trading, and market efficiency. *Journal of Financial Economics, 16*(2), 189-212.

Seyhun, H. N. (1988). The Information Content of Aggregate Insider Trading. *The Journal of Business, 61*(1), 1-24.

Seyhun, H. N. (1992). The Effectiveness of the Insider-Trading Sanctions. *Journal of Law and Economics, 35*(1), 149-182.

Seyhun, H. N., & Bradley, M. (1997). Corporate Bankruptcy and Insider Trading. *Journal of Business, 70*(2), 189-216.

Sharpe, W. F. (1963). A Simplified Model for Portfolio Analysis. *Management Science, 9*(2), 277-293.

Sharpe, W. F. (1964). Capital Asset Prices: A Theory of Market Equilibrium under Conditions of Risk. *Journal of Finance, 19*(3), 425-442.

Shostak, F. (1997). In defense of fundamental analysis: A critique of the efficient market hypothesis. *The Review of Austrian Economics, 10*(2), 27-45.

Spence, M. (1973). Job Market Signaling. *The Quarterly Journal of Economics, 87*(3), 355-374.

Steiner, P., & Uhlir, H. (2001). *Wertpapieranalyse* (4 ed.). Heidelberg: Physica-Verlag.

Stern, A., & Beresford, M. (2001). Financial services reform: full steam ahead. *European Policy Analyst*, 67.

Stotz, O. (2006). Germany's New Insider Law: The Empirical Evidence after the First Year. *German Economic Review, 7*(4), 449-462.

Su, D. (2004). Adverse-selection versus signaling: evidence from the pricing of Chinese IPOs. *Journal of Economics and Business, 56*(1), 1-19.

Sutton, C. D. (1993). Computer-Intensive Methods for Tests About the Mean of an Asymmetrical Distribution. *Journal of the American Statistical Association, 88*(423), 802-810.

Tebroke, H.-J., & Wollin, A. (2005). Directors' Dealings, Informationseffizienz und Handelsstrategien. *Swiss Journal of Business Research and Practice, 59*(01), 24.

White, H. (1980). A Heteroskedasticity-Consistent Covariance Matrix Estimator and a Direct Test for Heteroskedasticity. *Econometrica, 48*(4), 817-838.

WpAIV. (2004). *Verordnung zur Konkretisierung von Anzeige-, Mitteilungs- und Veröffentlichungspflichten sowie der Pflicht zur Führung von Insiderverzeichnissen nach dem Wertpapierhandelsgesetz (Wertpapierhandelsanzeige- und Insiderverzeichnisverordnung - WpAIV).* Retrieved. from http://www.bgblportal.de/BGBL/bgbl1f/bgbl104s3376.pdf.

WpHG. (2007). *Wertpapierhandelsgesetz - Gesetz über den Wertpapierhandel.* Retrieved. from.

Ziemons, H. (2004). Neuerungen im Insiderrecht und bei der Ad-hoc-Publizität durch die MArktmissbrauchsrichtlinie und das Gesetz zur Verbesserung des Anlegerschutzes. *Neue Zeitschrift für Gesellschaftsrecht*(12), 537-543.

Zweites Finanzmarktförderungsgesetz. (1994). *Gesetz über den Wertpapierhandel und zur Änderung börsenrechtlicher und wertpapierrechtlicher Vorschriften (Zweites Finanzmarktförderungsgesetz).*

Corporate Finance and Governance

Herausgegeben von Dirk Schiereck

Band 1 Sebastian Michael Gläsner: Return Patterns of German Open-End Real Estate Funds. An Empirical Explanation of Smooth Fund Returns. 2010.

Band 2 Patrick Ams: Directors' Dealings and Insider Trading in Germany. An Empirical Analysis. 2010.

www.peterlang.de